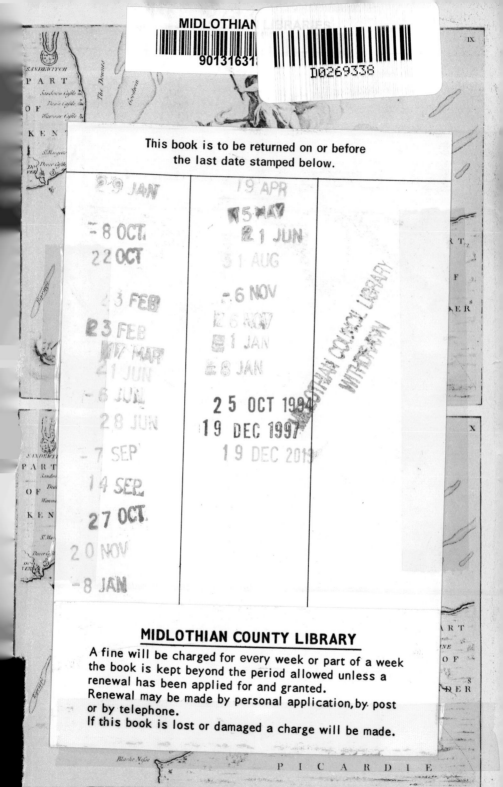

The Spanish Terror

MAURICE ROWDON

The Spanish Terror

*Spanish Imperialism
in the Sixteenth Century*

CONSTABLE
LONDON

First published in Great Britain 1974
by Constable and Company Limited
10 Orange Street, London WC2H 7EG
Copyright © 1974 by Maurice Rowdon

ISBN 0 09 458070 7

Set in 'Monotype' Ehrhardt
Printed in Great Britain
by Ebenezer Baylis and Son Limited
The Trinity Press, Worcester, and London

Contents

Illustrations

Spain and the Rise of Money

The sixteenth century was for Europe an epoch of fervent business, persecution and war. In that time the modern world as we recognise it came into being. Things changed faster than ever before and perhaps ever since. Even the industrial nineteenth century was less original in its changes; the basis of its work had been done three centuries before.

For some people 'the sixteenth century' means the beginning of Christian civilisation proper. They see the Middle Ages as a kind of passive incubation period, dominated and repressed by the Church, before the great liberating forces (called the 'Renaissance') which brought about renewed trade, voyages of discovery, new techniques of manufacture and the chastening of Rome.

But there is little evidence that a civilisation was created, though a quite new society was. Compared with the Middle Ages the sixteenth century had nothing tranquil and nothing wholesome about it. Small pockets of civilisation had arisen—Florence, Antwerp, Venice—but were now swallowed up in military occupation or affluence. They were piece-meal, brief and interrupted attempts at a civilisation for which Christendom as a whole did not seem ready.

The question arises, was a sustained Christian civilisation ever achieved, comparable to the great (and certainly sustained) civilisations of the Orient or the Mediterranean, where the smallest details of life seemed to refer to a divine illumination? Certainly mediaeval life was sustained; one generation saw much the same world as the one before it. But then Europe was still nursing its wounds after the chaotic dismemberment of the Roman Empire by barbarian tribes. There was something too guarded, too numbed about mediaeval life to call it civilised. Compared with the ancient civilisations the mediaeval world was starved of light; it never translated—it did not

9

dare to translate—its deep sense of the divine into the outwardly marvellous. It knew little about ancient Greece. But in the time of the Renaissance, during the fourteenth and fifteenth centuries, Europe did begin to look back, and to compare itself unfavourably with the ancient past. That was what produced the pockets of civilisation—notably Florence under the Medici. But they were soon engulfed in war and persecution.

The result was a disturbed society which still today fails to solve its problems or even to offer agreed definitions as to what these problems are. The problems certainly came into being in the sixteenth century. They were insoluble then, by their nature. And since they remain the basis of the world we live in now, there seems no more hope than there ever was of resolving them, except by the disintegration of the whole system of life adopted at that time and consolidated, with growing chaos, ever since.

Violence became basic to Christian life in the sixteenth century. It even seemed an essential condition of Christian survival. Yet thirty years before the century opened violence was neither expected nor thought necessary. When in 1479 Federigo of Urbino shattered some of the roofs of Colle Val d'Elsa near Siena with his cannons, in the war between Florence and the pope, the local population made a great cry about its being 'unfair'. Of course pillaging had gone on, but it had usually been the work of an eccentric, when not an accident. Niccolò Vitelli of Città di Castello, who devastated much of the Romagna during the same war, was known for his brutality, and everyone prophesied a sticky end for him. Less than half a century later there were new standards of violence which were more reminiscent of the barbarian period than anything else. Men became strangers to each other over trifling definitions of words—men in the same camp, the same court, the same Church. The divisions were so great that only one factor held sixteenth-century Christendom together at all and that was the threat of a Turkish invasion. Without this Europe might very well have reverted to its tribal condition of a millennium before. Yet by this time the Middle Ages were something to laugh at, presumably for having achieved a common and basically peaceful life throughout Europe.

Present-day society—whether we are talking about medical science or the printing of vast numbers of books in vernacular languages or communications or the banking system or exploration or racial and religious persecution or the arts and literature or state debts or techniques of war or espionage or the 'whitewashing' of human minds—was developed at that time. One factor underlay all these activities, a new factor for Christendom: money. Of course money had always been used. But now it had an unprecedented role. The fact that it went far beyond a mere symbol of exchange to become the *sine qua non* of power had a great deal to do with the violence. Great sums of money were borrowed by states at fantastic rates of interest, sometimes 50 per cent. This was for the financing of war, though it was still largely the polite war of mercenaries who hesitated to engage the enemy for fear of winning their battles and ending their contracts too soon. Now the armies had to do something highly impolite, and increasingly by fair means or foul; and that was to win sufficient territory and markets to pay back the loans plus the interest, in an escalating activity that created one empire after another.

These empires began with aggression and ended in inflation. The first great empire of this kind (quite different from the empires of Greece and Rome) was the Spanish. And it arose more clearly from the borrowing principle than from any factor of simple self-aggrandisement. The gold and silver bullion that poured into Spain from the newly won Americas financed Spain's hold on Europe, and through inflation it also reduced Spain to a secondary power in less than a century after its heyday. This new type of empire clearly rose and fell with remarkable speed.

Since then other empires have gone through the same process with varying degrees of speed. And they continue to do so. In this process the mother-country becomes overburdened with its far-flung responsibilities and in the end cannot compete with the power it has necessarily created (under viceroys and puppet rulers and in satellite states) in every part of the globe. Other countries, straining to nibble a piece off the empire, quickly achieve their end because their resources are less extended. They in turn close in and become great, before succumbing in turn to the crushing financial problem. It happened to Venice with her empire of 2,000,000 inhabitants and her outposts far down in the Archipelago. It happened to the tiny empire created by Florence under Lorenzo de' Medici with its satellite towns of Siena, Volterra, Pisa, Livorno. And later it happened to England, to France and Holland. In our day the empires have become huge zones of influence straddling continents and cutting across each other in intense financial and commercial competition backed by military programmes. Sooner or later the pressure on the centre grows too great, and financial uncertainty, the first sign of loosening grip, sets in. Thus the process has not stopped since the sixteenth century, it has simply become global.

As early as the fifteenth century the worst problem facing rulers was the financial one, and none of them solved it. This was the case with Lorenzo de' Medici, with Louis XI and his son Charles VIII, with the popes and the Holy Roman Emperor Maximilian, and with Ferdinand and Isabella of Spain. To send armies into the field you had to live on the future. And to keep them on foreign soil you had to live on even more of the future. The fifteenth-century state had to recognise its debt as permanent and inevitable and therefore legal. The idea of a national debt came into being. There was a Florentine saying at the time of Lorenzo de' Medici which declared, 'Unless Florence extinguishes her debt, her debt will extinguish her.' Her independence did become extinct after the great Medici era, just as Venetian independence became extinct when the Serenissima could no longer pay her bills. Thus the post-imperial generations have always paid the price for earlier glories in stagnation or servitude. The modern 'balance of payments' is the same debt, now under constant scrutiny, a gauge of the nation's health that changes with a speed known only to post-mediaeval society. But the scrutinising of a debt does not eliminate the violence of which that debt is the *alter ego*.

This viciously circular action of money and violence was a sixteenth-century phenomenon, though few men outside the monasteries noticed the connection at the time. Perhaps they did not want to notice. Certainly the wandering prophets who preached against usury, descendants of the so-called White Penitents, were considered embarrassing in commercial cities, and were often sent packing. Society was too busy chasing an interest rate it could never catch to listen to warnings from the monks. Once the legality of an interest rate was admitted (and the mediaeval world was for this reason careful not to admit it) you created a gap between production and consumption which no amount of effort could close. The loans tended to make aggression a necessity of survival. On the face of it the most commercial states were the most peaceful—England, Holland, Florence. The Medici party in Florence liked to keep the political balance in Italy because war disturbed trade. Yet the Medici banks were financing ambitious programmes throughout Europe at profitable rates of interest (though the debts were often not paid back). Cosimo de' Medici financed Edward IV of England in his wars to the tune of thousands of écus, and thus helped to lay the basis of the English state. The Medici, like all the great bankers of the time, were thus pursuing peaceful policies as essential to good business while their loans made peace impossible even for themselves (and indeed Florence was continually rocked by wars through most of the Medici 'reign' in the fifteenth century). The same was roughly true of every commercial state that came into being at that time. Anything like the old mediaeval stability was out of the question. One expansion on the basis of a letter of credit provoked another. You promised to repay the loan when you had won your war. Edward IV failed to do so and wrecked the Medici branch in London, just as the emperor Maximilian and his wife wrecked the branch at Bruges.

It was not that either letters of credit or interest had been absent in the Middle Ages. Merchants had charged interest under cover of their exchange-bills, arguing that the currency change involved was a matter of pure sale. In fact an argument had gone on all the time between the merchants and the theologians as to what constituted right business practice. Even when money came to be lent at interest on a big scale, as in the fifteenth century, the old laws against usury were not forgotten. The Medici would have been horrified to hear that they were usurers. So would the other bankers of the time. They were still 'money-changers'. Their interest masqueraded as legitimate compensation for risk or as a share in the profits.

The great change after the Middle Ages was the fact that governments began to borrow to put their policies into practice. These policies were not always within their means. It naturally provoked an expansionist state of mind, and grand dreams of future prowess. The pope himself was one of the chief borrowers, and the delicate political balance of fifteenth-century Italy was constantly disturbed by Vatican expansionism. The shady procedures that became accepted as good business practice, covering everything from tax-evasion to the manipulation of accounts (both were practised by Cosimo de' Medici as a matter of course, even while he was the real government of Florence), were less in defiance of the Church than in collaboration with her. It was wise of the first rich Medici to tell his sons to keep in with the pope at all costs.

At the beginning of the fifteenth century there were over thirty banks in Rome alone. By the end of the century there were little more than a handful, and even Medici fortunes were at a low ebb. During that century there seemed to be a great need for what we would nowadays call investment possibilities, without the possibilities being there. It partly accounts for the violent expansionism of the following century, and the first forms of colonial exploitation. The one investment-possibility open to princes in the fifteenth century (and one generously favoured by the Medici) was war. It rocked the foundations of society. The Church and the sovereign states were soon at war with each other, and within themselves, in what looked like a permanent state of unrest. It could even be said that from that time unrest became the distinguishing mark of the Christian world. The gap created by the interest rate—really a gap between present facts and future hopes—was, so to speak, the guarantor of this unrest.

Nowadays the chase to close the gap has descended the power hierarchy to the worker who, through his trade unions (comparable to states in the pressure they exercise), searches for new wage-settlements. But prices rise with wages, and the fact that modern society has turned into a kind of frantic animal chasing its own tail is now clear for all to see. It was not so clear in the sixteenth century when it began, or even in the reckless nineteenth century when it was thought that all you had to do was to consume more and produce more and the violence would stop. It did stop, but only for the relative few who happened at that time to be the maximum consumers. And even they—or rather their sons—were swallowed up in the greatest war there had ever been, a war which they could not understand. The 1914-18 war simply 'happened', like something outside human control, because no one understood the fearful secret of the commercial state.

Historically a line of increasingly spectacular development can be traced from the sixteenth century to the present day—greater speeds, greater populations, greater analytic knowledge. And this same line can be represented as an increasingly spectacular collapse. Its climax (or bottom curve) has been the two global wars of this century. The more riches, apparently, the more violence.

In the making of this new society the Spaniards played a leading role. The 'Spanish terror' that came about in the sixteenth century was not due to any special brutality on their part, although they were feared everywhere for just this. Other peoples and other soldiers could be equally cruel, and the *landsknechts* from Switzerland and Germany were invariably more so. Nor was the terror due to their ardent catholicism; protestants proved as unforgiving when their anger was aroused. In other words the plunge into violence was a general one, the Spanish role being simply that of the most powerful nation.

This was not only violence done to people and their property. It was a violent attitude of mind towards the whole of nature. In Peru the Spanish conquistadors managed in a handful of decades to ruin an agricultural system carefully built up over centuries and passed from one generation to the next, and to render almost extinct the fine breed of llamas on which Peru depended for its wool and, partly, for its meat. They tore down fabulous cities, they massacred where only friendship had been shown them, they turned the marvellous Inca road across the Cordillera mountains into an impassable track. The Christian seemed to lose his respect for man and beast and earth, and regarded them as endlessly expendable for market purposes; which is perhaps to say (and there is much evidence for this in the religious struggles of the time) that he had lost respect for himself.

Yet he showed an unbounded confidence. He began to feel he knew more than had ever been known before, though in fact there was not one aspect of his new knowledge, even the theory of the roundness of the earth and the so-called 'Copernican revolution', which had not been known to one of the ancient civilisations. The confidence was reckless precisely because it was narrow-minded. The Inca and the Aztec were seen as inferior because they looked different from Christians. It was therefore a small matter to murder them in cold blood or to go back on one's promises to them. Thus in the very confidence there was weakness. The Christian was not yet strong enough to respect the unfamiliar. His attempts to spread his civilisation were therefore rather grotesque, and disastrous to the peoples he 'civilised', bringing them disease and despair. It was clear that far from having a civilisation to spread, he did not even know what a civilisation was. He wrote about it and talked about it. Masses of books were printed about it. The talkative humanist movement penetrated every court in Europe, and did succeed in changing whole cities. But apart from a few marvellous decades here and there, the Christian civilisation was never actually *lived*. Men increasingly made the mistake of believing that civilisation was the way they lived just because they lived it. In our own day it is actually possible to talk of the 'harmful effects of civilisation' and mean air-pollution and nervous distress and cities which make human survival a miracle, and a medical science that chases the new diseases as pathetically as society chases the interest rate.

In the sixteenth century the needs of the market began to govern all other considerations, even those of human safety and survival. Few men of the Middle Ages could have predicted that one day the Christian's predations, industrial and military, would take a much greater toll of human life than the plagues. Even less could he have predicted that the society responsible for these predations would look on itself as a 'progress' on all former worlds, its immense destructions a kind of peculiar and unfortunate accident which would never happen again, at least until they actually did happen. Today the destructions would cease 'if' science could turn itself to entirely peaceful activities. The solution—the ideal world which so pre-occupied the humanists—continues to be just round the corner, while society continues to produce its shocks and accidents which no one is able to predict.

Again and again, in Italy, in Spain, in the restless principalities north of the Alps, the effort to promote a stable and 'universal' society under the Cross collapsed into bitter persecution, war, bankruptcy and assassination. Compared with the ancient religions, Christianity simply failed to define its mystical experience success-fully, perhaps because that experience was young and uncertain, perhaps because the conversion of the barbarian tribes of Europe had been intellectual rather than spiritual. Whatever the explanation, Christians seemed narrowly obstinate people whether fighting the hated 'infidel' or each other on points of doctrine. Obstinacy is said to be a mark of the weak. And much of the unyielding orthodoxy of the sixteenth century, whether catholic or protestant, was no more than the obstinacy of uncertain people. In that epoch the Christian came into close contact with other religions—the Hindu, the Arab, the Jewish, the Inca—and proved his own system to be by far the most intolerant and splenetic of them all. Far from having come of age in the sixteenth century, with the so-called Renaissance behind it, Christendom was still trying through turmoil and experi-ment to define the premises on which life should be based and about which Christ, addressing Jews whose system of life had been agreed and closely defined, had said so little. It looked as if the Christian *had* no way of life, and was desperately trying to find one. Many different peoples had been flung into the Christian net after the decline of the Roman Empire, and the spiritual government that came from Rome was too vague in the end, even too little agreed about itself, for the basically barbarian and tribal community of which it was overseer not to burst its bonds and experiment with its own definitions of Christ's words. The protestant sects were at-tempts at such a definition. But so was the catholic orthodoxy, which the protestant reform movement forced on the Church by a process of defensive reaction. It was, then, natural that people whose way of life was so unsettled should believe, in the old tribal manner, that what way of life they did have was sacred, and the best way of defining the 'Christian', and even civilised man. In the sixteenth century the idea of power replaced that of divine truth and even human goodness. For power too was an old tribal obsession. When the Peruvians gaped at the Spanish galleons, 'those palaces floating on the sea', and at the Spanish muskets which made such a fearful noise and caused distant objects to be shattered to pieces, the conquistadors took it to be a further proof of the blessedness of the Holy Mother of God.

Yet the Spanish effort to create a Christian empire from end to end of the globe—an effort started, with a certain amount of bewilderment, by Charles V, who was both king of Spain and Holy Roman emperor, and then systematically by his son, Philip II—was just as much an effort to make a civilisation as, say, the work of the Medici in Florence. But it became, through a series of colossal errors (mostly religious ones about the nature of the human will when satisfied that it was God's will), a pure struggle for power. Until well into the seventeenth century Spain was behind most of the murder-plots and intrigues that rocked the courts of Europe from time to time. Her machinations became a legend exaggerated equally by her friends and enemies. Her spies were everywhere. So was her gold. The world trembled at a word from the 'prudent prince', Philip. And the empire that he created seemed bound to last for ever.

Yet a century before no one could have predicted much of a future for Spain. It was a loose group of independent states and three different races, Jews and Arabs and Christians, living together in increasingly doubtful harmony. It was difficult to imagine these states, jealously resentful of each other, becoming the equal of France, let alone the centre of the biggest empire hitherto known.

But European life changed rapidly in the fourteenth and fifteenth centuries, and Spain's development into a nation was part of a general process which eventually dismembered the Holy Roman Empire. Mediaeval life collapsed. Or rather it evolved into something new—less uniform, more turbulent. During the Middle Ages Church law had regulated business life in a careful and, as we now see, wise way. The mediaeval rule of the 'just price' and the law forbidding usury ('the taking of money beyond the capital lent') were really recommendations for a healthy society. Indeed, the idea of health or *sanitas* was the key to mediaeval values, like the idea of renunciation on another level. Poverty was even something of an ideal. Beggars were rarely turned away from doors, convents were open to the weak and needy. Princes were buried in the habits of Minorite friars. They competed with each other to endow convents and charitable institutions. There was no lack of war, disease or social disturbance in mediaeval times, but a certain stability of ordinary daily life, unparalleled since, was achieved.

This was for a very good reason—security. The global organisation of the Roman world had fallen to pieces through terrorism, to which perhaps all global organisation lends itself in the end. Everywhere in Italy hill-towns came into being as a protection against the malaria and the brigands in the plains. The countryside became virtually deserted except during working hours. And this process was repeated in every part of Europe. It accounts for the massive crenellated walls, the stout gates of the typically mediaeval town. People clung together in fear. They tended to be drawn to the strong; crushing Roman taxes made it advantageous for the small landholder to incorporate his holding into that of a much greater man who could afford the burden. This produced identical centres of autonomous life all over Europe—domains where the knight, the priest and the peasant governed life at the three essential points of defence, thought and sustenance. The result was a descending scale of landed and military power which started at the top with the princes and lords of the manor and went down to the serfs or freemen. Each component was locked to the other by a common need for security. In this sense mediaeval society was a prolonged convalescence from one of the most spectacular declines in history, that of ancient Rome. Hence its—to us—unchanging quality; no one seemed much

interested in experiment. It was enough to survive and believe. All
the laws governing mediaeval society were therefore towards the
double end of preventing further turbulence and securing the young
Christian faith. Thus it was that the Church (the only global
organisation that survived the ancient Roman world) made the
essential laws and decided the essential attitudes. Christ meant peace
and therefore security. People had turned to the story of his Passion
with extraordinary relief, as though after a bad dream.

Such a society called for no great communications system. The
commerce of the Roman Empire (and thus its roads) had withered
in the years of decline. Money was relatively little used in the
mediaeval world. Agriculture was everything. No profit was made.
Each domain or 'villa' produced the amount of food it needed, not
the amount it could. Money was used but only at the local markets
which everyone to some extent needed. There were famines—every
harvest that failed caused one—but these were mild compared to
those that sometimes hit the post-mediaeval world. When a mediaeval
prince travelled from one of his estates to the other with his retinue
he lived on the land, and moved on when he had eaten and drunk
the year's supply due to him.

All this began to change in the fourteenth century. Church
authority collapsed. The papal states began to disintegrate until
only two of the Romagna barons acknowledged papal rule. For
almost a century the popes were resident at Avignon. In Rome the
leading families (the Colonna, the Orsini) fortified themselves in the
ancient ruins like tribal chiefs, while the populace, shrunk to fewer
than 20,000 people, trembled outside.

The monk became a figure of fun as he ceased to exercise his old
function as the local reservoir of spiritual vision (however much he
had often fallen short of this function in the old world). The peasant
began to be despised as an outsider, an attitude that survived in
Italy until a decade or so ago. More and more people acted on their
own interests rather than on faith. 'Liberty plucked Justice by the
nose', and men got to the top by murder and bribery. Intelligence
began to be a prized quality. With it you could make a fortune,
become a nobleman. In Italy you could change classes with remark-

able ease. *Parvenus* came to govern states—the Medici in Florence, the Visconti in Milan.

This turbulent reorganisation of life is called the Renaissance. Men had no further need of mediaeval security. Europe was on its feet again. After the uncertain days of the fourteenth century popes became little emperors in their style of life. The Vatican was a court. Popes were often members of important banking families, and took a lively interest in the new circulation of money. It was Eugenius IV who encouraged the Signoria in Florence to recall Cosimo de' Medici from his exile in Venice (1433), and to banish the ruling Rinaldo Abrizzi. Cosimo's father had always impressed on him the need to keep friendly relations with Rome, and perhaps the greatest *coup* of the Medici firm was getting hold of the papal account. Medici branches were responsible for collecting papal revenues, and a bad report from one of them to the Curia could lose a man his expected bishopric. On the other hand a Medici recommendation could bring interesting commercial preferments in its train. Cosimo advanced Nicholas V, when still a cardinal, large sums of money without security, and Nicholas rewarded him by renewing the papal account.

Borrowing, now encouraged and indulged by the Church, became the new hub of life. It meant new initiative and hope. At the same time the old health, the *sanitas*, collapsed. This may sound strange to anyone who has just compared the average mortality-rate in the eleventh century with that today. But longevity is no insurance against a rotten mind. The fact remains that compared with the old society the one that developed clearly in the fifteenth and six-teenth centuries had nothing certain about it, and nothing stable, and nothing—from the mediaeval point of view—sound. Profit was made everywhere. Vast dividends meant that society had to make desperate shifts and necessarily aggressive shifts to snatch propor-tionately vast profits. It produced a state of continual war. Other people's wealth was desperately needed by all. Change was therefore the theme of this new society. In the matter of costume alone nothing remained the same for twenty years at a stretch, so much so that we can identify any post-mediaeval epoch by its form of dress. The ancient world was no longer something to be forgotten and shunned. In fact it was 'reborn'—hence the name that historians have given to the epoch, the 'Renaissance'; and reborn as modern life.

Ancient Greece and Rome now seemed to shine with a great light. For centuries this light had been forgotten. There were growing contacts with the Greek Church, and thus Greek thought. An ecumenical council for the union of the Greek and Roman Churches was held in Florence in 1439. The doors to the ancient light were flung wide open. Mediaeval life, with its patient expectation of a Second Coming and its warning of hellfire, now looked like a dismal aftermath of those ancient marvels. Its humble church façades were dismantled wherever there was money to spend, and replaced with splendid neo-classical ones. The abbot of the Badìa in Fiesole begged Lorenzo de' Medici to build him a new façade as the present one was 'old'; that was already a criticism in itself of the previous way of life.

The idea of progress began to dominate the Christian view of the past; present society was an 'advance' on former society. By the nineteenth century historians were writing about the Renaissance as a great enterprise of liberation—America discovered, trade revived and the Roman yoke of ignorance thrown aside. In fact it opened with the most devastating plagues ever known; the first wave between 1347 and 1350 removed almost half the population of Europe and was soon followed by the Black Death. It introduced the most unthinkable religious persecutions since Decian times. The burning and torturing of fellow-Christians became a familiar sight. And society was now divided into 'nations' sometimes at peace with each other but mostly at war. Murderous Turkish armies stood on the Christian borders and sometimes encroached well inside. This was how far Christian life had 'progressed' from its mediaeval cradle. And, with increasingly spectacular wars and terror-systems ever since that time, the 'progress' seems to have gone on.

Nor did the Renaissance burst on the Christian scene like a sudden light. It was a process which had its roots deep in the Middle Ages. As early as the first half of the thirteenth century something like the later Renaissance courts had flourished under Frederick II in Sicily. He had taken a great interest in the medical schools of Salerno. He established the university of Naples where Thomas Aquinas studied. Learned Jews and Muslims shared his table with Christians. He patronised Leonardo da Pisa who introduced Arabic numerals and algebra to the Christian world. The first poems in the Italian language, based on Provençal models, were written by his courtiers, among them his bastard son Enzio. Even the later violence, the later frantic circulation of money were latent in mediaeval life, barely controlled by a Church whose leadership rocked unsteadily between popes and anti-popes, popes and emperors. The 'Renaissance' was not so much a movement of new ideas as a will to reorganise life; the avid search for ancient authors which characterised it indicated a need to hear their proposals for a life of happiness.

When we think of the Renaissance we usually think of Italian art and Italian city-life; and here, certainly, the rebirth was clear and unmistakeable. It was where the new expectation of happiness shone brightest. The artist in our sense came into being. Giotto (*c.* 1266–1337) and Lorenzetti (active 1327–55) and Perugino (1445/52–1523) are at once recognised by their styles. Men were thinking for themselves. The old numbed and guarded feeling had gone. There was a new concept of the 'complete' human being. The 'Renaissance man' made love, learned Virgil by heart, jousted, performed incredible physical feats. It was a stupendous burst of confidence. People felt like gods. This feeling was behind the daring skill of the Italian painters, and the daring skill of the geographers and seamen. It was a total manifestation. Printing, gunpowder, 'personality' in our sense came into being.

But if we look more closely we find that together with the self-confidence and self-reliance, so distinct from anything that went on in the Middle Ages, there was doubt too. The self-assertion may even seem to us an aspect of the doubt, as if the disappearance of the old mediaeval soundness had left a gap of inner experience. In the end doubt eclipsed everything else, until by the sixteenth century men were arguing and murdering about the meaning of the word 'transubstantiation'.

Paradoxically, the 'humanists' had more to do with this than anyone, though the society that actually came about would have pleased none of them. They were very clear about wanting to make a Christian civilisation. And at first it seemed as if they might succeed. Lorenzo de' Medici often used to say that without knowing Plato you could not penetrate the mysteries of Christianity or even be a good citizen. The two went together, and rulers like him, whose homes bustled with painters and thinkers and musicians, tried to make new cities in the light of the new thought. Most humanists believed in making the scriptures available to everyone, not simply to the clergy, as in mediaeval times; hence the invention of printing, to extend readership far beyond the monastery with its hand-written manuscripts. Humanists tended to see ancient Greece as the third-century neo-platonists of Alexandria had seen it, namely as a mar-vellous anticipation of Christ, a grooming of the ancient mind towards His arrival. Plato's 'perfect man', they argued, had indeed been realised in Christ. And society could be made—remade—on the basis of that perfection. Classical learning was so to speak the living text of that perfection.

Thus, far from visualising a secular society of the kind that actually came about, the humanists hoped for a more joyfully Christian one than ever before. Their thought was about the perfect or divine man, not mortal man. It had nothing to do with the later humanitarianism of the nineteenth century; no thinkers of that time were non-religious thinkers. The humanist attacks on the Church were about abuse, not doctrine. They never questioned Church authority. When Luther began doing this he turned from being a humanist into a man with a 'protest'—quite a different thing. But Church authority did suffer as a result of humanism. The doctrine of original sin which had given the priest a useful hold over the popular imagination did not tally very well with the idea of the 'perfect man'. Naturally the Church took fright in the end, and humanist thinking plunged the Christian world into a turmoil which it neither expected nor even dreamed of as possible.

At first the works of the greatest humanist, Erasmus (? 1466–1536), circulated with ease in all the courts of Europe and at the Curia itself. It was only when men inside and outside the Church began to question her *authority* that humanist ideas could get you tortured or burned alive. By this time Lorenzo de' Medici had been in his grave thirty years or more, and his city had become a Spanish satellite. By this time too it was no longer a matter of classical learning, no longer a discussion of the 'new' civilisation about to be made; it was a simple state of war. It happened with astonishing speed. Sir Thomas More's *Utopia*, printed in 1516, which laid down a few rules for this new civilisation, survived mainly as a name for social day-dreaming. The author ended his life in gaol. He was beheaded in 1536 for refusing to acknowledge Henry VIII as the supreme head of the Church in England. Five years before, Florence had been sacked by the same imperial troops who had sacked Rome in 1527, and this time at the request of the pope. He happened to be a Medici who wanted his city back again. In that act the 'rebirth' was smothered.

Yet perhaps this result should not have come as a shock to the humanists. One thing had always underpinned the long platonic discussions, the impeccable Greek texts at the printing presses, and that was money. Never before had thought and art depended so squarely on market operations. The two great commercial centres, Florence and Antwerp, were naturally and necessarily the two great centres of artistic patronage. Yet money in itself seemed harmless enough. It seemed, in fact, no more than it had ever been in Roman or mediaeval times, namely a symbol of exchange. But it now played a subtle and largely invisible role. It could apparently turn what looked like a brilliant civilisation into an inferno. Money was the principal ingredient of the Renaissance. Therefore it worked its effect. Murder and Benozzo Gozzoli frescoes, massacre and platonic thought, pillage and refinement went on side by side. Some of the finest church-frescoes were painted while the narrow streets outside clattered with the cavalry of a faction on its way to destroy another faction. With increasing refinement in its citizens the Christian world devised worse and worse cruelties. It was not accidental that gunpowder was developed during the Renaissance equally with the technique of the fresco, and that Leonardo da Vinci amused himself drawing multi-firing guns. The kinder and more educated the Christian became, the worse the wars he had to fight in!

It was natural that Italy should be the leader of this Renaissance, being the home of the ancient authority and in any case the most developed country in Europe. She had christianised the barbarian races of the Roman Empire and then—by means of Benedictine missionaries sent from Rome by Pope Gregory in the sixth and seventh centuries—she had unified them under one Church. She still had the ancient *savoir faire*. She quickly saw the possible new functions of money. The nascent capitalism of the Middle Ages lay in the weaver-merchant relationship, and this was most developed in Italy, especially in Siena and Florence. By the first half of the thirteenth century Florentine merchants were exporting cloth as far as the Orient, and importing wool from England. During that century Sienese and Florentine bankers were doing business in every part of Europe. Long before the Medici family came on the scene Sienese bankers like Musciatto and Guido were acting as money-agents for the pope, and as treasurers to princes. After the bankruptcy of the Sienese company of Bonsignori in 1289 Florence took over as the financial centre of western Christianity. The Florentine florin became the gold standard of the time, and the city became the greatest centre of cloth production in Europe. The rise of money was therefore a slow process. It soon became the major facet of government. Florence quickly destroyed her own landed nobility and devised a democracy where the elections were safely rigged on behalf of the chief business families, and where, apart from the dictatorship of money, everyone was free and equal. In this and many other respects Florence was the birthplace of the modern world. Lorenzo de' Medici never had an official position in the city, yet he was Florence's ruler, some said tyrant. His grandfather Cosimo de' Medici had manipulated the taxes to ruin his enemies and elevate his friends. He had prevented certain marriages, encouraged others. Lorenzo did the same. This does not mean that the Medici governed for themselves, any more than hereditary princes or elected politicians did. They simply did the ruling by financial means. Their system, and the fact that Florence on the whole welcomed it and thrived on it, meant that money had become synonymous with power. This was what made Florence the modern city *par excellence*. The recognition of that equation was slower in other places, but it came in the end. And in the meantime everyone in Europe was after Medici loans.

Where other parts of Europe flourished commercially (for example, in Flanders with her cloth industry) the capital funds nearly always derived from Italy. Social change was quicker in Italy than elsewhere. Nearly every Italian city had its tyrant who assassinated his enemies and bribed his friends while blandly patronising the arts. The Sforza of Milan owed their duchy to their peasant grandfather who had tossed his mattock in the air to decide whether he should join a passing troop of mercenaries. Sixtus IV, pope from 1471 until 1484, financed nephews who were either the sons of a shoemaker or the bastards of a friar (even they did not know which). One of these, Pietro Riario, a Carmelite friar, put the Curia on a level with the other courts of Europe not only in the matter of luxury but in genuine taste too. He spent over 200,000 ducats in the first two years of his cardinalate. His excesses so wore him out that he died at the age of twenty-eight. People said that had he lived he would have drained all Europe of its funds, by creating benefices for his relatives and friends. He was welcomed like a prince in Venice, Florence, Milan. His brother Girolamo, formerly a grocer's assistant (some say a customs clerk), took over from him and came to a violent end under the daggers of four of his own officers, after a lifetime of intrigue and aggression. Lorenzo de' Medici may have been behind his murder. Thus building projects, patronage, luxury and learning were all mixed up with plots and warfare. The latter paid for the former.

The Rome we see today was the work of the Renaissance popes— men like Nicholas V, who became pope in 1447. As a scholar he had been favoured by Cosimo de' Medici and given the San Marco library in Florence—800 volumes of Greek, Roman and Oriental texts collected by Niccolò Niccoli—to catalogue. As pope he not only rebuilt the Vatican and Castel Sant'Angelo (though he did

tear down half the Colosseum to do it), but rescued numberless
manuscripts from decay in monasteries. He founded the Vatican
library with about 5,000 of them, apart from saving what was left
of the papal library, shrunk by the journeys of former popes to and
from Avignon in the previous century. Pius II too was an ardent
humanist. 'Where letters die,' he once said, 'darkness covers the
land.' Julius II (pope from 1505 to 1513) commissioned Michelangelo
to paint the Sistine ceiling.

But Florence remained the centre of enterprise. The Medici were
bankers, rulers, patrons in one. Their political and their artistic
power was squarely built on the banking business started by
Giovanni, who died in 1429. His capital flowed to Venice, London,
Barcelona, Geneva, Bruges. But this was not a pure money-activity
—'finance' as it became known in the nineteenth century. It was a
total enterprise of investment which more and more, through
Giovanni di Averardo's son Cosimo, became government itself,
involving the arts as naturally as mercenary captains. Medici banks
looked for Greek manuscripts, bought French tapestries. They
recruited boys for the pope's choir.

Cosimo de' Medici used business agents, missionaries, preachers
and travelling friends to hunt down ancient manuscripts in every
part of Asia and Europe. Since eastern Christendom was falling to
pieces at this time under Turkish attack, and many Greek scholars
were coming to Florence as refugees, Cosimo could lay his hands on
Hebrew, Greek, Chaldaic, Arabic and Indian writings in great
quantity. These became the basis of the famous Medici-Laurentian
library in Florence. The platonic academy he started under Marsilio
Ficino was the first academy in Europe to depart from the accepted
methods of reasoning inherited from the mediaeval schoolmen.
'There is no employment to which I so ardently devote myself as to
find out the true road to happiness,' he once wrote to Ficino from
his estate at Careggi.

When printing, a German invention, was first heard of in Italy
around the 1460s it caught like a fire, and almost every town in the
peninsula had its printing press before the end of the 1470s. The
typeface developed in the Campagna near Rome was henceforth

called 'Roman' (as opposed to the German 'Gothic'), and that developed by Aldo Manutio, said by some to be based on Petrarch's handwriting, was called 'Italian' or 'Italic'. All this was not for the sake of publishing, much less selling, books, but to make sound editions of the ancient authors generally available, because they were thought to make a new life possible. Cosimo de' Medici once said that he went to his Careggi estate not to improve his fields but himself, in discussions with his friends. The best vehicle for this self-improvement was 'our favourite Plato's *De Summo Bono*', which he also called 'the Orphean lyre'. Rich men everywhere in Italy were thinking along the same lines, and spending fortunes on ancient scholarship not as a reclusive activity but as a means to a new civilisation.

No prince was long away from the company of writers whom he supported and encouraged. This was true of Alphonso of Naples as it was of Filippo Maria Visconti of Milan, perfidious and cruel though both of them could be. Princes longed to be immortalised in writing, and felt privileged in the company of men who spoke impeccable Latin and knew the Greek authors. The ambassadors of the day were learned men. Politics and learning were closer perhaps than they had been since the Greek city-state, which was so much the model for the Renaissance thinker. Gian Galeazzo Visconti once said that he feared a Latin despatch from Salutati (Florence's chancellor and a famous scholar) more than a thousand Florentine troopers.

The Medici family found its way not only to running Florence but the Church as well. Four Medici were popes after 1513. Money had clearly begun to assume an importance of its own, apart from the social (and increasingly the moral) standing of its owner. Aristocracies, churches, emperors fell on their knees before it. If you originated a successful business there was no limit—unless it was your own intelligence—to the power you could achieve. Such a thing could never have been said in the Middle Ages. That static world, closed to the seas, its ports in decay, a world turned in on itself for fear of Arab attacks from the Mediterranean and Norman attacks from the North Sea, was finished. The rules of the 'just price' and 'no bargaining', the old exclusion of 'foreigners' from a town's business, no longer worked. In a remarkably short time the Church had lost much of its previous function; it was possible for Machiavelli (a Florentine) to describe politics as something quite distinct from Church affairs and even from the human conscience. In the new society no holds were barred.

By the middle of the fifteenth century Italian capital had ceased to exercise its earlier monopoly. The new society was spreading fast, and finding its own methods. In the Low Countries, in England and France, in southern Germany (with its commercial contacts with Venice) new men of business came into being whose success depended on their powers of calculation and not on family connections or even on their standing in the local trade guild. They were distinct from the 'honest merchant' of mediaeval times. Wherever they appeared they were the natural enemies of the trade guild with its fixed prices and fixed wages, its restrictions on purchase and sale. Now even the Church itself was in a turmoil of change, since some of these new men were priests and cardinals. The fact was that no one could do without them. Charles V later secured his election as Holy Roman emperor by means of them. It was easier for a prince to borrow at the rate of anything from 10 to 50 per cent interest than to argue with an Estates-General or Cortes or parliament for revenue which it was unwilling (often unable) to give. Princes too wanted to be free. Jacques Coeur in France was one of the new men. He started with nothing and ended not only minting money for his king, Charles VII, but importing gold at tremendous profit to himself (1432). He owned 300 factories, some of them in England. He had houses in Montpelier, Paris, Tours. He became one of the king's closest councillors. There was too the Fugger family, based in Augsburg, with its silver mines in Austria, Bohemia, Hungary, and its many banks (the most important in Antwerp). It was they who financed Charles V in his imperial election, and in a good many of his wars. In the Low Countries the Laurin family profited immensely from their loans in high places, and their palace at Malines was extravagant enough for Margaret of Austria to buy it when she had become governess of the Netherlands. Jerome Laurin too had risen from nothing.

But, as in Italy, the commercial activity went hand in hand with the patronage of art, the embellishment of towns and the discussion of new principles of government; with shows of luxury and refinement and the production of printed books for the first time. Erasmus was born, an illegitimate child, at Gouda not many miles from the great commercial cities of Bruges, Antwerp and Brussels. The Low Countries or Netherlands were at this time in the hands of the dukes of Burgundy, patrons of the arts on the Florentine level. The Burgundian court was perhaps the most brilliant north of the Alps. It was greatly favoured by the shift of trade from Venice to the Atlantic seaboard which followed the discovery of the Pacific and the Americas between 1419 and 1502. Venice's port fell into slow decay, after being the trade and money link between Europe and the Levant for centuries. The Mediterranean was quickly eclipsed as the centre of Christian civilisation. The Portuguese and the Spanish began to buy their spices direct from the East, and at lower prices than those which had come to Europe in Venetian and Genoese bottoms. The port which profited most from all this was Antwerp. And if any one country wrecked both Charles V's and Philip II's plans to dominate Europe later in the sixteenth century it was the Low Countries, precisely because of their new wealth and spirit of independence. Thus money destroyed money. Antwerp could not only absorb the goods brought to it from across the Atlantic but fill outgoing ships with local manufactures, an advantage that the Spanish ports, with their old-fashioned restrictions on business transacted by foreigners, lacked. In a short time Antwerp was the greatest business centre in Europe. And the Spain-Netherlands relationship developed an importance that reduced Italy to a province and a battlefield.

Spain had nothing like Italy's refined and stirring background, nor the power of France just north of her border. She was not even a state until the end of the fifteenth century. She seemed geographically destined for a poor life. Less than half of her land was

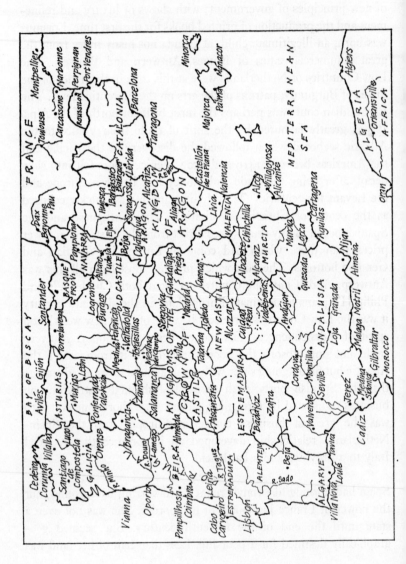

productive. One tenth was rock. There was no quick access to the north, because of the Pyrenees. Even communications inside Spain were difficult because of the high mountains that cut it down the middle, from the Pyrenees to the southern coast. Even her religion was not agreed, which meant a source of continual civil war.

Yet the energy was clearly there. In the fourteenth century Catalonia had had an overseas empire stretching as far as Greece. In Valencia there was a prosperous Moorish population. Castilian wool commanded an increasing market north of the Pyrenees. But the inner divisions kept Spain weak. There were five kingdoms— Aragón (later to include Valencia and Catalonia), Navarre, Castile, Portugal and Granada. The last was a wholly Moorish kingdom. Only a miracle, it would seem, could hold all these together. Yet the miracle happened.

It began with Ferdinand of Aragón's marriage to Isabella of Castile in Valladolid on 19 October 1469. Castile was by far the biggest state—two-thirds of all Spain. And it had over 70 per cent of the land's population. There were about 11,500,000 people in Spain at this time. In uniting the two kingdoms Ferdinand and Isabella created a new nation of nearly 10,000,000 people. The marriage contract, which was secret and based on a faked document of dispensation from the pope, made a single state of Spain possible for the first time. By the end of the fifteenth century Machiavelli was describing Ferdinand as 'the greatest king in Christendom', who had raised himself from 'a weak and poor prince'.

It was not done easily. Nor was the marriage itself an act of unification. Ferdinand, heir to Aragón's crown and already king of Sicily, was barely seventeen at the time, and Isabella only a year older. Neither was yet a reigning prince. Isabella's brother, Henry IV, still governed Castile, and was furious about her running away. As for Ferdinand, his father John II was still on Aragón's throne.

It was even a wonder that either of the young people was an heir at all. Ferdinand was John's second son. His Castilian mother (John's second wife) had carefully built up his prestige at court until his half-brother Charles, a much older man and of course the true heir, was more or less ostracised. In 1460 John had imprisoned Charles, and

2

proclaimed Ferdinand his heir, but there were such storms of protest outside the court that he had been obliged to release the prince
quickly. He then chose surer methods. The following year Charles
died in sound health at the age of forty. Everyone supposed he had
been poisoned.

Isabella too had profited from a murder in the family. At least, it
had been thought a murder. Another hale and hearty heir, this time
a child of fourteen, had died for no apparent reason. This was
Alfonso, her brother, found dead in bed in 1468 while her elder
brother Henry IV ('the impotent') was still on the Castilian throne.
Henry had got himself his unofficial title by failing to bring his first
wife, Juana of Portugal, to bed during the first six years of their
marriage. When a daughter was finally born to her in 1462 most
courtiers attributed it to the king's favourite, Beltrán de la Cueva.
The little girl, always known as 'Juana la Beltraneja', became the
focal point of a rebellion against Henry. His reckless incompetence
had been demonstrated again and again. Crime went unpunished
everywhere. The two noble factions, one for la Beltraneja and the
other for Isabella, virtually controlled the country. In the end Henry
acknowledged Isabella, after some lengthy negotiation. But that she
actually got the throne—and a husband of her own political choosing
—was due to her marvellous powers of persuasion and diplomacy.
These she inherited from her mother, Isabella of Portugal, who
brought the most powerful and enlightened people at court over to
her side.

It was a planned marriage with the humanistic idea of a united
Spain behind it. Cardinal Margarit, chancellor to John II of
Aragón, was one of several humanists round the king, while at the
Castilian court the archbishop of Toledo (who escorted Isabella to
Valladolid and incidentally faked the papal dispensation) did all he
could to advance the same views about a revival of the ancient
Roman concept of 'Hispania'.

The two kingdoms, Aragón and Castile, were formidably different
from each other. The Aragonese disliked the Castilians intensely,
despite the fact that Aragón's royal house had been Castilian since
1412 and both sides referred to themselves (though admittedly only

when abroad) as Spaniards. Castile's vast land holdings were in the hands of a few rich families like the Mendoza, the Enriquez, the de Toledos, the Guzmàn, the Valescoes. The soil was fit at best for grazing. But this was precisely Castile's advantage; it could turn endless miles of treeless waste over to sheep-grazing without much expense. A wool industry had grown up in the Middle Ages that had turned the towns of northern Castile into well-to-do commercial centres. By the beginning of the fourteenth century merino sheep had been introduced into Andalusia from Africa, and had made it possible for Castile to satisfy an increased European demand.

The Castilian felt a great contempt for commerce—and therefore for Aragón. In fact he despised most forms of activity except war. He was a knight, whatever class he came from. It was in Castile that the image of the Spanish infantryman as arrogant, brave and heartless came into being. United Spain, the Spain of the biggest empire ever seen, was a thoroughly Castilian affair.

This pride was due in great part to the so-called war of 'reconquest' which had gone on intermittently for three or four centuries against the Moors in southern Spain. Among all the invasions of Spain that had taken place the Arab or Moorish was perhaps the most successful. It had brought civilisation to the peninsula. In ancient times the Phoenicians, the Greeks and the Celts, the Carthaginians and the Romans had all invaded Spain, but none of them with such decisive results for the country's development. In the fifth century after Christ, barbarian tribes had poured into every part of the Roman Empire. Spain had been occupied by Vandals, Alans, Visigoths. When the Arabs landed on the southern coast of Spain in the year 711 they drove the now Christianised Visigoths far north into the Asturian mountains, where they remained during the subsequent four centuries of Arab rule.

Gradually the Visigoths managed, in battle after battle along their borders, to win for themselves a fairly large state—Asturias, Galicia, northern Portugal and León. It was the eastern part of León that became Castile, and the fiercest zone for Arab-Christian encounters.

It was natural therefore that Castilians should grow up thinking of life in terms of war, and of themselves as holy knights against the 'infidel'. Other independent states sprang up in the east—Catalonia, Navarre, Aragón. In 1085 the Christians captured Toledo (the pre-Arab Visigoth capital). But ten years later they were beaten back with heavy losses when they tried to penetrate further south. This defeat stung not only Spaniards but all of Christendom to a new interest in driving out the Arabs. The 'crusade', namely a war for Christ, started then. After a long southward march across the cold heights of the Sierrra Morena, in Andalusia, the Christians engaged with the Arabs and beat them at Las Navas de Tolosa (1212). That was the beginning of the Arab collapse in Spain. The Castilians took Córdoba twenty-four years later. In 1248 they took Seville. Granada was the last remaining Arab state.

This 'reconquest' was given a new emphasis during the reign of Ferdinand and Isabella. Much had already been made of it by the Church. When the Castilian priest preached holy war he knew that he had every class, however they might hate each other, behind him. And he had advocated it so passionately in the past that the Castilian soldier now tended to find holy war wherever he was, even when he was cutting another Spaniard's throat. It seemed to make little difference to him whether his enemy was a Netherlander, a Mexican Indian, a Muslim, a Christian heretic or simply someone he disliked. The fight was still a holy one. For the Cross and profit (namely land-grabbing) were early identified in Castilian history.

But by this time the 'reconquest' had lost much of its glory. It amounted to little more than skirmishes. Moors and Christians had intermingled and intermarried. The jealousies between one Christian and another were if anything greater than those felt towards the Arabs. Separate pacts against a Christian neighbour were often made. Christians and Arabs fought side by side. Arab customs were adopted freely. Spaniards wore long flowing robes and sat on the floor. They kept their women sequestered like the Arabs. A *duenna* or elderly chaperon guarded the women of a household much as if they formed a harem. The Castilian soldier took foreign women as concubines. Castilian kings kept harems unashamedly.

Now the 'reconquest' was useful again. It helped to create a new state by unifying the people. It helped to define the Spaniard. Under

Ferdinand and Isabella the first doctrine of 'pure blood' was put forward.

There was no better place for the launching of this racial war than Castile. The nobles were proud and rich and itching for battle. After their victories over the Arabs during the thirteenth century in southern Spain, new pastures had become available for Castilian sheep, which migrated there in the winter and returned north in the summer. Wool output had increased enormously. By the fifteenth century the nobility was so rich that it acknowledged no government but its own. Each estate administered its own often eccentric justice. As to the middle classes, they were docile enough, at least before Ferdinand and Isabella used their grievances. The Castilian kings were little more than puppets in the hands of the leading families. Lawless gangs pillaged and murdered in the Castilian hills. The retaliations of the landlords were swift and ruthless. But a certain amount of chaos was in their interests. Their private armies were the only effective police force.

Castile remained in a mediaeval state of mind long after the rest of Europe found it ridiculous. If during the later Reformation struggles there was hardly a pope whose heart did not warm at the thought of Spanish fidelity (however much he might fear Spanish arrogance) it was because Castile was the home of the passionately orthodox catholic. The air of Castile itself, shimmering with heat, seemed to talk about God. The mediaeval doctrine of renunciation seemed the soundest sense in its dry wastes, even in the sixteenth century. The Castilian was always ready for displays of fanaticism, again much like the Arab. Perhaps he had learned a certain extremism from close contact with the Muslim world. He starved his enemies as the Arabs did, he put them to the sword and burned their crops and houses. The idea of 'holy murder' may well have entered Christianity this way.

Castilian zeal was a terrible force, once released into the modern age. The persecutions of Jews and Arabs under Ferdinand and Isabella were its fruits. So were the persecutions of Christian heretics nearly a century later under Philip II, not to mention his military repression of the protestant Netherlands.

Aragón presented a very different picture, though not a more hopeful one from either Ferdinand's or Isabella's point of view. The Aragonese too had penetrated south in the reconquest, but with very different consequences for the Aragonese character. While Castile had absorbed Andalusia in the south, Aragón, together with Catalonia (which had been joined to it constitutionally in 1137), had absorbed Valencia with its eastern seaboard and the Balearic islands. While Ferdinand III of Castile had distributed vast holdings of Moorish land to his nobles and to the Church, the king of Aragón had made smaller divisions and left the Moorish population more or less intact. Most of Spain's eastern seaboard was in Aragón's hands, which naturally produced an interest in mercantile life and overseas possessions. The Catalan empire had included Sardinia and Sicily. Catalan ships, plying from Barcelona, were still doing business in the liveliest ports of the Mediterranean. It meant that the kingdom was dominated by a business class and not by land-magnates, and that Aragonese politics and psychology were worlds away from the Castilian, and that much closer to the rest of Europe. The Aragonese Cortes or parliament, with its division into four chambers representing the governing classes (one of them the Church), managed to keep its relationship with the crown rather like a business one. And the so-called office of the *Justicia*, unique in Spain, existed to prevent any abuse of power by either the crown or the barons. In Catalonia the *Diputacio*, a standing committee of the Cortes, fulfilled much the same function, though its origin was strictly a financial one. Even Sardinia and Sicily had their parliaments. There was thus a far more equal distribution of power in the Aragonese states than in Castile, and far less chance of friction between the king and the people, or of social chaos.

At first sight nothing could have been better than the unification of two kingdoms of such disparate character. But a Portuguese-Castilian union would have been better, in that it would have joined two strong lands. For Catalonia by the fifteenth century was not the Catalonia which had run a mediaeval empire. It was, in fact, an all but broken state, bankrupt and unenterprising. It had lost much of its trade to the Genoese, who had settled in the southern ports of Spain and scooped up the Castilian wool trade during its period of expansion. Also the Genoese had wrested the control of the Eastern spice trade out of Catalan hands, as well as that in corn. Several of the Barcelona banks crashed towards the end of the fourteenth century, and Catalan financiers had ceased to count at the Aragonese court, compared with Italian ones. The basic fact about Catalonia was its small population—in its heyday no more than half a million people. The Black Death between 1347 and 1351 (and then further waves of plague until the end of the century) had reduced the population to less than 300,000. There was a resultant shortage of manpower. Higher prices, and the fact that the peasants felt themselves to be in a strong labour-position, produced troubles with the feudal-minded lords, who wanted, because of the higher prices, greater dues than before. Riots started—really riots against mediaeval life. And the situation was not helped by the fact that the Castilian king of Aragón, Alfonso V, decided to take up residence in Naples, when that port was given to him in 1443. By a decree of his in 1455 the peasants (a third of the population) got the freedom they were after, though the Cortes forced him to suspend it two years later. He died in 1458 and was succeeded by John II, Ferdinand's father. He too favoured the peasants—and paid for his sympathy in a struggle with the nobility that amounted to a civil war and lasted a full ten years. When he died in 1479 the war was over and the crown more or less safe. But Ferdinand inherited a state exhausted by war and, compared with Castile, bankrupt. It was therefore Castile that decided Spain's future.

But the crown was equally weak in Castile. Ferdinand and Isabella had to deal with a double problem—that of uniting two kingdoms that did not want to be united, and that of giving them a king and queen they did not want either. Their strength lay in the fact that they saw the value of a united Spain, and considered it, as Italian humanists considered a united Italy, a thing of the future. Unlike the Italians, who paid for their failure to unite for another three centuries or more, they achieved their dream.

Isabella inherited the crown of Castile when her brother Henry IV died in 1474. Or rather, she declared herself queen. A court-faction had begun negotiating with Alfonso of Portugal, who hoped to marry her rival, la Beltraneja. It brought civil war to Castile. La Beltraneja was backed by Portuguese arms. Ferdinand took charge of the military campaign, with most of Castile's powerful families behind him. Powerful Jews in both Castile and Aragón were behind him too, perhaps because he himself had Jewish blood and they hoped (vainly as it turned out) that through him they would enjoy a safer future. Isabella won, mainly because of Portuguese incompetence, in 1479, one year after Ferdinand came to the throne of Aragón. Now they were free to deal with their two problems.

Chapter 2

The Holy War of Expansion

First it was necessary to harness energies that might be turned against them. They did this by the clever expedient of using the holy war. They carried it not only against the Moors in the south of Spain but against the Jews and Moors in their own midst. They even carried it against those Jews and Moors who were now Christians. And at last they carried it beyond Spain, across the seas to the Americas. The Spanish empire was simply an adjunct of this holy war.

The Castilians were less insular these days. Their wool trade now challenged England's. It brought them into contact with Genoese and Flemish merchants, and sometimes took them to the Netherlands. There was a small Castilian fleet, based on the northern ports (Laredo, Santander, Corunna, San Sebastian). It might have been predicted that one day, when their holy war in Spain was over, they would turn their attention overseas.

The crown lacked revenue after the disastrous civil war in Aragón. It needed to attach itself to a profitable enterprise, and the holy war of expansion was certainly this. Also the crown was insufficiently respected. It therefore had to attach itself to an enterprise that would be passionately convincing for every class of Castilian—and the holy war was this too.

But Ferdinand and Isabella also believed in it. That it brought them riches and perhaps the most powerful crown in Europe was simply an auxiliary proof of its rightness. An enriched crown was an enriched Church too. They had control of some important Church revenues (with the pope watching closely) and they could choose their own bishops. An increasing number of people was being drawn to their court for jobs, and a holy war enriched this side of court life by creating something like a central market of state and Church offices. Together the Church and the new middle-class interests behind the crown could help to tame the nobility, too. The result was a closer relationship between Church and sovereigns than anywhere else in Europe.

A less intelligent couple would soon have been pushed off the throne. They had to stop the great families from taking Castile's (and this now meant Spain's) affairs into their own hands. Their first step was to raze many of the noble fortresses to the ground. They prohibited duelling, a favourite system of the nobility for killing off enemies legally. The sovereigns also scooped many millions of *maravedis* into the exchequer in taxes which the nobles had until now evaded. Between 1476 and the end of the century they so arranged it that Ferdinand was elected Grand Master of three immensely rich knightly orders which had hitherto been the mainstay of the landed class. These were the orders of Santiago, Calatrava and Alcántara. The queen galloped from Valladolid through terrible weather to a convent 200 miles away when she heard that a new Master of Santiago was being elected, in 1476. She entered dripping with rain and announced that in view of the dignity of the order she thought only her husband eligible. The other two orders were brought under royal control in the same way when their Masters died in 1487 and 1499.

People still remembered how in 1464 Henry IV of Castile had had to restrain thousands of his people from leaving their farms and businesses to join a crusade against the Turks that was being advertised by the pope. This zeal had to be unleashed again—but in the hands of the crown. Castilian intolerance must be used to build a strong centralised state where before it had been the chief obstacle to it. The first campaign in the holy war was against the Jews.

Until the fourteenth century Castile and Aragón had been more tolerant of the Jews than most European states. Jewish wealth had been much needed. And then it would not have done to send them south into the arms of the equally energetic Moors, who already by long tradition employed Jews in their public service.

But during the terrible famines and the Black Death of the mid fourteenth century the Jews had become a useful scapegoat. The people had begun to listen to sermons against the 'infidel'. The Jews were often tax-collectors and money-lenders (they were often doctors, treasury-officials and honest merchants too). Resentment, once fired, called the Jewish doctor a murderer of the Christian sick, and the Jewish merchant an extortioner.

The Jews were persecuted because they were an important rival group, just as the Arabs were persecuted because of their possible connection with the Turks abroad. Both persecutions betrayed acute nervous symptoms on the part of the Christian. The people responded at once.

Towards the end of the fourteenth century the Cortes of Castile had decreed that Jews must wear a yellow patch over their hearts. But there had been too many Jews in high places for the decree to take effect. In 1391 there had been a series of massacres. In Seville alone over 4,000 Jews had been liquidated by the Inquisition. Fearful stories about Jews were current everywhere in Europe at this time. One of the most frequent was that Jews murdered Christian children in order to drink their blood. Another was that Jewish fathers baked their children alive in ovens if they showed Christian tendencies. Not until the eighteenth century did the Church officially establish that these stories were untrue.

The result of this persecution was that many, perhaps most, of the Jews in Spain became 'New' Christians or *marranos*, just as the Moors became *moriscos*. Some of them had married into powerful Castilian and Aragonese families. Thus Spanish blood became so mixed that no one—certainly no one in the aristocracy—could be sure that he was without a Jewish or Moorish strain. It added to the nervous awareness of there being some stain in the body politic. The Toledo riots of 1449 were worse than any before, and a decree of 'pure race' (*limpieza de sangre*) was passed in that city, barring anyone of Jewish blood from local office.

The 'new' Christians were never wholly trusted. It was said that they had changed religion for social convenience. The old resentment remained. And above all (this was perhaps the key to the later tragedy) the *marranos* themselves, especially those in high places, were so anxious to prove themselves 100-per-cent Christians that they denounced those of their own kind who appeared to lack zeal. It is even said that the converted Jews at Valladolid were the ones who persuaded Ferdinand and Isabella to use the Inquisition against their own race. Ferdinand, being himself part Jewish, responded to this with 'New Christian' zeal.

The *marranos* of Castile had settled down less well than the converted in other provinces. Many of them 'lapsed' into their old faith. Or rather, they seemed to lapse—which for the Castilian was the same. Surrounded by an unusually zealous and mystically inclined people, the Castilian Jews naturally felt themselves to be under close surveillance: some rebelled; others, trying to conform, behaved suspiciously. Those in high office were much resented by the nobility for daring to regard themselves as equals. Their wealth aroused increasing jealousy.

In 1478 Ferdinand and Isabella, hitherto tolerant of the Jews (one of Ferdinand's treasurers, Abraham Senior, had remained a Jew), asked the pope for a Bull which would give them control of a supreme holy tribunal or inquisition (meaning 'inquiry'). This was granted. The famous Thomas de Torquemada was made director-general of this body, with four subsidiary tribunals under him. He had absolute sole discretion (in consultation with the monarchs alone) over the choice of inquisitors or 'inquirers'.

It was an unpopular move. The clergy liked it as little as the ordinary people. When an 'inquiry' descended on a house it became usual for neighbours to keep their mouths shut. Ferdinand had to issue a decree obliging magistrates, none of them very keen on justice being dispensed by the Church, to co-operate with the inquisitors when required. In Seville, where the new powers were applied first, hundreds of *marranos* were rounded up and tried as lapsed Christians. The first *auto da fé* was held in Seville on 6 February 1481, and six Jewish 'heretics' were burned at the stake. By the end of the year over 298 others had been burned.

People were advised to inform on the 'lapsed'. A lapse was judged to be any sign of departure from Spanish norms of eating, blessing, slaughtering, mourning or dressing. The tribunal of the Inquisition published a list of the things a citizen should watch out for in his neighbour. If a neighbour dressed well on Saturdays instead of Sundays, if he cut the fat away from his pork, it could be that he had fallen back into Judaism. Even a man who turned his face to the wall when about to die could be condemned posthumously. The burnings became so frequent that special stone platforms were set up on the outskirts of Seville.

Naturally 'old' Christians were kept in a state of fright by all this no less than the 'new' ones. The charge of heretic could fall on anyone if his outward behaviour fell short of the norm. The rich were burned equally with the poor. The monarchs had found a way (not perhaps very much to their taste) of terrorising Spain into unity.

Of the 200,000 Jews said to be in Spain about 150,000 lived in Castile. It explains Ferdinand's success. The middle classes began to feel that he was their only protection against a Jewish *coup d'état*. But persecuting Jews was bad for business. Jewish financiers had been behind the 'reconquest', just as they were later behind Christopher Columbus's voyages across the Atlantic. Converted Jews had also played a great part in the spread of humanist learning, precisely as the Arabs had created a glittering civilisation in the towns of southern Spain. In the early Middle Ages Jews, Arabs and Christians had lived together harmoniously, had worked together on legal and scientific manuscripts. It had produced one of the most pleasant societies in Europe. Moorish Spain too had been expansively tolerant of other faiths, apart from a brief outbreak of Muslim fanaticism in the twelfth century. Toledo became a centre of translation visited by scholars from every part of Europe, and without the Arab translations of the neo-platonists of Alexandria there could have been no Renaissance. Arabic manuscripts had been rendered into Latin, and through them Aristotle, Euclid and Hippocrates had become known to the Christian world, together with the highly advanced Arab studies in medicine, astronomy and mathematics. The Renaissance therefore had its roots in the eleventh century. The first Christian victories against the Arabs of Spain stimulated the Christian world to a new interest in the ancient world; it had found the living link it needed.

The eviction of Jews and Moors turned Spain into the most bigoted place in Europe. It seemed to happen accidentally. The process of eviction, once started, gathered its own blind force. Men outside Spain began to see its usefulness. When Isabella complained to the pope that the measures against the Jews urged on her by Alfonso de Hojeda, prior of the Dominican monastery of St. Paul's at Seville, and by Thomas de Torquemada, were causing unjustifiable suffering, he replied that it was necessary for the security of Christendom. This same Sixtus IV died in 1484 of a fit of rage, when peace terms were announced to him ending his war with Naples. It was said of him that since he had lived by war he must needs die by peace.

Intolerance was in the air, and Ferdinand and Isabella were swept up in this by virtue of their Christian zeal. Everyone wanted to make the world safe for Christianity, even if it meant fighting other Christians; few seemed to see that the only place to make Christianity safe was inside, 'in the mild and milky soul'.

An act of violence helped Ferdinand carry the Inquisition into his own Aragón. The Aragonese Cortes, not understanding his political motive, had already tried to explain to him that an Inquisition was unnecessary because there was neither unrest nor heresy to speak of. He needed a scapegoat and this was provided in 1487 when an inquisitor called Pedro de Arlués was murdered in Saragossa Cathedral 'by two Jews'. At the discovery of the murder thousands of people fled the city for fear of reprisals. One of them, son of the queen of Navarre and nephew of King Ferdinand himself, arrived in Tudela and asked his friend Don Jaime for asylum. Don Jaime provided it. But someone found out and Jaime was tried for harbouring a 'new' Christian. He was flogged round the cathedral at Saragossa several times in front of a great crowd. The Inquisition moved into Barcelona.

Extending the Inquisition to Aragón helped define the Spaniard as a 100-per-cent orthodox catholic. Yet Ferdinand and Isabella were far from coldly calculating its effects. They were mortally afraid, like most of the people round them. The fear bordered on panic at times. Its cause was Islam. The Turkish advance into the heart of Christendom had begun with the conquest of Gallipoli in 1354. In 1396 a large

Christian army, drawn from every part of Europe, had been defeated by Sultan Bajezid I at Nicopolis on the Danube. His prisoners had included the duke of Burgundy's son and the Marshal of France, together with two sons of the French king. The news had staggered the Christian world. The first survivors of that battle to arrive in France were flung into prison for telling a palpably impossible tale. Thirty-four years later Varna on the Black Sea fell. Then Serbia was taken. In 1453 Constantinople surrendered, followed by Athens, the Aegean islands and Bosnia. Little wonder that Turks occupied the minds of kings and peoples alike. By the 1470s Turkish fleets commanded the Black Sea and the northern Aegean. In 1480 they even got a foothold in Italy, at Otrantro. In a country like Spain, where non-Christians freely walked the streets, suspicion and unease lay heavy on the air. Suppose there were a second invasion of Spain?

So the next step was the eviction of the Arabs. The attack against Granada began in 1482, three years after Ferdinand had become king of Aragón. Granada was the last Moorish redoubt. It had lasted until now only because of the quarrels that had divided Castile from Aragón and both from Portugal during the fourteenth and much of the fifteenth centuries. The Moors had profited from these divisions and even found occasion to stimulate them. It had made up for their relative weakness.

Now there were divisions on the Moorish side. 1482 seemed a good year for a last mopping-up operation. It was actually Granada's king, Mulay Hassan, who started the war. All his life he had dreamed of dominating the Iberian peninsula. Six years before he had refused to pay Ferdinand and Isabella his annual tribute. The previous year he had attacked a Christian post at Zahara on the Andalusian border. He had killed the soldiers and carried the women and children off to slavery. And now the Moors were in a state of civil war. Mulay Hassan was old and two of his princes, Yusuf and Boabdil, were in rebellion against him. Prince Boabdil had already declared himself king of Quadix, thirty miles from Granada. It was not long before Granada too recognised his authority, and the old king had to leave the city.

Ferdinand began bribing Boabdil, and even succeeded in giving him the impression that he was going to fight for him against his old father. As the Spanish army moved south in a series of planned battles and sieges a special terrorist army of 30,000 men scorched the earth and ruined the farmhouses. When Ferdinand captured Málaga after a bitter three-month siege he took the whole population into slavery. He hoped in this way to terrorise the rest of the Granada population into submission. In a few weeks he had defeated Boabdil's father. He now turned to the city of Granada. Boabdil had promised to open it to his troops in exchange for being recognised as its king. But he now saw the game Ferdinand was playing and decided to go back on his word. He fortified the city. After a siege Ferdinand took it with an army of 50,000 men, in January 1492. The earth all round was scorched. Some unintended scorching took place when the entire Spanish encampment caught fire; a candle in Isabella's tent was said to have caused it. A new city was built in its place, in the form of a gridiron. It was named Santa Fé or 'the holy faith'.

In contrast to his savage treatment of the Malagans, Ferdinand made no immediate attempt to Christianise the Moors of Granada or even to oversee their system of justice. His agreements with Boabdil even guaranteed freedom of worship. A strip of the southern coast was given to the Moorish king in compensation for Granada. No Christians who had married Moors were to be molested, even if they had also embraced Islam. Nor were their children. All this was secured by secret negotiation between Ferdinand and Boabdil before the siege ended. It was a cheap victory for Ferdinand. All he had to do now was dishonour the agreements.

He and his queen entered Granada with the greatest pomp. Four days earlier a silver cross had been placed on the highest tower of the stupendous Alhambra palace and crowds had screamed '*Castile! Castile!*' at the sight of it. The king and queen took up residence in the palace and held their first audience in the magnificent throne-room.

The first archbishop of Granada—at one time he had been Isabella's confessor—was Hernando de Talavera, by general recognition a mild and lovable man. He admired the Arab civilisation which had just been destroyed, and later succeeded in bringing over a great many Muslims to the new regime. He disagreed with forcible conversion and even asked his clergy to learn Arabic. The result was that the Moors trusted him, an important fact in the later rioting.

Things might even now have gone smoothly, the Moorish state might have become a Christian state, with fascinating results for the Church in Spain, had it not been for the daily pressure of the other Castilian bishops, chief among them Francisco Jiménez de Cisneros or 'Ximenes' as the history-books have called him. Greed played a large part in the pressure. Prominent Castilians were itching to lay their hands on Moorish land just conquered. Ferdinand's decree that no Castilian should grab more than 200,000 maravedis' worth of new property (about 10,000 dollars' worth today) was evaded by the men on the spot. The list of new landowners that went to the king and queen, with the size of their holdings, was a false one. The greater part of the new province fell out of the crown's hands in this way, and the powerful Mendoza family, with the Córdobas, were the chief beneficiaries.

Cardinal Ximenes, made archbishop of Toledo in 1495, was the centre of an increasingly aggressive group. He had not always advocated violence. He too had started as Isabella's confessor, but unwillingly: court life had never appealed to him, and he had left his Franciscan monastery with reluctance. But in Isabella he found an astute political intelligence which he felt the country (meaning the Church as well) needed. As archbishop he had begun a series of Church reforms on humanistic lines. He was the chief influence behind Isabella when she invited foreign scholars to Castile and endowed new universities and chairs in Hebrew and Greek. Like her he believed that the quality of Spain's priesthood could improve only if ordinands understood more about the textual sources of their faith. He was responsible for inviting the famous scholar Elio Antonio de Hebrija first to Salamanca University and then to his own university of Alcalá. Hebrija had been educated in Italy. Ximenes also advocated the polyglot bible.

But he came to see the Inquisition as the Christian's only defence against Islam. He argued that the defence-towers built by Ferdinand along the Andalusian coast were not enough. And he feared an armed rising in the bandit-infested Alpujarras mountains, between Granada and the sea.

The priests of Granada failed to learn Arabic. They even showed little desire to convert. They began to support Ximenes rather than Talavera. The middle classes favoured a strong central authority which would give them safe roads and a stable economy, and this too tended to strengthen the aggressive camp. More than the landed nobility, who had found the industrious Moors useful on their estates, the new commercial classes saw all Semitic Spaniards as their business rivals. There was also the naive idea that all you had to do to get rich was to scooop up Jewish and Arab businesses, whether you had their acumen and energy or not.

Talavera's Arabic bible was never printed. Ximenes made sure of that. Since Talavera spent less time at court than his enemies it was easy to work up feeling against him. The aggressive faction got its way in March 1492 in a decree of total banishment for the Jews. This was three months after Ferdinand and Isabella had signed their treaty with the Moors. An old wives' tale was circulated that a gang of Jews had stolen a consecrated Host with the idea of turning it into paste with the hot blood of a newly murdered Christian child. It produced a wave of popular panic, and Christian parents ceased to feel safe in their beds.

The Jews were forbidden to take gold or silver or cash with them. Their leader Rabbi Abarbanal begged Ferdinand on his knees in the Alhambra Palace to strip his people of all they possessed provided he left them their homes. The monarchs dared not show pity at this stage. The prevailing notion was that too much lenience had been shown towards the non-Christian. The time had come for action. Torquemada (who never travelled without a bodyguard of at least fifty men) would have done the job his own way, had he been allowed to. Which would have made banishment seem merciful.

Simultaneously with this decree preachers were sent out among the Jews to convert as many of them as possible. It could not be called a campaign of forcible conversion, but it was certainly a campaign of blackmail. Christians were forbidden to have any further contact with Jews. Jewish property was put up for sale, and since the owners were on the run it went for a song.

The richer Jews financed the exodus. They helped the poor among them not to be tempted to Christianity. The long procession left Spain singing. Their ships sailed to Africa, Italy, the Levant. Many Jews died from a plague that flared up in the ships. Others were sold as slaves. Some were murdered when they disembarked. Twenty thousand Neapolitans died from the plague brought to their shores in this way.

Ferdinand and Isabella meanwhile redistributed Jewish land among Castilians as they had done Arab land not long before. Their next move was to get rid of the last Moors. Of course the treaty stood in their way but there was no such thing as a crime of dishonour if it was done in the name of the Cross. The Moorish king's estates were sold from under his feet, and the money—80,000 ducats—was presented to him with a hint that he would be happier out of Spain. This was the first stage of total banishment. But Arabs were more dangerous than Jews. They were more likely to leave fighting than singing.

The long-feared revolt in the Alpujarras came in 1499. The forced conversions advocated by Ximenes had done a lot to provoke it. Rather than give the Arabs the Gospels in their own language he had offered them strong social incentives for becoming Christian. And this seemed intelligent enough in the light of the fact that not even 'old' Christians considered the scriptures their natural property. The new learning was doing much to break this down, but the idea of laying the scriptures before the 'infidel' before they were known to the Christian remained unthinkable. Three thousand Moors were brought to Ximenes in Granada for baptism. A mosque was consecrated as a Christian church. An Arab prince called Zegri did his best to stand firm against this unsavoury mass display but at Ximenes' order he was arrested and placed in a cell with the kind of monk who knew how to combine mystical argument with naked threat—a Jesuit in the bud. Within a few days Zegri too was baptised. About 50,000 more Arabs became *moriscos* in the following months. Ximenes had the Koran publicly burned. He ordered the arrest of 'lapsed' Christians in their hundreds, and the prisons were overcrowded.

But there were still many Muslims left. When the Alpujarras revolt burst on Granada Ximenes found himself besieged in the Alhambra Palace (Ferdinand and Isabella had already left for Seville). It was the mild Talavera who saved him. Indeed he saved the whole court from massacre by going out among the Moors and begging them to be peaceful. Ximenes more or less fled to Seville.

Yet the situation played into Ferdinand's hands. It gave him the excuse he needed to dispose of the entire Moorish population. He crushed the revolt in the mountains without much difficulty and offered those who surrendered the choice between conversion or banishment. This led straight to the decree of expulsion in February 1502. As for those Moors and Jews who had gone over to Christianity, they were for the time being safe. But forced conversion made them rather despise the religion behind it: many of them began to feel more deeply (though more secretly) Muslim or Jewish than before. It was clear that one day the 'new' Christians would have to go too.

All this derived from an idea deep in Church history—that there was a right way of thinking which could be clearly articulated in the form of a doctrine, and that any thinking outside this, if it touched religion at all, was 'heresy' or what we today would call sectarianism. As early as the fourth century the Church had taken its first step towards making sectarianism a punishable offence when it handed over the Spanish monk Priscillian to the secular arm for the punishment of death. This became the traditional method of the Inquisition —to 'abandon' the condemned man to secular justice, since the Church could not herself shed blood. In 1233 Pope Gregory IX had created the pontifical Inquisition, distinct from the Inquisition of the bishops which had existed from the earliest days of the Church. It meant an unprecedented control of belief. Only eighteen years before this a new Spanish order of monks had come into being—the Dominicans. Their special province was the examination of heretics. They were the first pontifical inquisitors.

It is difficult nowadays to conceive the horror aroused by excommunication. Orthodox ideas were now a social necessity in the strictest sense. It was possible to laugh at excommunication for a time. The republics of Venice and Florence had both been excommunicated by an angry pope. But no one felt comfortable under the Interdict for long. You were plunged into a complete social and spiritual despair. There was no hope for you. Bit by bit all the avenues of life closed to you. You were utterly alone.

On the whole Christians were agreed that the question of whether a man was fit for divine grace rested legitimately with priests. The fact that the Church was the greatest single landlord and tithe-collector helped to support this claim. The archbishop of Toledo, primate of Spain, was considered second only to Ferdinand and Isabella in authority. The Spanish Church had an annual income of more than 6,000,000 ducats. Its clergy were exempt from royal taxes. Abbots and bishops were often landed magnates with their own private armies. The state was naturally eager to collaborate with such a centralised and yet universal authority. It was when the state became more powerful, with the commercial development of the towns, that jealousy of the Church arose, and 'protests' were heard against what seemed the Church's unjust control of the mind.

One of the reasons why no protest shook Spain was that Ferdinand and Isabella managed the middle classes so cleverly. They offered them liberty from the landed magnates. They altered the royal council, which had hitherto been the governing medium of the big families. It was now to consist of a bishop, three *caballeros* or *hidalgos* (*hijo de algo*—'the son of somebody'), representing the lowest rank of the aristocracy, together with a number of jurists. The big families had no power over this new body. Their titles remained but were increasingly empty of real power. It was the royal council that now controlled the towns, at least those towns not *villas de señorio* or 'lord-controlled' (the lord being a magnate and/or bishop). In these 'lord-controlled' towns Ferdinand and Isabella encouraged the very people they tried to silence in the 'royal' towns, namely citizens who wanted to elect and be directly governed by their own officials. 'Royal' justice gradually became the central justice of the land. It was administered by lawyers and not by private families. The *Hermandad* or ministry of justice was maintained by taxes raised in the towns, and its police forces were directed against the lawless countryside of the magnates. Clearly everyone outside the big families craved for order, particularly the growing commercial classes, and Ferdinand and Isabella used this to advantage. Also the collecting of taxes was made more efficient, which meant that the king and queen were less dependent on the purse-holding Cortes than any of their predecessors.

All this contributed to an identification of the citizen with the sovereign. And the fact that Ferdinand and Isabella controlled the Church with equal skill meant that no 'royal protest' (the basis of the protestant movement in England) was felt necessary at court. In England Henry VIII created magnates out of the Church lands he seized, far from fighting a war against them. But Ferdinand and Isabella gained proportionately as the Church gained. Under their rule the *tercias reales* (the third part of all tithes paid to the Church in Castile) became a permanent source of royal revenue by a Bull of Alexander VI in 1494. And then there was the famous *cruzada* or 'crusade tax', money received from the sale of indulgences. This had originally been granted to them by the pope for the financing of their 'reconquest' in Spain. But it continued to flow into the royal exchequer after Granada had been won and the last Moor banished. Clearly no royal protest was likely against a Church that shared its income so generously. In Germany, on the other hand, the traffic in indulgences was the main immediate cause of the Lutheran movement. The money from this traffic filtered away to Rome, not into German pockets. And Luther won the attention of the German princes precisely because, like Henry VIII in England, they were not beneficiaries of Church wealth.

Once Granada looked safe for Castile, Ferdinand and Isabella turned their attention to the next phase of the holy war—overseas. They listened seriously for the first time to the wild-sounding suggestions of a Genoese adventurer called Christopher Columbus. He knew Ferdinand's private secretary and also one of Isabella's former confessors, a Franciscan, but his first appeals through them to the monarchs five years before in 1486 had fallen on deaf ears. At that time Ferdinand and Isabella had been busy with their war in Granada. Now it was a different story. Not that Ferdinand was any keener on private adventures abroad than he had ever been. But he now saw the chance of the crown financing and therefore profiting from an expedition.

Columbus's approach was characteristically Italian. He wanted to find the Indies and then become their viceroy, with a clause in his contract that would guarantee the viceroyalty to his descendants in perpetuity. He clearly had no idea of the holy war, and Ferdinand and Isabella would have none of it. They guaranteed him no more than the hereditary title of Grand Admiral, and he could take no more than one-tenth of the merchandise. They were prepared to make rich men but not great ones. They refused the wealthy duke of Medina-Celi's offer to finance the voyage, and Columbus found himself involved in a state enterprise which was also a military one. Being Genoese he accepted the terms, but living with Castilian zeal cost him many heartaches later.

In seeing the voyage as a holy one, Ferdinand and Isabella were much nearer the tradition of overseas discoveries than he was. In the first Portuguese voyages of the early fifteenth century, when Madeira and the Cape Verde islands and the coast of Senegambia were discovered, Henry the Navigator had had only one purpose in mind, apart from burning curiosity, and that was to carry the faith to every unknown part of the globe.

Those first voyages had brought the wide, square-rigged caravels of the Portuguese fleet into being. It was in these ships that Columbus sailed with a crew of eighty-eight men on his first voyage under the Castilian flag in 1492. The Portuguese Bartolomo Diaz had reached the Cape of Good Hope some years before and had seen the Indian Ocean. Vasco da Gama had then crossed the Indian Ocean and in two years reached Calicut in southern India. Columbus's plan was to reach these Indies by crossing the Atlantic; that is, round the other side of the world. He expected to find the other coast of India. In this he had the findings of Italian geographers like Toscanelli to work on. And they were proved right at least to the extent that there was land on the other side of the Atlantic, though it was not India.

The plan appealed to Ferdinand and Isabella on mainly two counts —that the expedition would make sailors of Castilians, and that a foothold in India would make it possible to attack the Turks from the rear. The Portuguese had already, in 1482, sent an expedition to the Canaries (discovered by the Genoese a century before), which made an ideal port of call on the way over.

Ferdinand and Isabella became more completely the monarchs of the western Indies than they were of Spain itself. In this 'New' Spain as it was called their control of the Church was absolute. They alone could choose its functionaries, and no papal Bull was valid in their colonies without their permission. The pope could speak to Mexico only through them. By a Bull of 1493 Alexander VI granted them the right to evangelise the West Indies alone. Eight years later, after the American mainland had been reached (Columbus found the Orinoco and the Isthmus of Panama), he issued a further Bull allowing them to take over the tithes imposed on the Indians. Later in 1508, the year in which Haiti became a wholly Spanish possession (indeed it was the first step towards the creation of a Spanish empire), Pope Julius II gave the Spanish king the right to choose functionaries there too. No Castilian priest could go to the Indies without royal permission. There was to be no papal legate. It was clear that Spain meant to be not simply the pope's rival in terms of power but a kind of new spiritual Rome. That desire was never clearly expressed. It was simply indicated from time to time, more particularly in Philip II's reign. It became a desire to Castilianise the whole world precisely as Sardinia and Naples and Sicily, the old Aragonese possessions, were being Castilianised.

Indeed Castile became the moral leader of the holy war everywhere. This is why Pope Alexander VI gave Ferdinand and Isabella the title of 'the catholic kings' in 1494, 'catholic' meaning universal. The Indies became Castilian property, not Spanish, and Isabella made it clear that she wished only Castilians to settle the Americas. Later in 1503 a monopoly in American trade was given to the Castilian port of Seville. Whereas the Aragonese Cortes was always harping on its rights and privileges, and angered Isabella more than once, Castile sent crusaders into the world. Their country was clearly an ideal place for building an absolute monarchy. Little wonder that Philip II was to feel much more Castilian than Hapsburg.

But Ferdinand and Isabella did more than build, in Machiavelli's words, a 'strong and centralised state out of their wars'. They brought the Renaissance to Spain, and the two activities were, far from being exclusive of each other, interdependent. Their wars like their pogroms were almost forced upon them by the nature of the times. They would certainly have preferred diplomacy and compromise if they could have achieved the same ends. It was a difficult matter, taming a virtually savage land like Spain without becoming savage oneself. Isabella was a serene, devout woman who never spared herself. Ferdinand was a military and sporting man. They complemented each other well. If they shared an ideal it was to make Castile not a centre of power only but the focal point of Christian civilisation on a level with states like Burgundy. On one great occasion Isabella, usually most austere in her dress, put on a magnificent costume of green velvet with crimson brocade, and changed it during the ceremony for another of cloth of gold. It was when Ferdinand received Burgundy's Order of the Golden Fleece in 1474. Her library, in her favourite palace at Segovia, was full of the Classics, the mediaeval poets, even Boccaccio. She disliked the fiendishly cruel game of bull-fighting which was then coming into vogue, and she tried to stop it. She gave her children what she herself had missed—a complete education, especially in the new learning. She engaged two Italians for this—Antonio and Alessandro Geraldini. One of her children, Catherine, became queen of England and surrounded herself with perhaps the most refined court St. James's ever saw, attracting the greatest humanists of the time, including Erasmus.

Isabella gave the printers of Castile special tax exemptions to encourage their output, and removed duties on books imported from abroad. Chivalric poems, many of them in praise of her, began to be written in Castilian for the first time. None of this seemed to contradict the holy war or even the Inquisition. The inquisitorial burnings were fewer in Spain than in France, Germany and the

Netherlands. The Inquisition was a corrective and not mainly a punitive arm of the Church. It imposed far more penances than death penalties. Its evil was orthodoxy. That was sweeping through all Europe at the time. Again this orthodoxy, like the holy war, was no contradiction of the new learning. In fact it arose from it, being no more than an argument that the Christian faith should be clearly defined for all to see. It was of course a declared part of the humanist objective to bring the gospels to the simplest people in their terms. Church frescoes by Giotto, Simone Martini, Gozzoli—lives of St. Francis, St. Augustine, St. Martin in graphic form, with brief captions under each picture for the guidance of the explaining priest—showed this clearly. But the explaining drained the simplicity. The orthodoxy smothered the humanity. In Spain it smothered the beginnings of a great civilisation. Yet Ferdinand and Isabella were trying to create this civilisation no less than Lorenzo de' Medici in Florence. The strong state they were building was for the Cross, not an end in itself. It was in the truest sense for the rebirth of Christian feeling. Was the alternative not a Spain of savages—or infidels? The deadly contradiction involved in such an enterprise (and written into the whole of the Renaissance) brought Spain and then the whole of Europe into a state of doctrinal turmoil and war that lasted for two centuries at least. Spain's leading role in this was simply the measure of her zeal.

Ferdinand's armies had not always been able to fight, though their guerrilla activities in the Granada campaign did give them useful training. In Italy, where he sent them in 1496, they seemed ridiculous in their light armour to their Swiss and French enemies. But their commander, Gonzalo de Córdoba, a veteran of the Granada campaign, learned quickly. He had to combine speed with heavier armament. He cleared the French out of Naples in two weeks and received the pope's blessing for it. The result of the two Italian campaigns, ending in 1504, was an army equal to any in Europe.

Simultaneously Ferdinand established resident embassies, not yet a usual practice, in the important European capitals—Rome,

London, Brussels, Venice and Vienna. Their job was to win friends. He persuaded Isabella that Castile could no longer be friends with France after Louis XI had invaded Catalonia and seized two of its northern counties, Roussillon and Cerdagne, in 1463. He got these back by diplomatic means, and then made an anti-French alliance with England.

At the same time he worked hard to make friends by dynastic marriage, and to secure the right heir for the Spanish throne. He arranged the marriage of his daughter Isabella to Prince Alfonso of Portugal, but Alfonso was killed in a riding accident. Isabella was then persuaded to take a second husband, this time the king of Portugal, Emanuel. She died in childbirth but her son Miguel survived. He would have inherited both the Spanish and Portuguese thrones, thus uniting the Iberian peninsula, but he too died, in 1500.

Ferdinand's best marriage *coup* was a double marriage into the Holy Roman Empire, giving his only son and heir, the Infante Juan, to Margaret of Austria, daughter of the emperor Maximilian, and his daughter Juana (who later went mad) to the Archduke Philip, Maximilian's son, called 'the Fair' because of his fine looks. There was no issue from the first marriage, since Margaret's child was stillborn and her husband died soon after. The second marriage was fruitful. The future Charles V was born. It was not a very sound step towards the Castilianisation of the world. A Hapsburg takeover now seemed a certainty. The marriage *coup* did in fact cost Ferdinand his throne.

This son of Juana and Philip the Fair would inherit both the Hapsburg possession of Burgundy (the Netherlands) from his father, and Spain from his mother. It was too much of a Hapsburg dream come true. Neither Ferdinand nor Isabella looked forward to Spain being swallowed up in a vast agglomeration of states north of the Pyrenees. If Isabella were to die before the Hapsburg heir came of age (which happened) Castile would go to Juana, who as everyone outside Spain knew was unfit to govern.

Isabella died in 1504. This at once rendered Ferdinand the king of Aragón and no more. Her will declared that he was to rule Castile

in place of Juana but only if Juana wished to remain in the Netherlands with her Hapsburg husband. Even then Ferdinand was not to
be king of Castile, only a regent for his daughter. It was a touchy
situation. Ferdinand had not only ruled Castile but, together with
Isabella, had groomed it to greatness. Now Archduke Philip was the
rightful king. And Ferdinand had to acknowledge his title. At the
same time he had the coins of the realm stamped 'Ferdinand and
Juana', as king and queen. Philip was determined, in so far as he
was determined about anything for very long, to inherit Castile in
the proper way. He disagreed with Ferdinand's anti-French policy
too. He disliked Spain, and he had little time for his Spanish wife.
He had tried to stop her rejoining him in Flanders after a visit of
theirs to Spain in 1500. Her madness in fact dated from this period
of frantic jealousy and loneliness, although she had always been
strange. During her husband's frequent absences she would spend
hours watching the portcullis for his return. She had violent fits of
screaming jealousy and one day wounded one of her serving maids
with a pair of scissors for having, so she supposed, seduced her
husband. When he died later she followed his coffin night after
night in processions by torchlight through the grounds of her
Tordesillas palace, opening it frequently to make sure that he was
still there. These macabre proceedings went on for months. She
was finally persuaded to bury him. She then retired to her room and
paid less and less attention to the outside world, and to her own
appearance.

Her son Charles, the future king of Spain and Holy Roman
emperor, was brought up in Flanders. Now that Isabella was dead
Juana must either govern Spain or allow the throne to pass to him
on his twentieth birthday.

There were enough high-ranking Castilians who hated Ferdinand
(the Córdobas were among them) to make his life dangerous at this
point. They were prepared to get rid of him even if it meant putting
a Burgundian who spoke no Spanish in his place. And there were
strong economic arguments for uniting northern Burgundy to
Castile, the chief among them the latter's booming wool trade which
needed efficient outlets. Already a great many Flemish merchants

had settled in Seville. And more Castilian wool was traded at Antwerp than at any single Spanish port.

Ferdinand's answer was to try to produce another heir by marrying Louis XII's niece Germaine. He calculated that if his son—supposing he had a son—was refused the throne of Spain he would at least become king of Aragón and be in a position to undo all the work of unification, or at least threaten to do so in the face of a Hapsburg takeover. But Germaine's son died some hours after his birth. The effect of this new marriage was only to alienate Ferdinand further from the great Castilians round him.

The Archduke Philip decided to come to Spain. Characteristically he was shipwrecked off the English coast and had to start all over again (10 January 1506). For a time he thought of making war on Ferdinand, but the two kings met in the summer of that year at Villafáfila, where they signed two treaties. The first declared that Ferdinand must give up Castile, the second that Juana was unfit to govern. On the same day, just after signing, Ferdinand renounced both treaties (this was quite usual at the time if the treaty was felt to have been signed under moral duress) and described his daughter's 'exclusion' from the throne as preposterous. He left Castile, and no one seemed sorry.

But in September of that year Philip died unexpectedly and Juana went irretrievably mad. Their six-year-old son Charles was in the care of Sieur de Chièvres, regent of the Netherlands in Philip's absence, and it looked as if Ferdinand had got his way after all. A regency to govern Spain was set up under Cardinal Ximenes, who appealed to Ferdinand to return to Castile 'to re-establish order'. Ferdinand did return, in his own time. Charles took over the throne in his seventeenth year, when Ferdinand died. It was also the seventeenth year of the sixteenth century.

Chapter 3

The First King of Spain

The news about Charles was disappointing. According to a Venetian diplomat his eyes looked as if they had been stuck on and belonged to someone else. His mouth hung open and he had trouble masticating and digesting. He was sickly pale. He stammered. His Hapsburg jaw gave him the look of an idiot. He had little conversation. He spoke French and Flemish and some Italian, and of course Latin, but seemed to know none of them thoroughly. As to Spanish and German he spoke not a word. For a Hapsburg about to inherit the Spanish kingdoms and possibly German-speaking lands as well it seemed not to promise the best future. There was one positive sign, and one that courtiers had little time for—his reserve. He was as much the opposite of what the Spanish were looking for in a king as possible. They wanted glory. And his character promised this less than anything.

He could not have been more polyglot. He had been born in Ghent in 1500 with Spanish, French, Burgundian, Plantagenet, Flemish, Portuguese and German blood in his veins, and probably some Jewish and Arab as well. In Flanders he had been in the care of an Englishwoman, Margaret of York, who was the widowed duchess of Burgundy and his great-grandmother. His education had been in the hands of several men, Adrian of Utrecht, Robert of Ghent, a Spanish humanist called Luis Vacca and Charles de Poupet (Lord of La Chaulx). The youngsters who shared his classroom were Maximilian Sforza and John of Saxony, as his pages of honour. His personal governor and Great Chamberlain was Guillaume de Croy, Sieur de Chièvres, a knight of the Golden Fleece. Chièvres was perhaps the chief intellectual influence on his life, even his model of what a statesman should be, combining knight, diplomat and ruler. Not everyone agreed about Chièvres' qualities. Sir Richard Pace,

English envoy to the republic of Venice, described Charles as 'an idiot surrounded by a corrupt council'.

In many ways Charles missed the Renaissance as an experience, which was why becoming one of its instruments perplexed him so. He was mediaeval, and the new society he had to govern seemed to take him by surprise. He borrowed money like any other prince of the time but he still thought in terms of the old *sanitas* which made usury indefensible. He dreamed of an empire that would spread across Europe from the Atlantic to the eastern borders of Hungary, but it was the mediaeval empire that Rome had made, namely a Holy Roman Empire, a spiritual community in the strictest sense. There were always humanists in his court but he did not think of their ideas as requiring a total reorganisation of life. He knew little about theology, less about mathematics. His faith was of the simplest and most robust kind. Nowhere was his mediaeval disposition clearer than in his struggle for those parts of Burgundy which the French had taken from his great-grandfather Charles the Bold (husband of Margaret of York) in the previous century. It was the basic reason why he could not beat the Turks and 'liberate' Constantinople as he always wanted to. Burgundy was a mediaeval concern. Erasmus tried to persuade him to give up some of these 'old rights' but he never agreed. He presented his son Philip with a modern state in spite of himself.

He had rather a serene nature, with occasional outbursts of anger which he quickly forgot. Unlike his son he never bore a grudge, and forgave more easily than he condemned. He was a forthright, rugged, careless man, yet underneath there was a quiet reserve which kept people at a distance. He was brought up with his three sisters, Isabella, Mary and Eleonore. Like many people used to a lot of attention early in life he was patient, listening and biding his time, always happy when a compromise was possible. It was from him that his son Philip learned his well-nigh obsessive inclination to delay orders and decisions. For Charles dynasty was the one valid guarantee of sound government, and a prince was therefore required to weigh his decisions carefully and slowly, since in the end no one else could help him. Both he and Philip were lonely men.

Titian's portrait of Charles gives him warm, observant eyes. He looks tolerant, steady, above all detached. He was a small man. The typical thrust-forward Hapsburg chin made his face slant strangely. Cranach's portrait of him shows this to the point of caricature. His grandfather Maximilian, on the other hand, found nothing Hapsburg about him except his love of hunting. Ferdinand of Aragón openly preferred Charles's younger brother, the Archduke Ferdinand, as a possible king of Spain. He even named the archduke regent after his death—until such time as Charles himself should arrive in Spain. The young Ferdinand had after all been brought up in Spain in his parents' household. His face was known, which was half the battle for a people like the Spanish.

On Philip the Fair's death the Estates of the Holy Roman Empire had appealed to Maximilian to take over the government of the Netherlands himself. He had appointed his daughter Margaret of Austria not only regent of the Netherlands but foster-mother to Charles and his sisters. Margaret had just been widowed a second time, the duke of Savoy having died when she was twenty-four and still childless. Henry VII of England had wanted her in marriage but she had refused, probably because she saw the importance of her political role in the Netherlands. When she settled there she brought advisers from Savoy and Franche Comté. Her closest minister was Mercurino Gattinara. He had been her state lawyer in Savoy, and was to become Charles's chief political adviser. Charles and his sisters called Margaret both 'mother' and 'aunt', and always spoke French to her.

Margaret's court did all it could to discourage Ferdinand of Aragón's prejudice against Charles. In October 1515 she sent down Adrian of Utrecht, Charles's best and least arrogantly Burgundian teacher, to argue with him. The result was a settlement not many weeks before Ferdinand died in which it was agreed that Charles should enter Spain without an army and that the ships which brought his court should return at once to the Netherlands with his brother Ferdinand on board as the new governor of that country. Just before he died Ferdinand of Aragón scrapped his 1512 will and recognised his daughter Juana's right of accession to the joint

Ferdinand of Aragon

Isabella of Castille

Juan de Torquemada, Director General of the Inquisition under Ferdinand and Isabella

Castile-Aragón throne and therefore Charles's right as well. He also stipulated that the regency of Castile should be in the hands of Cardinal Ximenes, and Aragón in the hands of one of his own bastards, the archbishop of Saragossa, until such time as Charles arrived.

Castilians were on the whole horrified that a foreigner was about to govern them. It was predicted that Charles would bring ruin to their country. He would squeeze Spain dry to make the Netherlands and the Hapsburgs rich, just as his father, Philip the Fair, had tried to do in his brief and disastrous reign. And then Charles's chief minister Chièvres loved France more than he loved Spain. Was not the Spanish inheritance much less important to the Burgundians than the Hapsburg one? To the Burgundians on the other hand it looked as if the Spaniards were making a great deal of fuss about a poor and out-of-the-way country which would never be great like their own. So the Castilians were right.

Foreigners competed to influence Charles the moment his future destiny was known. In fact a court war went on round him—between the Ferdinand of Aragón faction (anti-French) and the Castilian faction (pro-French). It resulted in friendship between Ferdinand of Aragón and the emperor Maximilian, both of them anxious to reduce Chièvres' pro-French influence on the future king. Ferdinand's paid agents had punctured Chièvres' arguments wherever they could. These same agents had also served to keep Maximilian informed about the royal youth's state of mind. When Charles was thirteen the intrigues came to a head in a decision, called the *Ordonnance* of Lille, to place his education in the hands of Maximilian, Ferdinand of Aragón and Henry VIII of England, through their representatives the Count Palatine Frederick (for Maximilian), Ferdinand of Lanuza (for Ferdinand of Aragón) and Floris Egmont, Lord of Isselstein (for Henry VIII). This *ordonnance* was Margaret's first political *coup*, a victory for the anti-French, pro-English element. She hoped that it would determine Charles's marriage too. At this time it was thought that he might marry Mary, Henry VIII's sister, thus binding the Hapsburg dynasty to the Tudor, and both to the Spanish possessions. England was a useful

3

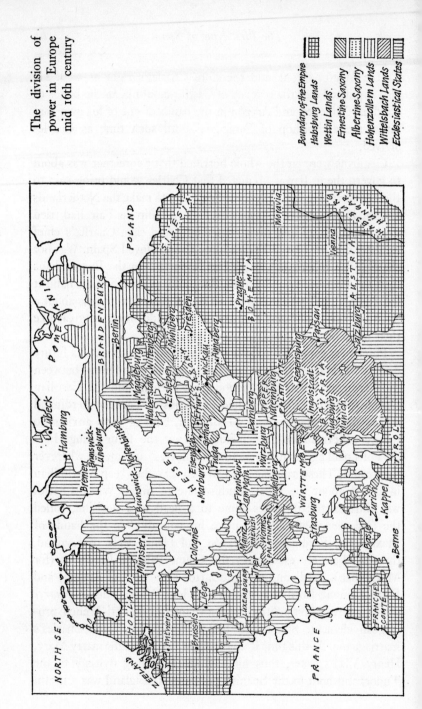

The division of power in Europe mid 16th century

Boundary of the Empire
Habsburg Lands
Wettin Lands.
Ernestine Saxony
Albertine Saxony
Hohenzollern Lands
Wittelsbach Lands
Ecclesiastical States

ally against France and a profitable trader for the Netherlands
ports. The English navy helped to keep the French off the Dutch
coast, just as it stopped the French getting a foothold in Scotland.
At first a French marriage had been planned with Claude, daughter
of Louis XII (who was also after the Spanish possessions). But then
Louis, under internal pressure, had given his daughter to the heir
to the French throne, the duke of Angoulême. So Charles was free
for an Englishwoman.

But Margaret was disappointed. Her father Maximilian was
negotiating a more useful marriage with another French or even
Hungarian heiress. The English found out about it before she did,
and Henry VIII promptly married his sister to Louis XII, whose
queen had just died. The Netherlands were bitterly disappointed,
hoping for a naval and commercial tie-up with England. The
ordonnance fell to pieces. And the Burgundian nobility, represented
by Chièvres, remained the chief influence on Charles's political
imagination.

He was declared duke of Burgundy at the age of fifteen, in a
ceremony at Brussels where he and his knights ate so much that
they had to miss Vespers. It was small wonder that he found Spain
austere later on, especially in the matter of pretty women. In Spain
you did not miss Vespers even if you were fighting a war. Ferdinand
of Aragón had always hurried from his victories to the nearest
church and flung himself down at the altar, dusty and sweating.

The Burgundians, when they arrived in Spain, seemed to their
hosts rather foppish and supercilious. At first it looked as if they
were going to shape Spain's political future. In fact the opposite
happened. Charles was turned from a Burgundian into a convinced
Spaniard. With his children he spoke not Flemish or even French,
but Spanish.

It was difficult to escape the atmosphere of mystical exultation in
Spain at this time, among the common people as well as among the
grandees. It was particularly difficult for a devout and warmly pre-
Renaissance man like Charles. The silent concentration within
convent walls could be felt outside too. Hernando de Talavera,
Alejo de Venagas, the Augustinian Alonso de Crozco, Luis de Léon

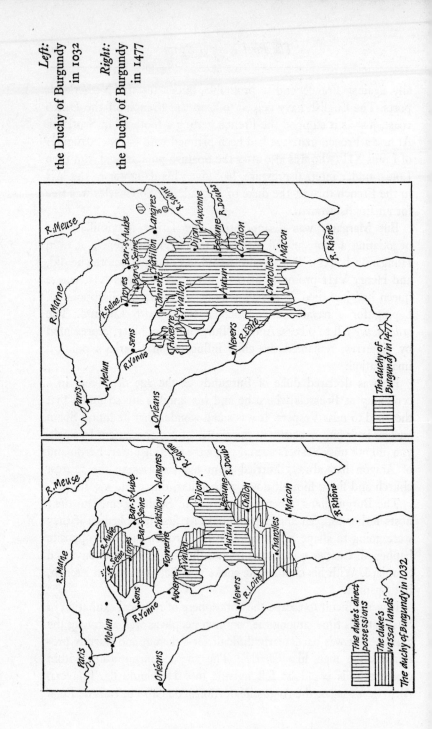

Left:
the Duchy of Burgundy
in 1032

Right:
the Duchy of Burgundy
in 1477

of Salamanca, Francisco de Osuna (St. Theresa's principal guide), the Dominican Luis de Granada—these names were known to everyone. The exultation came out in many ways. One of the ways was empire-making. It did not make for the best government. It is difficult for monks to govern.

Ximenes did his best to hold the country together until Charles arrived. The grandees, the urban middle classes, the priests, the *moriscos* were all in rebellion. All looked to the king's arrival to bring discipline to the others, while having no particular desire for it themselves. Pirates were threatening trade between Sicily and the Spanish ports, and there were rebellions in Sicily and Naples. The viceroy of Sicily had to leave Palermo in a hurry. Ximenes persuaded the pope to revive the old crusade tax on church lands and spent it on his fleet, since the pirates in the Mediterranean could be considered infidels, being under the Sultan's protection. Complaints were coming in from the Indies of Spanish maltreatment of the natives. It was not a promising picture for a youth of seventeen.

He was proclaimed king of Spain in Brussels on 14 March 1516. His mother was included in the proclamation as reigning with him so as to make no mistake about the accession. The Burgundian idea at this time was not simply to govern Spain but to unite her with the Netherlands. This made Chièvres' policy of friendship with France important strategically, if Franche Comté and the Netherlands were not to be cut off from Spain by a hostile wedge of France in between. The hope was that the combined Spanish and Netherlands fleets would dominate the Atlantic and the Mediterranean.

This shows how little the Spanish role was understood in the first months of Charles's reign. This role did in fact turn the Netherlands into a bitter enemy. But Chièvres' policy saw only the danger of a hostile France. A close dynastic connection between France and the Hapsburg empire was therefore necessary. The result was a treaty with the French (Noyon, 13 August 1516) by which Charles was to marry Louise, the daughter of Francis I.

None of this could possibly please the Spaniards. Anything Charles did abroad was wrong for them, but to marry a foreigner as well as being one himself seemed a double crime. Dozens of them took the journey to Brussels to persuade him to become king of the Spaniards to the exclusion of everything else. Others were disappointed by Ferdinand of Aragón's last-minute disavowal of Charles's younger brother, and his apparent acceptance of the Hapsburg takeover. Around the young Archduke Ferdinand intrigues were buzzing, the more so as he was only thirteen years old and could be twisted whichever way the grandees wanted. Charles sent word to Ximenes to isolate the child from his advisers, and this was done.

Ximenes now set about preparing a state for Charles to govern. It needed an army and he asked Charles's permission (at once granted) to set up a Castilian militia which would always be ready to put down revolt. In this he showed an uncanny understanding of the century, most of which he was not to see. He knew that the grandees had to have their claws finally trimmed, and that this was to be the chief social operation under Charles V and his son. His militia-idea was also the first clear step to breaking the autonomy, now the blistering pride, of the cities. It asked them to put up money for a common army—that is, for a force that could squash them at any time. At the end of the century Philip's treatment of Saragossa during the Antonio Pérez trouble, as well as his general policy of Castilianisation, proved how well Ximenes had understood the trend. The grandees of Castile were furious. The city of Salamanca told Ximenes' officers to go back where they had come from. The city of Valladolid forced his men to run away (in disguise) and then demonstrated in the streets. The fury began to look dangerous. Charles told Ximenes to hold his hand, thus showing that as yet he did not know the charm of ruthlessness for the Spaniard. Ximenes did know—and gave him a warning to the effect that, of all people, Spaniards should never be allowed to get away with rebellion. Philip II later applied Ximenes' rule; and he never regretted doing so.

The forty ships that brought Charles and his sister Eleonore from Flushing to Spain with their Burgundian retinue of 500 courtiers had a stormy passage through the Bay of Biscay and had to fetch up

on a rocky line of coast near Gijon at the foot of the Asturias. It was
a great disappointment for the Burgundians, as they had decorated
the flagship to dazzle their hosts. The king's topmast bore two splendid banners. Its sails had elaborate paintings on both sides. A picture
of the crucifixion on the mainsail was framed inside two pillars of
Hercules, with the king's motto *plus oultre* ('yet farther') hopefully
scrolled round them. The few fishermen and peasants who happened
to sight them thought they were pirates and gave the alarm. The
court had to abandon ship and cross the Asturias on foot with their
baggage, after fighting off a local army that had been quickly formed
by the terrified coastal villages. The Burgundian cry of *'Spain! It is
your king!'* was taken as definite proof of the Turks, until somebody
actually saw a Castilian banner. The plan had been to land at Biscay
in ceremonial glory, but the fleet had sailed a hundred miles off
course. But then nothing had been done on the Spanish side to
welcome Charles. The Asturians looked and behaved like savages,
with uncombed hair half-way down their backs. The plague was
raging locally and to make matters worse horses were unavailable.

The way south to the Castilian capital was long—150 miles of
mountain track in stifling September weather. The Burgundians
made no attempt to set up court before they reached Tordesillas,
where Juana, Charles's mother, still lived in permanent semi-
darkness. They even avoided Valladolid, a few miles north of it.
Chièvres was by no means anxious to meet Cardinal Ximenes, whose
possible influence on Charles he mistrusted. Ximenes was, after
all, Ferdinand of Aragón's man. Officially the excuse was the
plague.

The journey took weeks. When he arrived at his mother's castle
Charles went straight in to see her. He allowed no one to accompany
him, not even Chièvres, who was hanging about at the door in-
quisitively. He never mentioned his interview in the darkened room
as long as he lived. Many Spaniards still believed that Juana was
not mad, and his silence added to their conviction. She was clearly
being confined in the Tordesillas castle in the interests of the
Hapsburg succession. And of course a mad Castilian was in any
case saner than the sanest foreigner.

Ximenes died on his way to see Charles, at eighty years of age. Had he lived two or three years longer he might have prevented many of the Spanish-Burgundian misunderstandings that came about. As it was his death relieved Chièvres of the job of actively getting rid of him. In fact, a letter from Charles had been on its way to Ximenes, giving him 'permission to retire'. He never received it.

After the Tordesillas visit the court made a ceremonial entry into Valladolid, meaning again to blind the Spanish with splendour. They showed off at their jousts, so much that Charles had his knights separated by force after ten horses had been killed. By his sanction their weapons were uncovered—a veiled hint perhaps of the ruthless authority he might use against the onlooking Spaniards if he had a mind to. In this he was showing a new side of his character. According to Margaret of Austria he changed into a much harder man the moment he inherited the Spanish throne. For instance, when his sister Eleonore fell in love with the handsome Count Palatine Frederick, who had grown up at the Burgundian court and had received the Order of the Golden Fleece, Charles interfered at once. The one love-letter the count wrote her was filed as a state document, and the two youngsters were made to swear that they had not contracted a secret marriage and would forget each other. Strictly political ideas were already guiding Charles's personal life. He had other plans for Eleonore. She must become the queen of Portugal, by marrying her own uncle. This was what eventually happened. Charles also decided at this time to enter the lists as a candidate for the imperial throne.

His advisers kept Spanish ministers away from him as much as they could. He made his first mistake by giving Spanish bishoprics to Burgundians, as well as to Spaniards in the Burgundian court like Mota and Manrique who passed as Burgundians in proud Spanish eyes. Cardinal Ximenes' goods were confiscated. His archbishopric of Toledo went to a nephew of Chièvres, a youth of sixteen. It was a gauche and insensitive beginning. During 1516 and 1517 Chièvres got rid of the Aragonese followers of Ferdinand and the Castilian followers of Philip the Fair (under their leader Juan

Manuel). Pedro de Urrea, one of Ferdinand's followers, was given a job in Rome, and Juan Manuel was simply cold-shouldered out of Charles's court. The men who took their places were Spaniards, but Spaniards for whom provincial intrigues were outdated, a hindrance to the interests of both Aragón and Castile.

The demands made of the king by the Cortes of Castile in 1518 were amazing for their sense of independence. At the first session, under the chairmanship of Charles's Burgundian chancellor, Jean le Sauvage, a deputy from Burgos got up and spoke his heart. In a fierce tone he said that the presence of foreigners at the deliberations of the Cortes was an insult to Castile. Le Sauvage sent for him and told him that talk like that could end in confiscation of one's property. It could even mean death. The deputy replied that what he had said was entirely legal. He was supported unanimously by the other deputies. His property and his life were spared. In fact the Burgundians admired tenacity of this kind. Charles V swore respect for Castilian rights, in return for recognition as king. It was only the first lesson.

Other demands followed. The Cortes laid it down that no more benefices should be given to foreigners. The new sixteen-year-old archbishop of Toledo should be made to come to Spain. The king himself must learn Spanish and hold a daily audience. He should keep a firm hand on the Inquisition, and see that confiscated property did not go to the judges who confiscated it. Also there must be a sufficient number of witnesses for an indictment of heresy to be made. The king was advised to marry at once, and, it was demanded, his younger brother Ferdinand should not leave Spain until Charles's queen had had a child. Charles was addressed as 'your highness' and not by the title he preferred—'your majesty'. As for Juana (who to irk him *was* described as 'her majesty' in the Cortes petition), was she under lock and key, and genuinely mad? The Burgundians returned polite answers to most of these demands, and got the money they were asking for (600,000 ducats).

With the money in his pocket Charles moved on to Aragón. It was his second big mistake to spend more time there and in Catalonia than he had done in Castile, although Castile was the larger province

and had handed out the larger subsidy. He was received cere-
monially by the city of Saragossa on 9 May 1518. But here, in
Aragón, there was doubt that he would be recognised as king at all,
let alone given any money. He started off by vowing to respect
Aragonese liberties but very soon realised that almost nobody looked
on him as their protector anyway. His mother (most Aragonese
seemed not to know that she was incurably mad) and his younger
brother were preferred almost unanimously. Much resentment had
been caused by his refusing to let his mother be seen publicly, or
even privately, by her half-brother the archbishop of Saragossa.
There was only Charles's word that she was unfit to govern—and
he was a foreigner. The fact that he was a Hapsburg and related to
half the kings of Europe cut no ice at all. He had already sent
100,000 ducats out of what Castile had given him to Germany as a
first step to securing the electoral throne, should his grandfather
die. The Spaniards rightly saw themselves as financing foreign
ambitions. Burgundian speeches to the various Cortes, emphasising
how powerful Charles was in his foreign connections, were the most
sublimely tactless of any they could have thought up.

The Castilians at Charles's court resented the fact that the
Aragonese in Saragossa did not at once receive him with open arms,
since they—on whom everything Spanish surely depended—had
already done so. And they said as much. The Aragonese—who felt
that everything Spanish depended on *them*—gave them short
answers, and fighting started in the streets.

Charles got his recognition—and a very tight subsidy of 200,000
ducats. His court was still detested—particularly his chancellor,
Le Sauvage. But Le Sauvage's death in the summer from the plague
eased matters for a time. The Italian Mercurino Gattinara, who took
his place, was a very different man. He seemed to understand a
hundred different provincial points of view all at once, and to form
policies by means and not in spite of them.

In Catalonia the Cortes refused to recognise Charles until his
mother was dead. Chièvres began heartily to wish himself back in
Flanders, and many of Charles's court did actually go back, convinced that he could never hold so unruly and truculent a people.

It took Charles until May 1519 to get his recognition out of the Catalans. And the money—a fraction of what he had from the other provinces—only came in January of the following year. Yet—with that unpredictability which Spaniards could always command—Catalonia was much more favourable to him than either Castile or Aragón. The Catalans were quicker than anyone to see the advantages of a Hapsburg on the throne, perhaps because of their own imperial background. And then Charles himself had been learning fast. He was no longer the child he had been when his boat landed on the Asturian coast. He was wise enough to let Chièvres bear the brunt of bad feeling wherever possible.

Yet he was still mentally in Flanders. He spoke Flemish more easily than any other language. He still naturally thought of the Empire as an affair north of the Pyrenees. He still did not see—no one round him did—the degree to which Spain could participate in northern policies. The idea that a Spanish empire might come into being occurred to no one, for Charles had not yet taken the steps to make it possible.

But his choice of Mercurino Gattinara as his chancellor did mark a change of attitude. Gattinara was fifty-three. Like Ximenes he was incorruptible. That was a quality the Spanish liked in their leaders without necessarily asking it of themselves. He was a scholar in the humanist tradition—meaning that he saw beyond provinces and even courts, even Rome, to the problems of Christendom. Above all 'empire' meant a compact Christian civilisation for him, functioning through its independent parts. In this lay his chief influence over Charles later on.

The emperor Maximilian died in 1519. In the short term Charles's desire to take his place aggravated the Spanish situation. And Chièvres made it impossible for Gattinara to deal with it in his own way. The rumour got round that Charles would soon be leaving. Spaniards began to feel that they had put up money to benefit policies not their own. Again there would be a regent, this time a foreigner, Adrian of Utrecht. Charles's proposed visit to Valencia had to be given up, and this aroused bitter resentment there. He then summoned the Castilian Cortes to Santiago. There was no

precedent for assembling it so far from its base. But he needed more
money out of them, over and above the original 600,000 ducats
(which had been designed as a payment over three years). He also
tried to cut across the instructions traditionally given by the cities to
their representatives in the Cortes—by issuing direct ones of his
own. All the way from Calahorra to Santiago he saw discontent. In
Valladolid where the court stayed for three days during March 1520
there were brawls in the streets, and Chièvres was threatened.
Envoys arrived from Toledo to urge the Castilians not to go into
open revolt but to plan a revolution on a national scale. Only this
could have hurt Charles. As it was, one clear idea emerged from the
later sporadic risings—that foreigners were not wanted, though a
foreign king was. That was a big advance for Charles, and one that
luckily he understood.

The first signs of real trouble were in Castile and Valencia. In
Castile everyone from the highest nobility to the peasantry felt the
same resentment. The court got away from Valladolid only just in
time. The towns of Castile formed themselves into a Holy Junta, but
once Charles had gone the reasons for the revolt gradually became
blurred, and the rebels began arguing among themselves. The
nobles rediscovered their hatred for the business classes, and vice
versa. The fact was that no one had any government with which to
replace the king. Adrian of Utrecht failed to cope with the situation
—which was perhaps why Chièvres left him alone to cope with it.

The imperial crown was, by a tradition dating back to 1356, in the
hands of seven German electors—the archbishops of Trier, Mainz
and Cologne, the king of Bohemia, the duke of Saxony, the count
palatine of the Rhine and the margrave of Brandenburg. The election took place in Frankfurt-am-Main and the coronation in Aix-la-
Chapelle or Aachen. In the half-century before Charles was born
the Holy Roman Empire consisted of all the German-speaking
lands, a French-speaking area to the west of the Rhine and—
although somewhat shakily—Milan. It was the emperor Maximilian
who had turned it into a Hapsburg concern, nearly running Europe.
His marriage with the richest heiress of the time, Mary of Burgundy,

had served to make the Hapsburg grip all the more sure. His bor-
rowings, particularly from the Medici banks, did the rest. They had
started when he was still archduke of Austria. In fact he was the
most indebted prince in Europe. Mary's sudden death in 1482
caused the failure of the Medici bank at Bruges. She left her debts
unpaid, following in the footsteps of Charles the Bold.

In his battles in Switzerland and Italy Maximilian came off rather
badly, but a second *coup* in marriage-arranging brought about
another great addition to the Hapsburg lands in the form of Spain,
when he married his son the Archduke Philip of Austria to Juana,
daughter of Ferdinand and Isabella, in 1496. Into the Hapsburg
inheritance came not only Spain but its dependent states of Naples
and Sicily, as well as the American colonies. The strategic reason
for the marriage was the fact that France was attacking Italy and
challenging the Aragonese possessions there. Now, like Maximilian,
Charles saw France as the chief threat to the tranquillity of the
Empire, and the greatest obstacle to the realisation of a common
Christian society. That was why he clung to Burgundy and the 'old
rights'. He wanted Burgundy as a buffer-state between France and
Germany, or equally between France and Italy.

When someone at Margaret's court in the Netherlands suggested
that Charles's younger brother Ferdinand should be put up as an
alternative imperial candidate, Charles flared up at once. His determination surprised everyone. He wrote to Margaret—having sent
an envoy to her post-haste—not to think of any candidate but himself. Only he, with his Spanish inheritance, was strong enough to
maintain the Empire and the dynasty, and his grandfather's difficulties would only be repeated if anyone less powerful came to the
throne. Only under himself could Christendom hold out against the
Turk. These arguments were pressed simultaneously at the German
courts, in Spain and in the Netherlands.

His election was not a foregone conclusion. Maximilian had spent
as much money as he could afford on trying to make it so. He had
borrowed from the Fugger banking family. But Maximilian had
also 'promised' the imperial throne to Charles's uncle, Henry VIII
of England, and to Louis XII of France, though only for immediate

political advantage. Two electors had refused Charles's bribes—Frederick of Saxony and the Margrave Joachim I of Brandenburg, and both opposed Charles consistently in the Diet. The 600,000 florins he himself spent were not wasted, but they brought him less near to the throne than his rival Francis I of the rich Valois family. Francis (favoured in secret by the pope) was ready to spend 3,000,000 florins if necessary, and he had an army waiting on the German border to support his claim. Charles's agents were unable to outbid him. Henry VIII had no serious chance at all.

Threats of violence from the so-called Swabian League (which had its own army under the duke of Bavaria), as well as from the duke of Brunswick, tipped the electors towards Charles, and financial support from the Fuggers sealed the matter. In all, the Fuggers lent Charles 500,000 florins, and his total expenditure was 852,000 florins.

Europe was divided in its fear of the two main candidates. After Henry VIII himself, the English preferred Charles, while the pope wanted Francis as the lesser of the two dangers (though not at all as an ideal candidate). Henry VIII openly supported Charles, the pope then openly supported Francis, and both agreed secretly to do what they could (secretly) to prevent the election of either. Instead of keeping to this agreement the pope promised two German electors cardinal's hats if they supported Francis, though this had the effect of drawing the Germans as a whole closer to Charles. These were after all the first years of the Lutheran movement. In Germany there was an uneasy feeling that Francis was already too strong—and less likely than Charles to govern with impartiality.

Charles's influence was quiet but sound. He relied on Gattinara's powerful arguments, based on a calculation of the fears in other men's minds. He was the safest 'middle' choice for all. Gradually Francis's chances slipped, and on 30 November 1519 Charles was officially pronounced king of the Romans by the electors. Gattinara decided that his titles should be as follows, running in order of precedence: 'Roman king, future emperor, King of Spain, Sicily, Jerusalem, the Balearic Islands, the Canary Islands, the Indies and

the mainland on the other side of the Atlantic, Archduke of
Austria, Duke of Burgundy, Brabant, Styria, Carinthia, Carniola,
Luxembourg, Limburg, Athens and Patras, Count of Hapsburg,
Flanders and Tyrol, Count Palatine of Burgundy, Hainault, Pfirt,
Roussillon, Landgrave of Alsace, Count of Swabia, Lord of Asia
and Africa.'

His first political act after election was to visit England. He still
had to find a wife. The two kings met at Canterbury on the Whit
Sunday of 1520, and there were great celebrations. Henry's queen
at this time was Catherine of Aragón, an aunt of Charles's. On 1 June
of the same year Henry went to Brussels to meet Francis I. They
both protested friendship they did not feel. On 11 June Henry met
Charles again between Calais and Gravelines, and they agreed that
Charles should marry Henry's daughter, Mary. At the same time
Henry assured Francis through his envoys that Charles and not he
had raised the subject and that he had reminded Charles of his
(Henry's) friendship with Francis. For Charles, close association
with England meant political security in the Netherlands. He had
to make friends urgently, particularly against France. The Empire
he now headed could quite easily become simply a name. He was
still under twenty. His meetings with Henry VIII gave him his first
taste of political influence exerted personally.

He made his triumphal entry into Aachen on 22 October of the
same year. The electors met him outside the city gates. He answered
their speeches of welcome through the cardinal of Salzburg. Money
was thrown to the crowds. The procession included 400 cavalry
under the duke of Castelalto. There were Burgundians—knights of
the Golden Fleece—and Spanish noblemen, as well as the electors
and princes of Germany. It was a fine, warm day. That evening
Charles swore his coronation oath, in which he agreed to employ
only Germans in imperial offices, and to use either Latin or the
German language in official documents. He was never to bring
foreign armies into the Empire (namely, 'the German lands'), or to
reduce the lands in any way (but he *was* to try to increase them).
The coronation itself took place next day in the cathedral, where
Charlemagne himself had been crowned. Here Charles swore to

reverence the pope, protect orphans and widows and the Church.
On 26 October the pope's consent to his being called 'Holy Roman
Emperor' arrived.

In his early years as emperor Charles was opposed to all forms of
expansion. Wars were waged only in order to defend lands that
rightfully belonged to him, not for the acquisition of new ones.
He told the Venetian ambassador Contarini in 1529 that the rumours
about his wanting something like a 'universal monarchy' (which we
would nowadays call world-dictatorship) were slanderous, and that
he would in the course of his life prove it. He also pointed out to the
pope that the Empire—and peace inside the Empire—were necessary
in order to defend Christendom against the Turk. Erasmus defined
Charles as 'the protector, promoter and reformer of the religion of
the Gospels'. Paradoxically the protection he gave to the Empire
was the very thing that broke it up.

Protestantism and commerce thrived on the safety he provided,
and then, supporting each other, they began asking for independence. The new Europe was one of separate commercial states,
in need of one another because they were as yet weak, and in competition with one another in the hope of getting strong. They needed
the Empire for the temporary protection it gave them against each
other, but only for such time as they continued to be weak. Thus
throughout Charles's reign everything that strengthened the Empire
paradoxically weakened it at the same time, because it encouraged
the clamour for independence. In the end it forced him to rely on
Spain entirely.

And then life changed too drastically for mediaeval concepts to
work any longer. Machiavelli had published *The Prince* ('there is
one rule for business and another for private life') in 1513. Printing
—the factor which more than any other, more even than the voyages
of discovery, separated the Middle Ages from modern society—
had diminished the influence of Latin, hitherto the shared and
basically ecclesiastical language. Out of the 15,000,000 or 20,000,000
books printed before 1500 at least 12,000,000 had been in Latin. By
1530 books printed in the vernacular exceeded those in Latin by far.

Thinking and writing in the vernacular encouraged men to identify themselves with those who spoke the same language, and not with distant Rome, or distant Madrid, or distant Brussels. Nationalism was born. Correspondingly the Church had less and less access to people's minds as time went on, because people were no longer dependent on manuscripts (and therefore the monastery) for their reading. Humanism and then the protestant movement thrived on the printed book, which speeded up the exchange of ideas. The printed book penetrated frontiers, and turned ideas into the slogans of great movements. As commerce too developed it encroached on government, and the newly rich everywhere expected to see themselves represented rather than looked after from a paternal distance.

The Christian mind now calculated as it had never done before. During the sixteenth century statistics came into being. Logarithms were discovered. Arabic numerals took the place of Roman because they made calculation quicker. The human body was cut open for analysis. The first population censuses were taken. The mediaeval mind had on the whole accepted the material world as given and unalterable, and in the last analysis as uninteresting because unspiritual. Charles's patience and slowness were very much of this origin. But such was the force of the new age that he had to use its energies to defend the Empire, although its nature was against the empire. He had to use Spanish nationalism to fight and to subsidise his wars. He had to use 'New Spain' in the Americas because it was profitable. And so he created a national empire, a Spanish empire, because empire in his sense, supranational and divinely guided, was no longer possible.

He felt that the Hapsburg dynasty had a sacred function, meaning that he himself was the instrument by which God revealed His design. Both he and his son were devout as much for this reason as for any other: whole peoples depended on their being worthy of the divine transmission. They prayed for the right guidance. They asked of their confessors the utmost vigilance towards their failings. But it could not stop the encroaching dominion of secular interests. When American gold came pouring in Charles was no nearer

believing in foreign conquest than he ever had been, but the gold
meant that he could retain the Netherlands—the Empire's running
sore. The picture of Charles that gradually formed during his life,
as the 'new Hercules', was not a self-portrait.

Chapter 4

'The New Hercules'

Charles's sudden departure from Spain to be crowned the king of the Romans, of all things, was of course taken as an insult. Everybody joined in the Castilian riots—noblemen, merchants, priests. A mob threw a rope round the neck of one of the *procuradores* for Segovia (he had voted for the king's subsidy). He was dragged through the streets, and then hung. At Burgos a mob hung a rich French merchant who happened to be a close friend of Chièvres. The regent, Adrian of Utrecht, escaped to Valladolid. In Toledo the *corregidor* was thrown out, but 'in the name of the king and queen'. Already it was clear that the Burgundians and not Charles offended Spain. The risings were even a personal victory for him. Among the peasantry there was still loyalty to the 'old law', as it was called. The new society, in its first turmoils, was causing great anxiety among the old tradition-based classes, the Church dignitaries and the peasants, and some of the grandees. So the crown remained the only stable element, a promise of things as they had been. Charles's sudden departure looked like an abandonment of moral responsibility.

Adrian was reluctant to act. In July 1520 he sent a thousand men to put down the riot in Segovia. They were thrown back. He sent reinforcements. There was bitter fighting in the streets. The chief market town of the district, Medina del Campo, was burned to the ground by his troops on 21 August because the inhabitants refused to give up their guardianship of the royal arsenal there. This touched off the fiercest resentment yet—even Valladolid rose. The castle of Tordesillas was taken over and Juana was made 'queen of the revolution'. It looked as if Charles might never be able to return. The revolutionaries entered Valladolid (allowing Adrian of Utrecht to escape) on 28 September 1520.

But then the movement began to lose force. Old Castile was solidly behind the revolution, but the Andalusians (so despised by the Burgundians) formed a royalist confederation. Granada and Córdova remained loyal. The revolutionaries laid down decrees as to what should be done—but sent messengers to Charles to ask for his approval of them. His answer was to suspend the collection of the second subsidy of *servicio* which had been squeezed out of the Cortes at Santiago. It was also agreed that no more offices should be given to foreigners. The admiral and the constable of Castile would now join the foreigner Adrian as co-regents.

The rebels, under a grandee called Padilla, not only asked Charles to come back; they suggested what in fact took place in his son's reign—'he can govern the whole world from these provinces'. They asked that the *mercedes* or grants of lands to settlers in the Indies and even to Spaniards in Spain should cease. An emissary was sent to Charles at Worms, to put their suggestions for the future, but he took this very coldly, which meant that Chièvres and Gattinara knew by now how safe the Spanish crown was. The rebels could be relied on to quarrel among themselves (in fact Padilla was replaced for a time as leader by Pedro Giron).

The co-regents Charles appointed were Don Inigo Velasco, constable of Castile, and Don Fadrique Enriquez, admiral. The constable reconquered Tordesillas, pushing the 'Holy Junta' of rebel cities down to Valladolid. The rebels now found a new and more demagogic leader in the bishop of Zamora, a grandee by the name of Antonio de Acuña. Under this 'devil of a bishop' peasants and monks plundered the convents and burned the farms. The regent Adrian contacted the pope, and Acuña was denounced as the 'Spanish Luther'. The French faction at the Vatican, who were egging the rebels on, denied that the bishop was anything of the kind. Meanwhile Padilla was captured by Velasco the constable, and Valladolid was reoccupied. Then Toledo fell. It was the last Castilian city to give way, defended heroically by Padilla's widow. The bishop of Zamora was captured on his way to France. Five years later he was tortured and garrotted after murdering his gaoler and trying to escape from prison—the Simancas castle in Navarre. Meanwhile the

French had crossed the Pyrenees and were besieging Logrono. They might easily have driven a wedge between Castile and Aragón. But the Castilians, by their victory at Valladolid, were now free to face the north. With help from Aragón they routed the French on 29 June 1521, and Navarre returned to Spanish hands.

In Valencia there was a quite different state of rebellion. Feeling there had nothing to do with dislike of the Burgundians—who had not been to Valencia anyway. It was much more a social movement, and its first leader hoped to make of Valencia a new republic like that of Venice. The riots were caused by an outbreak of the plague, when the rich and noble classes fled from the city, leaving it in the hands of a quickly formed Germanía or brotherhood. The Germanía announced that the days of the 'nobility and the heathen' were over, and that there would now be 'one king and one law'. They subjected the *moriscos* working on the grandee estates to forcible conversions. The grandees were spurred by this to agree for once among themselves, and they began putting down the riots. In March 1522 the rebel leader Viçenc Peris was captured. As in Castile and Andalusia, aristocratic support was essential for the success of a revolution, and this had everywhere been withdrawn. The nobles—Charles's chief source of aggravation—had finally come over of their own accord.

Charles returned in the summer of 1522 when Spain was already at peace again. He no doubt wondered what miracle had prevented the rebels from joining up with the French (on whom he had just declared war). He badly needed peace in Spain.

This time he stayed seven years. He built himself a palace in Granada. He 'became a Spaniard', though his total residence in Spain did not amount to more than sixteen years out of a total of forty years as Spain's king. But he retired at the end of his life to the Jeromite convent of Yuste in Estremadura, in the south-west. This was how far he had become a Spaniard. No other country could satisfy his religious yearnings, always veering between ecstasy and the most intense melancholy. And he saw to it that his children,

especially Philip, should feel that Castile was the only place in the
world fit for kings and princes.

Gradually his court began to lose its brilliant Burgundian character and take on the rather parched and ascetic look of the country
round it. The fornicating and beer-drinking Fleming in him was
tempered with Spanish austerity now, though he continued to eat
too much and too richly. Above all, Spain was becoming a haven of
rest for him—the opposite of what he had expected in the early days.
It was a rest from disloyalties and frictions north of the Pyrenees.
And then Spaniards had an undeniable attraction for popes and
monarchs. They understood kingship. Charles's Spanish advisers
addressed him as *Sacra Caesarea Majestratis*, an infectious style for
a king just turned twenty-one. They now loved the thought that an
emperor was among them.

One of his first acts on returning to Spain was to rationalise the
social hierarchy. He confined the number of grandees to twenty-five,
choosing the most notable families of Castile and Aragón. These had
no place in the royal council, but could remain uncovered or hatless
in the king's presence, and were addressed by him as 'cousins'. The
lowest rank of the aristocracy—the *caballeros* or *hidalgos*—were the
more numerous and politically active. They were sometimes in
business. Many of them were poor. They prefixed their names with
'Don'. They farmed the royal taxes, and filled the treasury posts.
Like the grandees they were exempt from royal taxes and could not
be imprisoned or tortured. The result was that everyone wanted to
be a *hidalgo*, unless he could be something higher. They tended to
be more loyal and more reliable than the grandees or the so-called
segundones or sons of grandees. They were the lawyers, the political
secretaries, the functionaries. Loyalty meant a livelihood for them,
which it did not for the grandees or the *titulos*, the other titled rank.
Ferdinand had felt safer with the lesser aristocrats for this reason,
and had greatly increased their number. Charles followed him in
this. More and more the privilege of *hidalguía* was put on sale. In
this way commerce slowly undermined the power of the great
families, and served to underpin royal authority.

No Germans were to sit on Charles's council (his becoming Holy

Roman Emperor had seemed to threaten this, in Spanish eyes). It is interesting that of his two most important secretaries, Lalemand, lord of Bouclans, a Fleming, and Francisco de los Cobos, a Spaniard, the Fleming was arrested after six years and disappeared from public life, while Cobos became secretary of state and Charles's top financial brain.

Charles also introduced a new system whereby instead of visiting each kingdom of Aragón at about the time he needed a fresh subsidy, he called the Cortes of Aragón, Valencia and Catalonia together in one place. The Cortes of Castile had a permanent deputation at his court. He constantly explained not only his internal but his imperial policies to them, so that very soon they had a sense of leading Europe, as well as being the pioneers of Europe's new enterprise in the Americas. Their closeness to Charles may have been responsible for the fact that he began to govern more and more personally. This was 'the Spanish manner' pure and simple. Often a decision was left in the air because he insisted on taking it himself. One of his ministers complained to Margaret of the Netherlands that Charles would not take advice. Sometimes decisions were taken too quickly. This was all the more dangerous as Charles showed signs of lacking confidence, and often hid it under a forced and unconsidered decision. Only Gattinara rescued him from the worst effects of this fault. Later, in 1523, his councillors (Gattinara, La Roche, La Chaulx, Vega) took the line that he must avoid the trivialities of government himself. A royal stamp or seal would take the place of a personal signature. His council took to meeting in a room close to his each day, to break their information and advice down to simple briefs, which were then presented to him. Minutes of everything they talked about were kept.

To establish his authority at once Charles sentenced 250 rebel leaders to death at Valladolid on 2 November 1522. A few years later he was excommunicated for ordering the execution of the bishop of Zamora, and spent some months in misery before being absolved. Members of the so-called Holy Junta were also executed. But many of the sentences were not carried out, especially when they involved the confiscation of great estates. Charles acted with decision, as he was expected to, but then allowed mercy in the application, again as he was expected to.

As to his marriage, it was becoming clear that having renounced his promise to take a Frenchwoman he would now—under the Spanish spell—have to renounce his promise to Henry VIII too. He began to make political excuses for his close alliance with England to the king of Portugal, who was anxious for him to marry his daughter Isabella, and who offered a stupendous dowry of a 1,000,000 ducats, payable when the agreement was signed.

But meanwhile there were other worries. Chièvres had always been against war with France. Gattinara on the other hand argued that Francis I must be dealt with, as the first act of Charles's reign, otherwise as emperor he would get a reputation for timidity. And—another bone of contention with Chièvres—Charles must establish himself firmly in Italy; he must drive out the French and build an alliance with the pope. Chièvres died from the plague at Worms in May 1521. From that point Gattinara's astute arguments carried Charles with them.

Since April 1520 Don Juan Manuel, a Castilian grandee, had been Spanish ambassador in Rome, and had skilfully played down Leo X's fears of a big empire north of the Alps under a young king. But Leo still favoured the French; their recent success in Navarre made it seem quite likely that Francis I and not Charles would soon be the first power in Europe. He would be an effective counterweight to the Hapsburg domination. Leo also feared Spain as much as he needed her. Spanish soldiers had restored the Medici dynasty in Florenec. Leo was after all Lorenzo de' Medici's son, and since his father's death had seen his city fall into French hands. Francis I was being intractable over the papal claims to Ferrara. The idea of joining up with Charles to get rid of the French from Milan began to appeal to Leo. Also Charles's power in Naples was useful against Turkish pirates. The Neapolitan coast had already been plundered. Above all, Charles could hold down the detested Luther. This argument—pressed hard by the clever Manuel—weighed most.

Charles had turned out less of a dynastic firebrand than Leo had feared. He already showed that he enjoyed politics. He sat in council every day. Francis on the other hand showed that he still enjoyed hunting parties, and his country was really in the hands of his mother, Louise of Savoy.

In the end—because Francis threatened to invade Naples—Leo asked Charles for an offensive alliance, and then it was Charles's turn to waver. But Gattinara's policy won. He urged that failing to check Francis now would put Charles on the wrong foot for the rest of his reign, and throw away the friendship of Switzerland, the pope, Venice and England. Also a war to settle Italy was essential, to keep France out of that country, to secure it against the Turks, and to make sure of the papal alliance (that is, papal compliance in imperial policies). On 21 May 1521 the alliance was signed. It was agreed that Francesco Sforza's rule in Milan should be re-established with 16,000 Swiss troops. Charles was to hand over Parma and Piacenza to the pope, when he had conquered them. He was to take the Medici dynasty under his protection. In return the pope was to receive Charles and crown him. Naples was to be recognised as belonging to Charles, in return for a grant of 10,000 ducats for Alessandro de' Medici, and the same amount for the Cardinal de' Medici. To a man who believed in dynasty as Charles did, this did not seem strange.

It meant war against France on two fronts—in Italy and in Burgundy. For Charles was also fighting for his claims as a Valois—against Francis's claims as a Valois. And Francis felt so encouraged by his recent successes in Navarre that he refused Wolsey's offer of mediation. Henry of Nassau, for Burgundy, took Mouyon and besieged Meyières, while the French supported the duke of Gelderland and lord of Sedan (Robert de la Mark) against the Empire. Francis was clear about his objectives in supporting de la Mark—he wanted to pin Charles down in the Netherlands and weaken him in Italy.

Against the French were the papal armies, the Spanish and Neapolitan armies, and Swiss and German *landsknechts* (though the Swiss tended to fight on both sides). Gattinara urged Charles to get a victory quickly for its publicity value. He had after all the best general—Henry of Nassau. The expense was far more than Charles could afford. Subsidies were called in. There were difficulties in Hainault and Artois. French trade with the Netherlands—hitherto, before becoming part of the Empire, a neutral area—had stopped. Nassau had to withdraw from Meyières (September 1521). On 22 November 1521 a treaty between Charles, Henry VIII and the pope was signed. Charles agreed to marry one of Henry VIII's daughters, after all, and to do all he could to ensure that Cardinal Wolsey became pope if Leo should die. He also gave Wolsey as large a pension as the cardinal had hitherto been receiving from the French. Henry VIII had decided to throw in his lot with Charles because of the French victory in Scotland, where the duke of Albany, his old enemy, had been made regent over James V.

News came that papal and imperial troops had occupied Milan and that the French had fled. Tournai fell in December of the same year. That was the publicity Charles needed. Together with the flight of French troops from Navarre it put him on the right foot for the rest of his reign. The 'new Hercules' began from there.

When Leo X died in December 1521, and Charles's old tutor and regent in Spain, Adrian of Utrecht, was elected pope, it looked as if God was putting Rome as well into his pocket. Charles suggested just this through his ambassador at the Vatican—'God Himself has made this election'. But the new pope found the Spanish ambassador Manuel's address to him offensively full of advice, and said as much. Manuel claimed that he and the emperor had 'worked hard' for Adrian's election, which Adrian knew to be quite untrue. The discussion gave the first inkling that the two men, emperor and pope, were the advocates of very different interests, however close they had been as tutor and pupil.

Adrian was not nearly as anxious as his predecessor to form alliances against France. He withdrew papal subsidies from the imperial army. At the same time the Swiss, under French influence, changed sides and clamoured for battle against the Milan garrison which they had helped to establish. On 27 April 1522 they attacked the Spaniards and the *landsknechts*, and were beaten back in a very bloody battle. The French withdrew but took some garrisons in the duchy. Though Genoa surrendered to papal troops, it was not the best moment for the new pope. But he continued to support Francis, and he continued to tell Charles that he would not renew the agreement made with Leo. Nor, he added, could he understand England's new hostility to the French. Uppermost in his mind was the urgent need for Christendom to defend itself against the Turks, who might very soon be at the gates of Vienna. Charles's answer was that Francis intended to make war in Italy—to take Milan and, if possible, Naples as soon as he could. And this was suddenly proved in Rome when Cardinal Medici (on Charles's side) intercepted some letters written to France by Cardinal Soderini, leader of the French delegation to the Vatican. Soderini's letters urged Francis I not only to renew his attacks in the Lombardian plains but to stir up trouble in Sicily. Adrian ordered Soderini to be arrested on the spot, and the cardinal was flung into Castel Sant'Angelo.

The pope now swung over to his former pupil. He made Charles a few concessions, among them the right to consider the knightly orders of Santiago, Alcántara and Calatrava as under the Spanish crown, which they already were in all but law.

Charles was conscious of having no money. The war had already made a gigantic debt. Yet he had acted hesitantly, and had not won a crippling victory over the French which he might well have done by concentrating his forces on one front, instead of dividing them between Burgundy and Italy. He had failed to pay the German princes for his election (the promised bribes), and they were complaining. Wherever he turned he found problems. Gattinara pointed out that Charles's grandfather Maximilian had been called 'the bad gardener' because he was here, there and everywhere in his exploits, and had never learned to 'harvest' at the right time. He advised Charles to centralise the imperial finances. And he must 'win the hearts' of the Spanish, and give the impression that he was building a great army even when he was not. From Italy, once he had established himself firmly there, Charles must launch a massive attack on the Turks. Gattinara added a threat of resignation if Charles continued to delay and leave his affairs to the accidents of time.

Thus everything continued to press personal power on Charles. He was quickly becoming the axis on which the powers of Europe, from London to Budapest, turned. Gattinara advised him to win Venetian friendship. He prepared his speeches to the Spaniards, and did more than any other minister to reconcile the differences that still hung over from the period of rebellion. In his speech to the Castilian Cortes in July 1523 Charles confessed that he had made mistakes, and that these were due to his youth and his ignorance of Spanish affairs. He said he would stake his life and everything he had on the preservation of the Christian faith. This speech had a great effect, in that the Castilians felt that they had become the leaders of the war against the Turks. That was Gattinara's cleverest stroke—to harp on the holy war. In doing this he was drawing Charles into the dark Spanish net as well.

Charles was helped by luck again. Incensed by Adrian's arrest of his representative Cardinal Soderini, the French king did an unprecedented thing. He issued a pamphlet declaring that he would punish Adrian, as Philip the Fair had punished Boniface VII. This was bringing up old murders. He then stopped his payments to the Vatican. Adrian consulted with Henry VIII and the viceroy of Naples (Charles de Lannoy). He entered an alliance on 3 August 1523 with Charles, Henry VIII, the Archduke Ferdinand (to whom Charles had given the Austrian lands of the empire, as he had given Hungary to his sister Isabella), the duke of Milan, and the towns of Florence (under the Medici), Genoa, Lucca and Siena. The army they raised was placed under the command of the viceroy of Naples. So in fact Adrian endorsed everything that Leo had done, only more so. Charles could not have been more satisfied.

Not only this but subversion was being planned in the French army. Its commander-in-chief, Charles de Bourbon, was one of the most powerful landowners in France. He had a grudge. His wife had died childless and some of his lands had passed to Louise of Savoy, the queen-mother, which filled him with resentment towards the royal family. Word got to the king that Bourbon was planning revolt, and Francis tried to get him to come to Paris. But Bourbon, pleading illness, stayed on his estate on the Upper Loire. Charles V and

Henry VIII began secret negotiations with him, in the hope of chasing Francis off the throne. Like many conspirators they spent much of the time checking up on each other's (often doubtful) loyalty. After six months they agreed (August 1523), and a contract was signed by Bourbon, Henry VIII, Ferdinand and Charles V. Henry VIII's interest was to get the French throne—to which he had a claim—for himself. In return for services rendered, Bourbon was to have Charles's sister Eleonore as a bride. Charles was to send troops to Narbonne, that is to invade France, and place 10,000 imperial *landsknechts* at Bourbon's disposal. Henry VIII was to land about the same number of troops on the Normandy coast. The arrangements look very modern: armies ready at three points to make a pincer movement across France at the first news from the capital of a *coup d'état*.

The *coup d'état* failed to happen. It was a fact that Bourbon had no influence beyond his own estates, and no political party. This had been known to all three parties to the contract. Francis, on the other hand, had a following that cut right across the large estates. He centralised the new reality, 'France', in himself no less than Henry VIII did England. Charles V, like the pope, represented quite a different order of things. He dealt in many languages. He conducted wars in Italy with Spanish troops and German money. He fought battles for Burgundian rights—they were losing battles. Ultimately French national feeling would disrupt Burgundy and draw its French-speaking people into one centralised unit based on Paris. As for Bourbon, he was simply a great man in the mediaeval sense, and relied on a homage which had not been exploited because it had been taken for granted. The *landsknechts* advanced down the Marne to Chaumont but nobody seemed to know what they were doing. English troops got to Compiègne and, seeing no reason why they should be there, started ravaging the countryside. Spanish troops crossed the Pyrenees to Sauveterre but too late to do anything, supposing that anything remained to be done.

The situation was not made easier for Charles by the sudden death of Adrian in September 1523, perhaps from overwork. No one knew what the next pope would do to the anti-French alliance.

In November of the same year Cardinal Medici became pope as Clement VII, which looked good for imperial interests, especially as these had done a lot to get him there. The opposite happened. He refused to endorse Adrian's contract. He wanted peace, and in the spring of 1524 he sent the Archbishop of Capua on a tour of France, England and Spain to mediate it. There seemed every chance of success. The idea was mooted that Charles should swop Milan for the small Duchy of Burgundy (in French hands), and for that part of Charles de Bourbon's property which had gone to Louise of Savoy. As the French had failed in their latest Milan attack (1524) it seemed likely that they would listen. On the other hand, giving property inside 'France' to 'foreigners' would naturally be hard for Francis I. Charles also required him to renounce his claims to Flanders, Artois and Naples. Francis listened—and asked to have Charles's sister Eleonore as his bride. Charles agreed. It was also suggested that Charles should be given Francis's daughter Charlotte, with the Duchy of Burgundy as the dowry. It looked as if Europe was mending itself by means of an old formula—dynasty.

But the war went on, and the dynastic dreams were quickly blown away. The French lost battle after battle in the plains of Lombardy. The Spaniards won Fuenterrabia (24 March 1524). These imperial victories offered Charles the hope that he need not mediate via the pope or the English or anybody else, only ordain. In August of the same year his troops based in Italy advanced north and occupied Aix-en-Provence and laid siege to the port of Marseilles. They were hopelessly beaten back, and returned to Italy only just in time, as they were in danger of being cut off from their Lombardian bases. Francis himself led the troops who harried them. He rushed on south to Milan—and took it.

Charles was now as much in need of a settlement as Francis had been a month before. The pope fell over himself with surprise. He even made a quick treaty with Venice, in December 1524, so as to hold the new French menace in the north. And the following month, in 1525, he felt obliged to come to terms with the French so as to avoid chaos up and down the Italian peninsula.

Charles's situation had thus taken a complete turnabout in less than three months. He blamed himself for poor judgement. Since Chièvres' death he had relied on himself more and more. He knew that lack of money was his chief weakness. He found Henry VIII rather a poor ally. Wolsey intercepted a secret agent's letter suggesting this, and barred the imperial ambassador de Praet from Henry's court while Henry himself was negotiating a marriage with the Scottish crown. Charles felt that everyone, friend or enemy, had one objective where he was concerned—to keep him as weak as possible, realising how strong he *could* be. Having commitments all over Europe, he was accumulating vast debts while smaller men like Francis, able to husband their resources and confine them to one field of action, scored hits along his too-dispersed front. And it was natural that one small man should continually join another. Charles felt he had so far done nothing magnificent—only made a series of careful moves. He must do something great. And he decided that this great act would be a personal visit to Italy. He would clear up the mess in person, and be crowned by the pope.

His possible marriage to Isabella of Portugal began to mean two things for him—first, a way of reconciling the Spanish to his second departure from Spain, and secondly, a way of financing his trip (with the promised dowry of 1,000,000 ducats). Also Castile and the other provinces would probably be glad to give him extra grants to make the marriage possible. This calculation involved the worry that Henry VIII, foiled of marrying his daughter to Charles, would give her to Francis, and a powerful Anglo-French (necessarily anti-imperial) alliance might result.

In Lombardy the imperial commander-in-chief persuaded his men to carry on fighting without pay. The exchequer was empty. The army was close to mutiny. Then they were suddenly saved by Francis's rashness. On 24 February 1525 he left his strongly fortified position before Pavia, and attacked the imperial army in its unready state. But his ammunition ran out during the battle, and the imperial side swooped in on an exposed flank. Francis himself surrendered to Lannoy and was taken prisoner. So Charles was back on top again, for the moment. In an extraordinary way his desire to go personally to Italy was fulfilled without any work on his part. Lannoy wrote to him that he must come immediately—a better moment for his crowning in Italy would never occur again.

When the astonishing news reached Charles's court at Toledo he was the only one to keep his head. He felt that successes should not be celebrated with jousts but silent gratitude. He allowed only masses. But, though he kept his head, he did think that Pavia was the end of his troubles, just as Henry VIII thought that it meant his own coronation in Paris. Gattinara urged quick action. The duke of Milan should seize Piacenza while the duke of Ferrara should seize Modena; and Charles could arrange to be looking the other way. It was the first time Gattinara had argued for the kind of two-level action that was to become more and more accepted in state-craft, and almost the definition of 'diplomacy'.

But Charles did nothing. Not only was he particularly slow to reach decisions when pushed, but the wonderfully slow (because unworldly) rhythm of Spanish life was having its effect on him. Lannoy brought Francis I down to Spain as Charles's prisoner. Francis refused to listen to any suggestion that 'French' provinces be handed over to the Empire (Louise of Savoy was governing in his stead). He knew that Charles's victory had re-awakened Europe to the dangers of Hapsburg domination. Even now alliances began to form against Charles. It seemed that he could gain nothing from a victory, especially as the Empire was now increasingly looked on as a Spanish affair. Even as early as the 1520s there was a new sense of the Spaniard as the soul of arrogance, and the natural enemy of independence everywhere.

The pope did make an alliance with Charles and Henry VIII, and promised to make Gattinara a cardinal. But it was only a cover for his other moves. The duke of Milan (whose friend-ship Charles threw away by delaying his investiture) began negotiating with other elements in the Vatican. Florence chose the French side. Like most Italian states she feared the French less than the Spanish, if only because Francis had just got a bad beating.

Meanwhile there was treason in the imperial command in Italy— and almost a *coup d'état* in Naples. The pope was at the bottom of

Charles V, Holy Roman Emperor and King of Spain.
A portrait by Titian

William de Croy, Sieur Chievres, Charles V's Burgundian tutor and his chief minister at his accession

Fugger 'the Rich', famous Burgundian banker who helped finance Charles's election as Holy Roman Emperor. Pictured here with his assistant

this. The imperial generals who had won Pavia were Pescara, a Neapolitan Spaniard, and Morone, a Milanese. The Vatican already knew that the latter resented Spanish infiltrations. The pope therefore worked on him while Morone himself worked on Pescara (Spanish heir to the Pescara and Vasto estates on the Adriatic side of Italy). The pope pointed out that Charles was penniless. Morone told Pescara that, as a Neapolitan, he could easily get a rebel movement going down there, and then lay hold of the crown of Naples for himself. He argued that Charles had passed him over for other officers on more than one occasion in the past. But Pescara gave the whole show away to Charles in a series of letters (having sworn secrecy to Morone). During his first interview with Morone he had contemplated arresting him at once, but had decided that by biding his time he could learn a lot about anti-imperial designs in Italy. He sent all Morone's letters on to Toledo.

The trouble was that Charles (or rather Gattinara) did not believe him. There was always the chance that Pescara was grinding an axe of his own. In October 1525 Pescara suddenly arrested Morone without a brief from Spain. Six weeks later he himself died. In all this time there had not been a word of acknowledgement from Charles. Gattinara was proved wrong in his distrust of Pescara. But Charles never rewarded the man's widow, Vittoria Colonna. This apparent ingratitude was typical of him. Even Gattinara was not rewarded generously, not as Henry rewarded Wolsey. But then Charles did not cut off Gattinara's head, either.

Henry VIII and Charles were to administer the post-Pavian peace together, so to speak. But Wolsey was as anxious to stop Charles getting any more powerful (by taking the duchy of Burgundy from Francis, and establishing himself firmly in Italy) as Gattinara was to see that Henry did not get the French crown. At once, of course, Francis became a necessary pawn in the game, by being the only safeguard against either side. Two English diplomats came to Toledo to talk to Charles, and to celebrate the Pavian victory with wild celebrations. Their job was to put Wolsey's 'Great Project' before the emperor. This was to the effect that if Charles married Mary of England after all, she would bring to him as her dowry the French

4

crown. To get the crown Charles and Henry had to make another war in France.

But Charles had no money for war, and in any case wanted to marry the Portuguese princess. He broke off negotiations. At the same time he felt he could secure the French crown for the Hapsburgs more surely through his sister Eleonore (by marrying her to Francis) than through the cunning and variable Wolsey. Wolsey at once began negotiating with the French queen, who gave him a personal gift of 130,000 soleils and Henry VIII nearly 200,000 soleils. Sir Thomas More signed the alliance at the end of August 1525. Charles, trying to do much the same thing, got nowhere, because his demand for the duchy of Burgundy always stood in the way. Francis was kept at Jativa near Toledo, but the only time the two kings met was when Francis had a serious hunting fall. Otherwise Charles kept away from him. He staked his claim to the Burgundian provinces and left it at that. He turned down Francis's offer of 3,000,000 talers in gold as a ransom, as well as the renunciation of all claims to any part of Italy or Flanders or Artois.

Francis then tried to escape, but failed. The negotiations went on month after month. It was Lannoy who concluded them (the Treaty of Madrid, December 1525). Francis was to set aside some money and 500 soldiers for Charles's use, and to provide a fleet to get him to Italy. He was to give up his friendship with Navarre and Gelderland. He was to marry the emperor's sister, Eleonore. He was to join Charles in a crusade. His two elder sons were to be brought down to Spain as hostages while he returned to Paris to put the treaty into effect.

But behind the scenes, some months before, Francis had taken an oath that he would observe no agreements made while imprisoned. This oath was repeated with his own ambassador present the day before the treaty was signed (14 January 1526). Gattinara refused to put his seal on the treaty. A month later Charles met Francis again at Illescas, and Francis agreed solemnly to observe the clauses of the treaty. He became a free man again on the frontier at San Sebastian (17 April). He again made a solemn guarantee, this time to Lannoy, his captor.

By this time Charles had got Isabella of Portugal as his wife (she was twenty-three), together with her vast dowry. Their wedding was celebrated with solemn and unsparing Spanish pomp in Seville. They then went to the Alhambra at Granada, and took up residence. But Charles had serious work to do. Francis (as Gattinara knew he would) defected from his solemn promises. De Praet, ambassador to the French king after his withdrawal from the court of St. James's, had reminded Francis again and again of these promises during the journey north. Eleonore waited in Spain, at Vittoria, as Francis's future wife, but no news of him came. An imperial emissary went post-haste across the Pyrenees. Francis sent a message down to Granada to the effect that, as the Treaty of Madrid had been published in Italy and in the Netherlands previous to his arrival in Paris, his Burgundian subjects were in a restive state and he would need time to cool them off before ratifying the treaty. Lannoy, in disgrace, asked leave to withdraw from Spain back to Italy (he was with Eleonore in Vittoria), as Gattinara—who found him a nuisance —had always wanted him to do. But now Gattinara forced him to stay. He even ordered him to go to Francis personally and have it out with him, which he did. The French king told Lannoy that the treaty was null and void, having been signed under duress. Apart from that first clipped statement about the treaty he treated Lannoy with courtly respect during his stay, and even offered him all Bourbon's confiscated territories, which he refused. Everyone expected Charles to banish Lannoy from his councils, but he did not. He insisted instead that Francis should become his prisoner again, to prevent a large-scale war. There was of course no chance of this and he had to concede that Gattinara's policy had been the right one, in that it had always insisted on Italy being given first place in imperial calculations. For in Italy the most damaging anti-imperial alliances could be formed, and conversely the most advantageous friendships.

Francis now made an alliance with the pope, the Duke Sforza of Milan, Florence and Venice. As for Henry VIII, he supported Francis's action and asked Charles to release the two French princes who were being held as hostages. The effect of this sudden Holy

Alliance against him was to make Charles feel warmer towards the Lutherans, realising that only in Germany lay any hope of a solid and faithful friendship north of the Pyrenees. The German princes, feeling themselves to be part of a general European scene for the first time, with shared interests that had to be defended against the pope's, now united with Charles in a number of alliances (1525 and 1526). Charles wrote to Ferdinand, his brother, of his plan to 'forgive' the Lutherans and to hold a council of the Church to decide on what condition they would be received back into it. A General Council was the pope's daily nightmare as he feared that it might draw attention to the fact that his election had been illegal. As to meeting the Lutherans, he was losing far too much money in Germany (since the princes had seized Church lands there) to make it even thinkable.

Meanwhile war had started again in Italy—the same story as in 1524 and 1525, only fiercer and certainly more damaging to the civilian population. The pope had to face a choice between French and Spanish control of Italy. He chose to go on supporting France, despite the imperial forces in Naples under Lannoy which were ready to march north.

In all this changing of sides everyone forgot about the Turkish menace in Hungary. Even the Archduke Ferdinand forgot. He now had Milan—which Charles had asked him to attack—on his mind. In the meantime the king of Hungary was killed in a skirmish with the Turks at Mohacz and left no heirs. Ferdinand himself was then elected king of Bohemia on 24 February 1527. This meant more territory for the Hapsburg dynasty. As for Hungary, Ferdinand tried to get himself elected there too. He declared the election of John Zapolya, the Voivod of Transylvania, to be 'illegal', and simply a nationalist manifesto. This meant he had to declare war there too, financed by Bohemia, with the Turks still pressing from the east. But it gave him the excuse he wanted to withdraw troops from Milan.

Charles was meanwhile urging the pope to come over to his side and 'save Christendom'. He again threatened a General Council of the Church. Francis was simultaneously asking the pope for Naples in return for 'liberating' Italy. But Clement was embarrassed at this moment by a revolt led by the Colonna family. In September 1526 the family's private army marched on Rome, took it, and forced him to bless them for doing so. All the nationalist and would-be nationalist forces were converging on the one place least equipped for national cohesion—the Vatican. The imperial army in the north was coming down under Charles Bourbon and Frundsberg. The pope had, in fact, suddenly become everyone's enemy, through vacillating too long.

The result was the terrible sack of Rome by Charles's troops. These troops—Spaniards and Germans—still had not been paid, and were longing for plunder. Their leaders, Frundsberg, Lannoy and the prince of Orange, tried to hold them back, but the southwards advance through Tuscany continued. The pope offered money. The army demanded twice as much. On 6 May 1527 it stormed the city. Charles Bourbon was killed, the prince of Orange was wounded. Army discipline collapsed. The men poured into the city, smashing everything. They laid siege to Castel Sant'Angelo. The orgy went on for months. It was beyond the power of Charles to stop it. As for the pope, he could have prevented it by paying the army its price, after 'selling a few cardinals' hats' as he had been advised to, but this he refused to do.

Charles and his court tended to see the sack as an act of God. But Henry VIII and Francis I now openly became friends and decided on war to 'liberate' the pope. A few days before the sack of Rome they had reached agreement by means of which Henry would finance Francis's new war in Italy to the tune of 32,000 crowns a month. It looked as if Charles's new prisoner—the pope—would bring him as few advantages as his previous one (ironically the pope had the same gaoler as Francis—a man called Alarçon).

Gattinara (holidaying between Monaco and Genoa) wrote to Charles that he must deny responsibility for the sack of Rome. He must also press for the desirability of a General Council of the Church to bring in ecclesiastical reforms (this to take the wind out of the sails of extremists on both sides—the Lutherans and the papists). Most of Charles's advisers, including the brilliant secretary Alonso Valdes, were of the same mind. Charles also insisted (doubly cautious now through experience) that a few cardinals in the pope's entourage, and the city of Bologna, be held by imperial forces as hostages against the pope revoking his promises after release. It was the most bare-faced blackmail. The pope was being asked to pay for what had amounted to a mutiny in the imperial army, whereas he should have been indemnified.

Charles came off as badly with this second prisoner as he had with the first. In fact, precisely the same thing happened. The rest of Europe went over to the prisoner. Everybody wanted to 'liberate' the pope. This provoked de Praet, now back in Spain, to urge that the pope should be set free anyway, to prevent others trying to do so. Clement was therefore released from Castel Sant'Angelo (on Charles's security conditions) just before Christmas 1527. Negotiations started in Orvieto, to which safe town, high on its cliff, the pope was smuggled dressed as his own major domo. Both England and France were determined that he should not obey Charles's demands and that no council should be held. Their concern was not to discourage reform in the Church—the problem of reform played no part in their calculations—but to prevent any suggestion that Charles had the Church in his hands. Wolsey, cunning and rash as ever, hit on the idea of getting all those cardinals who were not under Charles's sway together at Avignon, thereby splitting the Church down the middle and getting himself elected pope while Clement was still virtually behind bars. He had an extra interest in becoming pope at this time because Henry VIII was pressing him to clear the way at the Vatican for his divorce from Catherine of Aragón (he wanted to marry Ann Boleyn and, aside from that, the queen, being Spanish, was none too popular in England).

By 1527 the English divorce plan was known everywhere in Europe, and Charles's feelings towards England were at their coldest. Gattinara advised him to negotiate with both England and France but secretly to arm against them. This is what he did. But as the other side knew perfectly well what was going on no one made any attempt to come to an agreement.

England and France declared war on Charles on 22 January 1528. Charles's answer was strikingly mediaeval; he would fight a duel with Francis, who had behaved like a rat. Francis's answer—sent through his heralds—was that Charles only had to state the time and the place. Charles's advisers cooled him down. A duel would leave the problems precisely where they had been before, and reduce his standing as a 'universal' monarch. Instead Charles asked Ferdinand for support, but failed (the Turks were too near Vienna). Ferrara and Mantua went over to Francis I. Then the duke of Ferrara was asked to become commander-in-chief of the imperial forces and promptly changed sides.

Gattinara now drew up a plan by which ships from Portugal and the Netherlands and Castile would invade England. Guillaume de Montfort got ready to take an army of 6,000 *landsknechts* across the Channel. But Margaret, with her policy of friendship towards England, based on the fact that the trade from Netherland ports would be exposed to the English navy, scotched the plan with determination. Later on, in 1530, she suggested a joint meeting of Charles, Ferdinand and herself, to review the problems of the Empire and measure them against its resources. This came to nothing. They remained separate rulers, in constant contact but never formulating an overall imperial plan. The important change that did come about gradually was that Charles used his Spanish subjects to represent him abroad, sometimes together with Burgundians (as in England), sometimes alone (as at the Vatican, Venice and Genoa).

Imperial troops (now under the bold and dashing Antonio Leyva) held Milan against the French and Venetians, but mostly because the French abandoned the siege in order to march south to 'liberate the pope' (in fact to try to win back Naples). The province of Apulia was under French control within a month. They were suddenly close to Naples. Genoese ships were said to be approaching Naples with the idea of blockading it. The imperial garrison there was under the prince of Orange, at this time twenty-five years old and in Charles's opinion too young to be given the viceroyship. He made a series of jabs at the French (who were weakened by plague) but land skirmishes were useless against the blockade from the sea. Then there was a sudden stroke of luck in the defection of the Genoese

admiral, Andrea Doria, who had not been paid by the French. His
ships simply left harbour. Orange put Leyva into the attack again
and broke the French lines. The French commander Lautrec died,
and troops on both sides moved north again. Naples was saved.

But a new French army swept into Lombardy. Against it a
Spanish army disembarked at Genoa (now opened to the imperialists
by Andrea Doria), and it dealt the French such a blow on the outskirts of Genoa and at Landriano that Francis was forced to negotiate again. He had offended the pope by showing how much more
he cared to own Italy than liberate the Vicar of Christ. Clement was
at last convinced that he had to befriend Charles. He made Francisco
Quinones (general of the Franciscans and once Charles's confessor)
a cardinal. This was not done to please Charles so much as to make
sure that Quinones understood the papal point of view in the coming
negotiations. Realizing this, Charles sent Miguel Mai in Quinones's
place as ambassador to the pope.

Mai was an astute man, a good judge of character. A political
prelate like Clement was an open book to him. When the pope
suggested that he himself should visit Spain Mai saw at once that
this was a ploy to stop Charles from coming to Italy. Mai cleverly
suggested that Charles would forget about a council and deal with
the Lutherans in other ways, provided he could be assured of the
pope's close friendship. Clement changed course. He was ready to
concede a great deal if he could be spared a council. The Peace of
Barcelona was signed on 29 June 1528. Charles was to keep Naples,
and Clement was to get Ravenna, Modena, Reggio, Rubiera and
Cervisa. Charles and the imperial troops were absolved from the
sack of Rome. They were to unite against the Turk (who was
advancing up the Danube).

Meanwhile Margaret was cleverly arranging the terms of a peace
with her sister-in-law Louise of Savoy, the mother of Francis I. It
took a year and emerged under the unofficial title of *Paix des Dames*
(the two women met at Cambrai) in August 1529. Francis was to
waive all claim to Naples, Genoa and Milan, and recognise Charles's
right to Artois and Flanders. But there was no advance on the question of the duchy of Burgundy. The duke of Gelderland and Robert

de la Mark, Francis's warring allies, were disarmed. In fact it was the Treaty of Madrid all over again. Francis's sons, still hostages, were to be released. He was to pay 2,000,000 soleils in ransom money. At last he was to marry Eleonore. And Francis was to pay Charles's debt to England.

Altogether Charles must have felt that God had shown His hand unmistakably. Wolsey was at the beginning of his fall from power. The pope was now persuaded that he must stay on friendly terms with the Empire. Other Italian states—notably the Venetian republic and Milan—felt the same need, and treaties with them were negotiated. The English were now official friends too, by the armistice of Hampton Court signed on 18 June 1528. Francis even went beyond the Cambrai treaty and suggested giving an army of 60,000 foot to Charles for use against the Turks. The imperial ambassadors took this as another of Francis's fervent promises which would come to nothing. Like Charles they were not too confident that he would even keep the Cambrai agreement. There was a great celebration in Paris.

Charles began his journey to Italy (Portugal and Castile sent forty mule-loads of gold to Barcelona to help finance him) and arrived in Genoa harbour on 12 August 1529. In December he made a triumphal entry into Bologna to meet Clement VII for a series of talks. They planned an appeal to every Christian state to join forces against the Turks. One of the first items of news to come from Ferdinand during the journey was that the Turkish advance had been halted outside Vienna. On the debit side, some people said that Francis was only waiting for the release of his two princes as hostages to start a war again. Clement had refused to countenance Henry VIII's divorce, and Henry might easily join France again in another rash campaign designed to humble him.

While in Bologna Charles began to feel that he had too many pressing commitments—meeting Ferdinand in Germany for the settlement of the whole Lutheran question was one of them—to allow time for his being crowned in Rome. He was aware that Ferdinand needed help now or never against the Turks. He therefore decided that his crowning should take place in Bologna. The pope's sigh of relief could be heard all over Italy. As he told some of Charles's enemies at the time, he was quite happy that the emperor should hurry on to Germany, as he would certainly spend what was left of his money there. On 22 February 1530 the pope crowned Charles king of Lombardy. Two days later he crowned him king of Rome in the cathedral of S. Petronio. Three thousand *landsknechts* marched through the streets of Bologna bearing banners, seven abreast, with 3,000 Spaniards behind them in files of five, and last of all 3,000 Italians, also in files of five. Despite the presence of the pope, the ceremony had little of the religious about it, and nothing joyful. It was a military display. Understandably, Clement had had his fill of *landsknechts* and Spaniards. For the unpleasant experience of crowning Charles he demanded his portion, which was the sack of Florence so that the Medici dynasty could resume control there.

Charles obliged and Florence was cruelly sacked. The city never again recovered her astonishing powers. A whole civilisation was eclipsed in that long bitter fight which ended in burning and plunder. It was perhaps the first act of what came to be called the Counter Reformation, for which almost anything new and imaginative smelled of heresy. It was also the first step of Charles's holy war, though at the time it looked as if he was simply obliging an ally. It meant that the humanist discussion as to what civilisation should be was cut off, and the starkest power considerations substituted. A grimmer, more philistine Italy, stranger as much to its own Renaissance monuments as to the ancient ones, came into being. As later events were to show, it was also the first act of Castilianising the whole of Italy and not simply the states of the south.

As a further part of his bargain with the pope, Charles was to give one of his own illegitimate daughters, now eight years old, to the new duke of Florence—a Medici in name if not in capacity.

Gattinara (now a cardinal) died when the imperial court reached Innsbruck to meet up with Ferdinand. And six months later Margaret of the Netherlands died too. Charles was alone for the hardest struggle of his life: that with the protestants.

Chapter 5

The Protest Against Rome

The protestant movements of the sixteenth century always harked back to doctrines from centuries before. Although we know these movements specifically by the names of their leaders—Luther, Zwingli, Calvin—they were widely and intensely popular. It took little to turn a few words pinned up on a church door into a national manifesto. And this was for a very good reason: that they were first and foremost, like all 'heretical' movements before them, protests against Rome, against the long arm of ecclesiastical authority. The Hussites (active in Bohemia in the early fifteenth century, like the Lollards in England and the Vaudois in Savoy) had maintained that a communicant should receive not only the bread but the wine as well (at a time when only the clergy took both). This so-called 'Utraquism' was allowed to the Bohemian people for a time, which shows how little the doctrine itself troubled the Church. But then the pope of 1462 denounced it as heretical, and an uprising had been the result. Thus the doctrine had come to express an attitude of defiance against Rome, and anti-Roman feeling had swamped the simple matter of bread and wine. This was the nature of most 'heresy'. It talked doctrine as a means of liberation.

Men were therefore prepared to murder and torture and denounce each other for doctrinal arguments which look to us now like wilful hair-splitting. The political speeches of our epoch, on which wars are fought, may look as incomprehensible to the future. The point is that their arguments are signs and symbols of something else: power. No protestant movement could escape this identification; a doctrinal protest against Rome always ended in a struggle for power. And this struggle in the sixteenth century preoccupied Charles V and then his son Philip II more than any other. And more than anything else it brought their empire tumbling down.

At the beginning of the fifteenth century two papal officials had exposed as fakes the main documents on which the pope's right to govern Christendom rested (the 'Donation of Constantine' and the 'Isidorean Decretals'). A century before that there had been a movement advocating the severance of Church from state, which meant denying the pope his worldly function. John Wycliffe had argued for the disendowment of the Church, and had called the pope an anti-Christ. By the sixteenth century the indignation of kings, philosophers and churchmen had become a popular indignation that begrudged the Church her taxes and privileges.

Since Charles's privileges as emperor were tied up closely with Rome's, he would obviously be the loser from any successful 'reformation' of the Church. For this very reason the reform movement attracted other princes. Some of them had already achieved a degree of independence from the Church. Francis I, by a concordat of 1516, had been allowed to nominate 620 major preferments in France. And he was less free in this matter than the English kings, even before Henry VIII formally cut himself off from Rome. In both France and England lawyers and bankers and merchants were beginning to find that their king and not a prelate was the more useful of two allies. Monarchs and princes were naturally protestant, in that they begrudged a distant control over their finances. John Wycliffe's success in England had been due to resentment of 'foreign interference'. John Huss, inspired by Wycliffe, won a well-nigh dictatorial hold on the Czechs through their resentment of the Germans who had been pouring into Bohemia since the twelfth century, and who seemed to personify the Roman Church. In the same way Luther found no difficulty in getting the German princes behind him. And the German explosion was all the more violent because the princes could only be 'represented' to the pope by the emperor. Lacking direct access to the Vatican, they remained bound by the old privileges, unlike the French and English kings. From being the Empire's most loyal subjects they therefore became the principal source of its destruction.

The pope and the Curia were hated inside Italy quite as much as elsewhere ('a gang of scoundrels', Francesco Guicciardini called them, writing at this period). Venice was an all but protestant republic. But in Italy the papacy was a vested interest. Money that should have been used by the pope for the whole of the Church was increasingly used inside Italy, to maintain his tenuous *status quo* at home. The grand Rome of the Renaissance was built with funds that came from every part of Europe. The College of Cardinals was swamped with Italians. Sixtus IV in the previous century had granted indulgences for souls in purgatory to get himself out of financial trouble. The most fearful crimes could be redeemed with down-payments. Indulgence-pedlars went from town to town, playing on people's fears, and were a usual sight everywhere in Europe. They often spoke bogus Latin to impress the crowds. They bought off local priests with gifts. Little wonder that, according to Erasmus, an ordinary man felt insulted if taken for a priest or monk.

There were many other corrupt practices—the sale of dispensations for marriage; the sale of ecclesiastical offices for many times the value of their stipends; the delegation of duties by bishops to badly paid chaplains and registrars; as well as the accepted practice of making children 'princes of the Church', with vast estates attached to their titles. It was natural that free commerce should be the chief spur of the Reform movement. In concentrating on its Italian politics, the papacy lost touch with what was happening in the rest of the world, not least commercially.

In any case Italy had already passed through its reform movement in the person of Savonarola in the previous century. The Church and the state of Florence had at first found him useful for a 'revival' of Christianity against the humanists. They had then burned him alive. The Italian listened to an ardent reformer only to the point where he let the *status quo* alone. The moment Savonarola took over the government of Florence and began denouncing the Vatican he was in danger as much from the people as from the pope. For papal government was too useful to be ruined. Lorenzo de' Medici had learned as a young man that it was best to make alliances against the pope when he looked too strong but to rush to his defence when he looked too weak. If there was a national feeling at all in divided Italy it lay in this vested interest in the pope's survival. In the end it was always the Italian people who sided with the pope against his attackers. They, and not their rulers, feared his interdicts.

In Germany it was a different story. The particular indulgence campaign that provoked Luther to pin his ninety-five theses on the door of Wittenberg Cathedral in 1517 was the last straw in corruption. To raise a large sum of money for the twenty-four-year-old Hohenzollern prince, Albert of Brandenberg, who wanted to become archbishop of Mainz (he already had Magdeburg and Hulberstadt), an indulgence was granted for his territory. Half the funds were to go to the pope and half to the Fugger brothers, who were his accountants. The Dominican friar Tetzel went round the country 'rattling his box', as the protestants said. Luther's attacks increased. In 1519 he repudiated papal authority altogether. The following year he began to advocate national churches independent of Rome. The papal bull declaring him to be a heretic appeared in the summer of 1520. It required him to recant at once, on pain of excommunication. From a humanist desire to reform abuses in the Church, a movement had come into being to subvert the Church altogether and to bring about a secular society. Nothing could have been further from humanist ideas. Princes and their courts outside Germany began to turn against the 'protest'. But inside Germany protestant princes seized Church lands. Only later did they find that the riches thought to accrue to the Church from these were not so great after all.

'I fear the worst for the unfortunate Luther,' Erasmus wrote in September of 1520; 'so does conspiracy rage everywhere, so are princes incensed with him on all sides, and, most of all, Pope Leo. Would Luther had followed my advice and abstained from those hostile and seditious actions! . . . They will not rest until they have quite subverted the study of languages and the good learning.' Luther had gone too far for most humanists.

In Spain their number was dwindling as the cry of 'heresy' was heard more and more. A Spaniard called Zuniga tried to brand Erasmus as a heretic and as the cause of Lutheranism (1520–2). Had he succeeded, Erasmus might well have ended at the stake, since the

Netherlands were now a Spanish possession. Yet, hitherto, the university of Alcalá in Spain had been a centre of Erasmian teaching. Now the Inquisition began to 'examine' Erasmians. And in 1537 it banned the works of Erasmus in the Castilian language altogether. His Latin works were expurgated. 'Lutheran' quickly came to mean something near to a devil in the Spanish mind. The inquisitors smelled one wherever they went.

In 1520 Luther put out his appeal 'to the Christian nobility', in which he said that God had provided the Germans with a young ruler who might satisfy their hopes. He meant Charles. It was a difficult situation because Luther had princes behind him who were, of course, Charles's electors. When the special papal ambassador at Charles's court, Hieronymus Alexander, asked Frederick the Wise to hand Luther over to him, Frederick refused. He maintained (prompted the day before by Erasmus) that Luther had already agreed to appear before judges in public. Also, he said, it was one of Charles's election promises not to condemn a German unheard. But Leo was after Luther's blood.

Chièvres supported the papal nuncio. Gattinara was closer to Erasmus. Charles wrote to Frederick that he should bring his Luther with him to the first Diet (a meeting of the German Estates) since his coronation, at Worms. But then he withdrew the offer, when the nuncio pointed out to him that the papal Bull on the subject had set a time limit of sixty days on a free hearing for Luther, and that this had elapsed. The Diet opened on 29 January 1521. Mostly it was taken up with other business, but the Lutheran problem was at the back of everybody's mind. The Estates held out; Luther should not be condemned without a hearing. Alexander accused Charles of vacillating, which was the case. He could not afford to alienate Frederick the Wise, nor could he afford to alienate the Church. He also knew that both Erasmus and Frederick were good catholics. His confessor, Father Glapion, even told the Saxon chancellor that Charles believed in Luther's reforms. As for the pope, only Luther's book *On the Babylonian Captivity of the Church* had made him angry. Charles's advisers worked hard on Frederick to bring him over. Gattinara joined in. Alexander had skilful arguments to hand.

He was clear and sound in his exposition of Church law, and perhaps his protestant hearers even agreed with him. But the situation had gone too far. It was now a matter of nationalist feeling.

On 19 February the Estates insisted that Luther must have a safe conduct and look after his own defence, *in the interests of the German nation*. And in the following month Charles ordered Luther to appear—on a safe conduct. Luther arrived at Worms on 16 April. He was escorted all the way by knights. One reception after another was given for him. The papal agent, Alexander, had to bribe the local printing presses (busy putting out Lutheran tracts) to get his own arguments printed. When Luther appeared before the Diet he asked —in a low voice—for time. Everyone was disappointed. But two days later he made his speech, in which he clearly laid down that conscience, and nothing that the Church ordered contrary to it, must be a Christian's guide to action. Charles answered with a speech in French. He said that 'a single monk' must be wrong if he stood against all Christendom. Therefore the imperial power must be thrown against that monk. He was sorry that he had delayed taking action until now. Luther's speech had made the matter clear. He had no alternative, Charles said, but to crush heresy. The speech was translated into the other languages and published.

But the actual edict against Luther was not published until 26 May, although it was put before the emperor to sign before 12 May. Charles was still shy of drastic action. But he signed it. Heresy had been 'dealt with', and everyone forgot the matter. Nothing happened. Luther returned to Saxony, and Charles returned to Spain.

Luther had a hard time controlling his followers. Andreas Carlstadt and Thomas Müntzer longed for spectacular action. Müntzer advocated violent methods to get rid of the 'ungodly' before the coming of the New Jerusalem. Luther called them both the 'heavenly prophets' and preached against them in 1524. Carlstadt later became a Zwinglian. Müntzer became a prophet-leader in the Peasants' Revolt, and was tortured to death in May 1525. There were also prophet-weavers from Zwickau, who influenced a number of top

Lutherans for a time, including Carlstadt. Luther's robust sanity brought them back on the whole, and kept the movement in a manageable unity. But so many unbridled natures round Luther were a constant spur for him to go to extremes. Considering this, he kept a remarkable control. His 'rage' was shared all over Germany.

Gradually he extended his hold among the powerful. Albert of Hohenzollern, Grand Master of the Teutonic Knights, disbanded his order under Lutheran influence. A duke of Prussia accepted his teaching in 1525. A year later landgrave Philip of Hesse did the same. Two years after that the duke of Brunswick, the count of Mansfield, the duke of Schleswig and the margrave of Brandenburg-Ausbach came over to his side. In 1534 Nassau, Würtemberg and Pomerania joined too. And in another five years the princes of Saxony and Brandenburg also decided for Luther.

Charles's handling of the movement continued to be hesitant and even rather sympathetic. It was his brother Ferdinand who came out against Luther and put the Empire's point of view out-spokenly. At the Diet of Speyer in 1529 (called by Charles to 'hear, understand and weigh the opinion of every man with charity and love, and in this way to achieve again one Church and one State'), Ferdinand made his own proposals before the official ones had arrived. He rejected the idea that the Estates had the right to reform the Church in their own way. He hinted that the protestant sects would be suppressed by force if necessary. This provoked the Zwinglians in the south of Germany to their 'protestation' of 17 April in the same year. By this document the princes of southern Germany laid down that each man had the right to decide how best to save his own soul. It was drawn up by the Saxon chancellor Brück, and signed by the margrave George of Ausbach, the landgrave of Hesse (Philip), the elector of Saxony, the prince of Anhalt and the duke of Luneburg, and by sixteen towns. It was the original document of what came to be called protestantism. On its simply expressed idea, referring to no church and no dogma, the whole disruption of the Empire and of Europe was based. Hitherto the argument had gone on inside the Church. Now the papal authority was waived, not simply challenged.

Towards the end of the same year the young Philip of Hesse managed to get reforming theologians together from every part of Germany to argue out their differences, largely on the question of the sacrament. Luther attended. But when it came to a discussion (at Schmalkalde in December 1529) as to what political action should be taken, Philip failed to hold them together. They were united in opposition, but in utter disagreement on doctrine. The elector of Saxony even began to think of abandoning his protestant friends.

Another Diet was arranged to take place in Augsburg in 1530. Charles arrived there on 16 June, full of the conviction that loyal catholics far outnumbered the protestants and that if the Lutherans could be put down the whole protestant movement would fizzle out and the other sects would return to the Church. Luther was now in Coburg. Charles was presented with a protestant 'Confession', and he toned down the answer prepared for him by his advisers. He wanted peace with the protestants, but if they did not come to heel he had nothing against force either. His answer was presented to the Estates in the form of a 'Confutation' a month or so later. Negotiations went on from there. Melanchthon (who had written the 'Confession') prepared an answer to this, called the 'Apologia'. It was really stating the same position as before but in firmer terms. Charles knew that only a General Council of the Church could save peace in Germany. But the protestants were well aware that the man on whom a council depended was the man most set against it.

The Diet of Augsburg changed nothing—it even made retreat for either side less easy than before. At the same time Charles was prevented from threatening force again by the fact that he could not rely on his own side, the catholic princes. They were clearly frightened men, whereas the protestant elector of Saxony exuded confidence. In a rash speech delivered in September, the catholic Elector Joachim of Brandenburg asked the other side fiercely what free interpretation of the Gospels had given them the right to seize lands belonging to other people? The catholic estates were so frightened at this clear statement of their own position that some of them wanted to offer the elector of Saxony an apology for it.

At this time Charles was anxious for his brother Ferdinand to be elected as King of the Romans, which produced an interesting political schism that cut right across the protestant-catholic struggle and showed that nationalist feeling was common to *all* the German princes. The catholic Bavarian dukes, William and Louis, even made an alliance with the protestant princes of Saxony and Hesse, in the autumn of 1531, to scotch Charles's proposal.

The elector of Saxony asked officially that Ferdinand's election as King of the Romans be at once rescinded and that a general toleration be issued for the Lutherans. Also the lands seized from the Church should be confirmed to their new owners. The Bavarian dukes came out against Ferdinand even more openly by forming an alliance with his Hungarian rival John Zapolya (who was friendly with the Turks). That was how far doctrine counted when interests stood in the way.

The Estates did support imperial policy in one thing. They got together an army against the Turks. Italian, Netherlander and German troops (these last under Count Palatine Frederick) were sent to Ferdinand's support. The Turks were pushed back in Styria and western Hungary, but the imperial commander refused to help Ferdinand against Zapolya on the domestic front.

Charles entered Vienna as a victor, but only in the formal sense. There was no sign anywhere that the Hapsburg interest was safe. The Empire seemed, suddenly, to be on the point of collapse. It had no friends.

In alliance with the king of France the catholic princes of Germany, led by the Bavarian dukes, seized Württenburg (the province connecting Franche Comté, Alsace and the Tyrol) as the first stage of an attack on the Hapsburg dynasty and thus (though they did not see it this way) on the Empire. Even Charles seemed unaware of the loss. Yet Württenburg was an ancient Hapsburg possession. Only Ferdinand could have taken the necessary quick action, but he was too tied up in Hungary with troubles of his own. Instead he traded Württenburg for recognition of him as King of the Romans. That meant acceptance by the German protestants. He also got the landgrave of Hesse to fight for him in Hungary. Meanwhile the catholic ex-king Christian of Denmark had failed to dislodge protestant Frederick from the Danish throne by force, or to restore the Church there. With typical folly he accepted Frederick's invitation to talk over their differences in Copenhagen, and was thrown into prison, where he spent the next twenty-seven years. In Sweden, too, protestantism was successful. As for Henry VIII of England, he was urging the emperor to persuade the pope to grant him a divorce from Catherine of Aragón, in return for declaring himself part of the Empire—which useful possibility Charles had to reject with horror.

All this tended to drive Charles still further into his own nationalism. He was now more safely established in Spain than anywhere else. Belonging to Spain had another advantage, which he did not recognise for a long time as being of more than incidental importance, but which became (together with the Turkish threat) a principal means of keeping the Empire and therefore the Church together: the wealth that poured from 'New Spain'. It was American money that saved Charles, and made it possible for him to build a new kind of empire centred on Madrid. The money was in the form of gold and silver bullion.

Chapter 6

Paradise and Gold

In 1492 Columbus had written home from Hispaniola (Haiti), about
the Indians he had found there: 'So loving, tractable, and free from
covetousness they are, that I swear to your Highnesses, there are
no better people, nor a better country in the world.' He had been
wrecked on the Haitian coast and owed his survival to them. He
left a small colony of Spaniards behind who began to behave with
diabolical cruelty. The Indians exterminated them. A second
Spanish colony was set up and, by the middle of the sixteenth
century, there were hardly more than 150 Indians left, out of
hundreds of thousands. The white man had brought his diseases
with him, notably smallpox and measles. And then there was the
yellow fever or 'black vomit'. Haiti's story was a miniature version
of what happened in Mexico and Peru.

Not all Indians were tractable, even before the Spaniards came.
But, whether they were tractable or not, nothing deterred the
Castilian. He brought to the Americas an astonishing—indeed a
fearful—zeal which made even the blood-obsession of the Aztec
people seem pale. Hernando Cortés was thirty-six when he landed
at Vera Cruz with about 500 men (and only sixteen horses) to subdue
the Aztec empire with its 7,000,000 inhabitants, in 1518. He achieved
his end, just as another adventurer, Francisco Pizarro, one of the
bravest and most heartless rascals ever to have walked the earth,
subdued the neighbouring Inca empire in Peru with a force less
than half as large.

The Castilian apparently did not know what it was to feel a sense
of defeat when faced with the infidel. If he flagged it only needed
the famous Castilian war-cry ('St. Jago and at 'em!') to send him
dashing forward again. God, having a vested interest in the conversion of the infidel (or, failing that, his destruction), simply could not

afford to favour the other side. Thus it was that millions of Indians, the bloody and warlike Aztecs as well as the peaceful Incas, watched these unpredictable invaders—who murdered in cold blood one minute and talked about the love of Jesus another—with increasing awe. It seemed to them as if something had happened in the Mansions of the Sun to eclipse all humanity except these 'bearded ones', whose coming from 'the direction of the sunrise' had long been predicted by their prophets. One of these, telling the Aztec emperor Montezuma of the imminent destruction of his empire, could hardly be understood for the tears that clogged his throat.

Quetzalcoatl, the 'plumed serpent', had been one of the principal gods of the Toltecs, a Mexican people earlier subdued by the Aztecs. This god had been 'banished' because, it was said, he refused to approve of human sacrifices, which were an essential element in Aztec worship. In the great Aztec city of Tenochtitlan (Mexico City) it was usual for thousands of young boys and virgins to be sacrificed at the altar during special dedication ceremonies which lasted for days on end. The blood ran down the temple steps in great congealing channels, setting up, together with the piles of corpses, an unbearable stench. The priest plunged a dagger into the victim (who almost never uttered a sound) and then quickly tore out the heart while it was still beating—all done, according to a watching Spaniard, in the time it took to make the sign of the cross. The body was then thrown down the temple steps so that its arms and legs could be chopped off. These were later eaten. The sacrificial priests had their hair permanently matted with human blood, and a stench of sulphur and decomposing flesh surrounded their persons. Blood and gore encrusted their robes so thickly at times that they could hardly walk. They had skulls embroidered on their cloaks, and their fingernails were unusually long. Mostly they were young men from noble families. They never married but, so it is said, went in for homosexual practices among themselves, and sometimes dressed up as women.

Human blood was smeared freely on the temple walls and on the idols, since it was believed that the Sun—in its divine and in its physical capacities—would cease to give heat unless continuously replenished with blood. At least four or five humans were sacrificed each day, apart from the great dedication ceremonies. The idols were often made of a paste consisting of various types of seed and human blood.

Now the banished Toltec god who had disapproved of this had travelled after his banishment towards the east, probably to Yucatan. He had gone on a magic raft. And on this raft, it was said, he would one day return. The 'plumed serpent' had a white skin and a full black beard. None of this would have troubled the Aztecs had it not been for the fact that the great Aztec god of war and the sun, Huitzilopochtli, supported the prediction, and added that the Aztec nation would one day be entirely destroyed. He had prophesied that 'the children of the Sun will come from the east, rise up against me, take me by the feet and cast me down'. The 'children of the Sun' would be under the leadership of the plumed serpent Quetzalcoatl, and their arrival was due in 'one reed year'—that being a special year in the Aztec calendar which occurred irregularly and after long intervals. 1363 had been a reed year; so had 1467. The next was 1519. That was when the Spaniards under Cortés arrived. It was natural that the Aztecs should at once recognise him as the 'plumed serpent'. He was nothing less than a god for them. It accounted for the awed generosity with which he was received. The first stories to reach the emperor Montezuma, of the appearance of 'a terrible round thing in the midst of the waters' carrying men with white skins and black beards must have thrown him into alarm, although it was not customary for an Indian monarch, Aztec or Inca, to betray the smallest degree of fear or concern to his subjects. When Hernando Cortés came ashore on Good Friday, 22 April 1519, he happened to be dressed in black. The pictures of the plumed serpent's arrival that had been painted for generations past had always shown him to be dressed in black.

Montezuma sent the Castilian god messengers loaded down with gifts. His hope was to propitiate the god, and perhaps make him take to his magic raft again. He little knew that this particular Castilian serpent was a very greedy one, who liked to lay his hands on other people's possessions and call them his own, particularly if

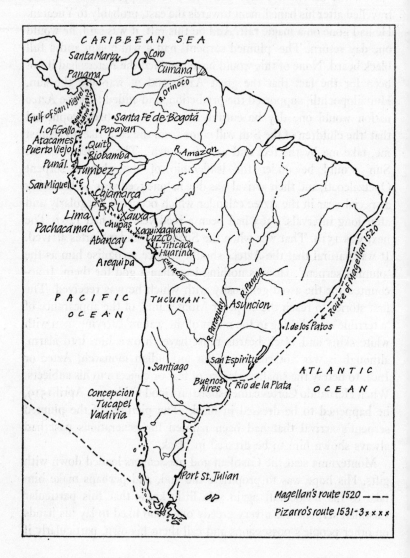

CARIBBEAN SEA

Santa Marta
Coro
Panama
Cumana
R. Orinoco
Gulf of San Miguel
Santa Fé de Bogotá
I. of Gallo
Popayan
Atacames
Quito
Puerto Viejo
Riobamba
R. Amazon
Punál.
Tumbez
San Miguel
Cajamarca
PERU
Xauxa
Lima
chupas
Pachacamac
Xaquixaguana
CUZCO
Abancay
L. Titicaca
Huarina
Arequipa
CHARCAS
PACIFIC
TUCUMAN
OCEAN
R. Parana
Asuncion
R. Paraguay
I. de los Patos
Santiago
San Espiritu
ATLANTIC
Concepcion
Buenos
OCEAN
Tucapel
Aires
Rio de la Plata
Valdivia.

Port St. Julian

Magellan's route 1520 — — —
Pizarro's route 1531-3 x x x x

Route of Magellan 1520
Route of Pizarro 1531-3

they glittered with gold or silver. And the more messengers Montezuma sent, with increasingly valuable loads, the more he was loading the dice against his own survival.

Cortés cleverly set about winning over the local people, who were not Aztecs but Totonacs and Tlaxcalans. He found much resentment against the Aztec. No Castilian serpent could have failed to use it and direct it against the lavish host who was daily sending him treasure and whom he was asking—through ambassadors—to receive him. In the delay between his arrival and Montezuma's invitation he managed to stimulate a state of civil war. This, far more than any strength of arms, even more than the superior power of Spanish armour and shields and firearms over the Aztec arrows and spears, was what won him Mexico. In Peru, where the Indian was not only more united but more peaceable, Castilian tactics were the opposite: those of brute force.

When Cortés began his 250-mile march inland in August, he had several thousand Indian warriors with him. The journey took him eleven weeks, with some battles with other tribes on the way. The emperor's nephew, the prince of Tetzcoco, came to meet him on the edge of the first of the three (partly salt) lakes that entirely surrounded Tenochtitlan. He was carried on a gold litter, by eight of his highest noblemen, in much the same style as the Inca prince later seen by Spanish soldiers in Peru, with servants going in front to sweep the path before him. Cortés and the prince then went on together. Huge crowds assembled to gaze at the first white men, and the first horses, they had ever cast their eyes on. The Spaniards too had something to gaze at. They had never seen such a splendid land: garden after garden of heavily scented flowers leading to a marvellous city reflected in water (later to be totally destroyed, with regret, by Cortés). There were wooden drawbridges which, as the Spaniards saw with alarm, could be slid out of position without difficulty. The Indians travelling with them had warned them that the emperor had every intention of slaughtering them once he had them inside the main square. They were wrong. Cortés and his men were received with great splendour. Montezuma descended from his litter in gold slippers, supported by two noblemen in such a way that his feet barely touched the ground as he moved towards Cortés.

The first hostility shown was weeks later, and on provocation, after Cortés had confiscated the imperial treasure and taken Montezuma prisoner as a hostage 'against any possible rebellion'. It was easier to subdue an empire in partial rebellion than one which received him with mysterious kindness. Pizarro later had the same problem in Peru, and solved it in the same way.

Meanwhile the governor of Cuba had sent a detachment of other Spaniards to grab Cortés and end his private adventure. But this turned to Cortés' advantage. He defeated the Cubans and made them join his army. He then returned to the city to find that the Aztecs were laying siege to the palace where the emperor was held. This was for a very good reason, that the officer who had been governing in his place, a Pedro de Alvarado, had rashly slaughtered a number of Aztec noblemen during one of their wild dances to celebrate the war-god. Cortés sent the emperor out to address the people and advise caution. He did so, but he was pelted with stones and died five days later. Cortés then thought it best to have all the noblemen belonging to the emperor's entourage murdered, and this was done. Their bodies were thrown into the street outside, where the screaming and wailing of their bereaved women became a terrible sound, deafening the frightened Spaniards inside the palace. Many of Cortés' men had been killed or wounded by now, and their powder —the principal instrument of terror on the Castilian side, used as much to create confusion as to kill—was running out.

Cortés managed to escape from the city that night—the 'sad night' as later Spanish chroniclers called it, though it was one of relief for the Indian inhabitants. The drawbridges had been taken away, which meant swimming with full equipment across the deep channels, closely pursued by five or six thousand Aztecs.

Cortés lost about 800 men that night, and nearly all the gold he had stolen from the imperial treasure. The cypress beneath which he is supposed to have wept is still there, with a chapel near by to endow the spot with sanctity. Beyond him lay an army of half a million Aztecs, waiting for him to reach the edge of the lakes. A miracle saved him, as it was to save Pizarro in a similar situation in

Peru. During the ensuing battle his men happened to kill the Aztec commander-in-chief, and that—from the Indian point of view—was the end of hostilities for that day. They simply retired. Cortés was therefore able to move on to Tlaxcala, where the people were loyal to him, and set up his headquarters there.

Many of his men wanted to withdraw to Vera Cruz and treat the whole expedition as a simple reconnaissance, but he refused on the grounds that it would show weakness to the enemy. Instead he planned revenge on the capital city, Tenochtitlan—in fact, its obliteration. He sent to Haiti and Cuba for reinforcements and then began a new branch of activity: shipbuilding. In a few months twelve brigantines were ready for use on the lakes. The move began in April 1521 and it was not long before he had surrounded the city. Then he waited to attack. He despatched a message to the young emperor, a nephew of Montezuma's brother Cultlahuac (who had died of smallpox after a short reign), to ask if he would become a subject of Charles V freely, or would fight for it. The emperor refused even to answer, and Cortés at once cut off all access to the city along the causeways, as well as stopping the water-supply.

About 4,000 canoes came out to meet his ships. But a light wind helped the brigantines to bear down on them and crush them virtually against the walls of the city. Cortés then pitched camp in two towers on the outskirts. The siege lasted for seventy-five days, almost every one of which was occupied with fighting. The losses were very heavy. On one day alone Cortés lost fifty-three men. Almost every day the Spaniards could hear the great 'snake-drum'—a vast drum of stretched snake-skin audible for many miles outside the city, which was sounded for the fearful human sacrifices. It meant that their captured comrades were being made to dance naked in front of the great altar, crowned with feathers, before they were laid down on the altar slab for their hearts to be torn out. These sacrifices could even be seen from some of the Spanish positions. And all day a massive noise was kept up on the Indian side—drums and shell-trumpets, war-whoops and piping. A terrible stench of dead bodies and sewage escaped from the city. Twice Cortés was nearly captured, and would have lost the battle had the Aztecs been content to kill him. But the object of battle for them was to take prisoners, and then to sacrifice them. They preferred Cortés alive to Cortés unsacrificed. Rations were now desperately short on both sides, but the Aztecs, like the Indians on the Spanish side (reckoned to number almost 200,000 by now) fared better because they ate their own dead.

The Spanish boats managed to find an unblocked canal that led straight into the heart of the city, and Cortés began to set light to everything he could find, though it was not always easy on account of the water. What would not actually burn, his men knocked down. The emperor still refused to sue for terms, even when the Spaniards placed a cannon in the main street. Cortés ordered the main temple to be stormed and the houses all round it to be put to the flame. He felt particularly sorry about burning down a small palace where Montezuma had kept a delightful collection of birds.

Thousands of the Aztecs inside the city were dying of hunger and disease, and their bodies were heaped up in the streets, deliberately out of sight of the Spaniards, who would otherwise have known the full extent of their weakness. Then the emperor and his commander-in-chief were captured. A thanksgiving mass was said, and Cortés refused to oblige the emperor by driving his dagger through his body, as he had asked.

In a short time the city was entirely rebuilt, in the Spanish style, with Indian forced labour. Many of the workers starved to death during the operation, or succumbed to one of the imported diseases. There were also outbreaks of typhus, a disease which had always been known in Mexico. But unlike typhus the European diseases were nearly always fatal to the Indian, once caught. In 1576 over 2,000,000 of them died from smallpox alone.

It meant the collapse of the Aztec empire. The provinces began to send their ambassadors to Cortés, bearing gifts and vowing homage to an emperor they had never seen, Charles V. Cortés had played the part of the plumed serpent well.

Peru was a very different country, the Incas a very different people. But the results for themselves of Christian invasion were much the same.

The Inca (the name of Peru's emperor or 'representative of the Sun') had extended his hold to the northern coastal region of Peru only at the beginning of the previous century. Thus his empire included what is now Ecuador, Peru, Bolivia and northern Chile down to the Maule river: namely about 2,200 miles of coastline. This coastal strip, about forty miles deep, was barren desert where little rain fell, but the Cordillera mountains that divided it from the rest of the continent yielded numberless streams, so that with an elaborate and carefully maintained irrigation system it was made fertile. Canals stretched for great distances, carrying water from mountain lakes. One aqueduct was sixteen miles long. There was a rich variety of produce: maize, potatoes (sweet and sour), tomatoes, beans, oca, quinoa, mandioca, squashes, cotton and all kinds of fruit including bananas. Among the plants were guava, chilli pepper (cayenne), quinine, tobacco, cocaine. There were lima and kidney beans, alligator pears, agave. Good soil was carried up the hillside to terraces where no irrigation was needed. Quinoa could grow on very high ground. Gold was mined, but equally it was washed from the gravel of streams flowing from the Cordilleras. Silver was mined in great quantity. An achievement that won unreserved Spanish admiration was the Cuzco–Quito road that penetrated the mountains and crossed gorges and rivers from north to south of the empire. Galleries were cut into the rock, and powerful suspension bridges made of creeping vines or withe-ropes with branches laid across them to form a platform with braided hand-rails, crossed the turbulent rivers. Ravines were filled up, and steps cut into sheer rock.

Cuzco was the heart and capital of the empire, where pilgrims came from every province to worship at the vast Temple of the Sun. The name actually meant 'navel'. It stood 11,380 feet above sea-level, and the first Spaniards there swore that there was no city on earth like it. Near the temple was the fortress, its wall 1,200 feet long, made of vast unmortared blocks of stone measuring nearly forty feet long and eighteen feet high, with a depth of at least six feet. These were dragged immense distances.

The Inca was the source of all civil law, just as the High Priest was the only judge in religious matters. Laws hemmed the Inca's subjects round in the most meticulous way, determining their work and place of residence and even their wives, without appeal. There was no property in Peru, no trade, no money. Each of the four provinces was ruled by a governor, representing the Inca, who owned the entire country and so to speak portioned it out to his subjects for their lifetime. There were few criminal laws because there was little criminality. Rebellion was regarded as sacrilege against the Inca's divine person; he was the Child of the Sun and any offence against him was punishable by death. Not only the guilty man but his family and even, sometimes, his village were exterminated.

The Inca never went to war, it was said, without just motive, and he regarded barbarity or ignorance as sufficient motives. In other words the atmosphere was quite unlike that in Mexico, where a bloodthirsty priesthood had become divided from the civil arm, and both were divided from the people. When the Inca took over new provinces he trained new rulers for them at Cuzco, together with their sons, and then sent them back to govern. All food, wool and stores of any kind were distributed to the people from central sources, a portion of them being kept back for the Inca and the nobility. Revenue came to the crown in this way. Everywhere in the country there were stores. Storehouses marked the whole road from Cuzco to Quito, for the use of the army or ambassadors when on the move—a fact to which the Spaniards several times owed their lives when advancing across country to hound the people who had put them there.

At the death of an Inca his favourite wives and concubines struggled to be buried with him. It is said that as many as 4,000 servants and courtiers were sometimes entombed with him, for the privilege of accompanying him to the Mansions of the Sun. Life was not given up easily but, on the other hand, it was not clung to either, which meant that, while perhaps less righteously cruel than the Spaniard, the Indian could dispense with someone else's life or his own more easily.

For all Indians, Mexican or Peruvian, the universe or reality was so to speak transparent. Every object in it was alive. The world throbbed with magic, though not magic in the Christian sense, as a dark practice separate from worship and religious thought. To the Indian, the visible world could be seen through to the divine or dark source that was its inner nature, though the Indian did not emphasise the dark side or give it a separate power perilously near to the power of God, as did the Christians. There were spirits, and these spirits often had to be propitiated. You never chewed your cocoa leaf when in the fields or on a journey, without remembering to spit it out before all the goodness had gone. Maize was sprinkled on the sea. Sacred objects at home were given seeds or maize. Every object had 'eyes' too. It could hear you and see you. It was useless therefore to tell lies, since everything you did was at once known. This was why the Indian never lied in his confession (the invading Christians were astonished to find evidence of what they had always thought to be their own inimitable system of self-redemption). For the Indian priest who heard the confession had special eyes too, with which he could divine the truth about you. And apart from the eyes of things and the eyes of priests, there were 'the seven eyes' of the Supreme God, like the 'seven eyes of the Lord' mentioned by the prophet Zachariah in the Old Testament. It is a mistake to see the Indians as 'sun-worshippers'; the egg was for them equally a symbol of the divine source, and neither the sun nor the moon (the latter often worshipped in preference to the sun since it seemed more amenable and feminine), nor the egg, took the place of the universal spiritual source of everything, God Himself.

In the Inca play *Ollantay* the High Priest divines that General Ollantay has fallen in love with one of the Inca's daughters, because 'knowledge tells me what is hidden from the common man'. The general, discovered, asks him to plunge a dagger into him. There was no lying or hedging or withdrawal from a guilty position, because everything was seen and known. The separation between the 'material' world and the 'spiritual' world that came about in Christian thought as a result of bifurcating reality too sharply into good and evil, light and darkness, could never have come about in the Indian system. That was why, when a man left his home for a time, he had no need to bar the door. In fact he left it open, with a branch across the entrance, to show that he was away.

The High Priest was usually a brother or uncle of the Inca and lived in the country just outside the city so that he could 'contemplate the stars and meditate upon them'. He lived a simple and ascetic life, quite unlike that of the Aztec priests. He had eight-day fasts, but no more was allowed; as in the Hindu religion, excesses of any kind were discouraged as producing too great an attachment to the world, through either pleasure or pain. As for human sacrifices, the Incas had gone a long way towards ending them, so that now a llama was substituted for a particular person (and given that person's name), and even small clay figures could be used to bury in the soil or fling into a ravine instead. There were no bloody scenes on dedication days, and the priesthood was only feared for its powers of prophecy and divination. The god of war was not given such paramount importance as in Mexico, nor did it have to be assuaged with the blood of prisoners. Therefore war was not prized as an end in itself. Compared with Mexico, the land of the Incas was peaceful, thriving, composite: a land which did not expect the vengeance of a 'plumed serpent'.

The sun was, so to speak, the warmth of God pouring over that society. The moon was the sister-wife of the sun, and Venus was his page. Thunder and lightning were his ministers. The rainbow was a fleeting physical appearance of God Himself. Everything had an essence, called *mana*. There was a llama *mana*, a maize *mana*, a source that had to be worshipped and, especially for the common people, pleased. Peru had many nuns, called Virgins of the Sun, or spiritual brides, under *mamaconas* or abbotesses who instructed them in religion. They spent their time making fine garments for the Inca and his family. They were on the whole chaste and pure. Any girl found with a lover was buried alive, her lover strangled. Her village was then razed to the ground. Nor would the villagers attach any blame to her; the event was simply part of a divine system being enacted without reference to individual life. The entire concept of individuality was in fact missing from Inca society, and the

Spaniards, children of the Renaissance, were often astounded to
see an Indian woman pass a screaming child by without even glanc-
ing at it. An accident would simply be reported to the authorities,
but no help would be given to the victim. All initiative stemmed from
the Inca, whose conduct and standards were quite different from
those of other people. He could even choose concubines from the
Virgins of the Sun. That was the only union they were allowed, for
the simple reason that it was a divine one. After such a union they
did not return to the convent, but were sent home to live in special
comfort, receiving gifts from the Inca until the end of their lives.
They were not allowed to marry or touch another man.

The chief divinity was called Pachacamac, creator of the world.
His temple lay about twenty miles north of Lima. He was not
originally an Inca god. But he had been kept by the Incas after
central Peru was conquered, and Lima had become the Mecca of the
Peruvians. It was perhaps this mutual respect for each other's
divinities that knit the separate nations within that country into one
consciousness.

On the whole the invading Christians showed no such respect,
and conducted religious wars which the Inca would have regarded
as unthinkable. Since respect for alternative religious systems was
not taught in Christendom the ordinary Spaniard simply saw what
he called 'barbarians' when he arrived in the Americas. Many
people in Spain—certainly most of those in authority—would have
condemned his cruelties, and they did, strongly, when they heard
about them. But the intolerance had come from religious education
in the first place. By now the Christian had come into contact in his
various voyages with the Hindu, the Muslim, the Jew and the Indian
of the west, and he had proved his system to be incomparably the
most intolerant of them all. We must remember that Constantinople
under the Sultans still had a Christian patriarch for a time, and that
more than one Sultan showed great esteem for the Jews. It is difficult
to avoid the conclusion that the Christian mind lacked religious
depth compared with that of other peoples, if it could close itself
off so implacably from experiences foreign to it. In fact, as the
Spaniards came to know the Indians, after colonisation had started,

5

their first disapproval gave way to appreciation, sometimes to fervent admiration, and then to bitter guilt.

Warnings had been sounded by Spanish missionaries years before. In 1510 Friar Pedro de Córdoba had founded the Dominican order in New Spain. He had preached fervently on behalf of the Indians, to prevent 'conversion by the sword'. And the bulk of the Inquisition's work in the Americas was the maintenance of some kind of moral order among the Spaniards, not the Indians. Much of it was simple punishment of blasphemy. One friar, writing home, criticised the way in which the Spaniards attended divine worship, coming in late and discussing contracts in loud voices, while the women laughed and gossiped. He compared this with the zeal and devotion the Indians had shown 'in the temples of their demons', as he called them, before their 'conversion'.

In fact the 'demon' played a minimal part in the Indian religious system, and much less than in the Christian. The festival of the summer solstice in Cuzco, for instance, drew Indians from every part of the Empire. After a three-day fast thousands of them, superbly dressed, assembled in the square before the main temple to await the Rising of the Sun in complete silence. The instant it appeared on the horizon there was a great shout and the music of pipes and horns and drums began. This was the 'barbaric' music heard by the Spaniards. In other words it was unfamiliar to them.

Like the forward troops of all invading armies Pizarro's men had no time to observe the civilisation around them, even if they had felt inclined to do so. Later it was noticed that the Inca people had quite as advanced a medicine as the Christians. Their use of herbs was more meticulous. They grew tobacco and cocaine entirely for medicinal purposes. It was usual to take snuff against colds. Blood-letting was done, and operations were carried out with a sharp flint said to be less painful than the Christian lancet. Even trepanning was performed, with a piece of obsidian in most cases. But when you have come looking for paradise and gold, with an emphasis on the gold, you are not likely to lose time watching the other skills of the people who produce this gold in such fantastic quantities. In one of the portraits of Francisco Pizarro, in the Palace of the Viceroys at

Lima, there is a large cross embroidered on his jacket and cloak. It looks strangely like a dagger.

Another factor, apart from hunger for gold, urged Pizarro on to drastic action: the unofficial nature of his enterprise. He was in increasing conflict with the governor of Panama. He wanted to seize hold of Peru at whatever cost to its people as soon as possible. With an empire in his hands not even a Christian emperor could overlook his claims. Wherever his ships moored he and his men were shown the greatest kindness. From the sea he saw every evidence of a thriving civilisation—good roads and fertile, irrigated land along the coast, together with an obviously contented people. The further south he penetrated the kinder the Inca people seemed to become. At Tumbez, when he anchored off the island of Santa Clara, the people came down to the edge of the water to gaze in wonder at the 'floating castle'. They then sent out boats loaded down with bananas, maize, pineapples, coconuts, sweet potatoes, plantains, game, fish, and even a number of llamas. Pizarro and his men gazed at this 'little camel' as the Indians called it with great interest, since it was the first time they had seen one; later the breed became almost extinct through their reckless depredations. The town chief came with one of the vessels and was received on board. He wanted to know why the Spaniards had come, and from where. Pizarro told him, through an interpreter, that he was the subject of the greatest prince on the earth and had come to extend that prince's government over this land, 'lawfully'! More than this, the inhabitants of this land were in 'darkness', since they worshipped an evil spirit (not that Pizarro knew anything about Inca worship, or even very much about his own). He would gladly lay before the chief and his people all he knew about the only true God, Jesus Christ, so that they too could be saved. The chief said nothing.

On his return to Santa Cruz (in 1527), after his second reconnaissance expedition which penetrated to the ninth degree of southern latitude, he found that an Indian woman of rank had prepared for his visit with special arbours interwoven with heavily scented flowers, under which he and his men were given a sumptuous banquet, with music and dancing. As a special favour, Pizarro let her too into the secret of his voyage south, as he had done the chief of Tumbez, and he was even good enough to unfurl the flag of Castile. The lady and her people thought it a great joke, which indeed it was, considering he had no right to be there. He simply could not get them to take what he said seriously and—luckily for them—he decided to leave it at that for the time being. And at Tumbez he took on board a handful of Peruvians, one of them, Felipillo, as great a rascal as he was himself, as later events showed.

It was natural that, in the course of time, Indian suspicions should be aroused. In Pizarro's third expedition (1531) there was plenty of fighting. But in the end this was to his advantage. It was easier to convert the Incas to Christianity in his sense—namely, to seize their treasures and turn them into a labour force—if they took him seriously. Nothing was more difficult to subdue than laughter and kindness. Indeed, he had to force the Inca people to fight, after their emperor Atahualpa had exhorted them all to show the invader every consideration. And he had to murder Atahualpa. Much later, after the settlement of the country, Spanish missionaries did their best to undo the damage. But since they too believed in the destruction of the Inca religion, by the terms of their own faith, they could only complete the conquest.

At this time the Inca Empire was divided between two rulers, sons of the last Inca, Huayna Capac, who had died in 1525. One of them was the rightful heir, Huascar, and the other an illegitimate but favoured son called Atahualpa. On his deathbed Huayna Capac had divided the Empire between them, and appealed to the two brothers to keep the peace. Huascar was to rule in Cuzco, Atahualpa in Quito. The result was naturally enough (after five years of peace) a state of civil war, which only came to an end in 1532 a few months before Pizarro arrived. Atahualpa had got the upper hand in a very bloody battle in the plains of Cuzco, after laying waste much of his brother's territory. He showed his brother every respect but confined him to a fortress at Xauxa. He was now sole emperor. The official Spanish story goes that he invited to Cuzco all the nobles formerly under his brother's rule, together with the entire royal family, in order—he promised—to divide the empire up more satisfactorily. Instead, so it was claimed, his soldiers massacred them all, including his own aunts and nieces. Many of these cold-blooded executions were said to have been enacted in front of Huascar.

All this is on the testimony of the best-known historian of the Incas, Garcilasso de la Vega, who was born in Cuzco in 1540, the son of a European father and an Indian mother, herself related to the royal family. The extraordinary thing about the story is that Pizarro's cold-blooded massacre of the nobles later in the same square of Cuzco was exactly like it, and the whole thing reads like an official rewriting of the facts in order to mitigate Pizarro's otherwise unthinkable callousness. But there is a contradiction in that Garcilasso testifies later in his account to the fact that nearly 600 people of 'pure blood royal' were in good health seventy years after the 'massacre'. Not only this but Atahualpa spared the lives of his greatest rival, Huascar, and also of his younger brother Manco Capac. Clearly no one would have taken the trouble to wipe out the whole of a royal family and yet leave its chief protagonist.

Pizarro fought his way through the interior—against Indian guerrillas and bitter cold on the heights—to Caxamalca, reaching it on 15 November 1532. He sent a small embassy into Cuzco to contact Atahualpa. The Inca came out to meet them, and Hernando Pizarro (Francisco's brother, a less violent man who later befriended Atahualpa) gave him a dazzling display of horsemanship. He dashed all over the square and then charged full gallop towards Atahualpa and his attendants, pulling up so close to the emperor that foam from the horse's mouth flecked his robes. The Inca did not move an inch, though his attendants did. It was Castilian humour with a sting in its tail. The story later went round that Atahualpa had every one of his attendants put to death that evening for showing fear before strangers. Like the 'massacre', this story tallied neither with his personality nor with later events. At that first meeting concubines from the royal harem came out into the square with golden cups full of *chicha* or maize-beer for the visitors. They drank it but did not dismount. Unsuspectingly Atahualpa promised to return the visit.

Pizarro's plan—his 'council of war' as he described it to his officers—was to get as many of the emperor's followers into the square at Caxamalca (unarmed of course) and then to massacre them. He gave orders that the emperor himself must not be touched, only kidnapped. Saturday, 16 November 1532, was a bright warm day, and the Spanish camp was up long before dawn, preparing its positions. Horses and men were to be out of sight, secreted in the great halls around the square, and in the hidden lanes. They were to bar all retreat. The signal for the massacre to begin was to be the discharge of a cannon. The soldiers were given a hearty breakfast, and bells were placed on their horses' breastplates to frighten the Indians. Muskets would do the rest. The Spaniards knew by now that gunpowder was the key to their strength, even more than their iron swords and shields (iron, like horses, being unknown to the Indians). They had once or twice given displays of their marksmanship, and seen that magical powers were attributed to them. It was half the battle, when you were fewer than a couple of hundred against thousands.

When everything was ready Mass was said, and these simple Castilians prayed to their Lord to make the murder of these innocent people successful. Everyone cried, 'Rise, Lord, and judge thy cause!', in the words of the Inquisition. It was perhaps not such a far cry from the Aztec idea that God had to be assuaged with human blood. The Castilian idea was that God preferred a dead man to a heathen.

The Spanish camp waited for Atahualpa's column to appear. They waited a long time, in silence, in growing tension. Then at noon Atahualpa was seen on the horizon in his golden litter, held above the shoulders of his followers, surrounded with every pomp, which had taken half a day to prepare. The Inca sent a message forward that he would be entering Caxamalca with fully armed soldiers, in the same manner as the Spanish embassy had approached him the day before. For the moment Pizarro agreed, though it looked like the end of his plan. Attendants swept the path before the emperor, whose litter was open. It was a brilliant display of clothes and ornaments, flashing in the sun. They then pitched tent, surrounded by regiments of soldiers, who followed suit in the neighbouring fields. The emperor sent another messenger. He would stay where he was for the night, as it was growing late. He would enter Caxamalca in the morning.

The Spaniards had been at their stations at least eight hours by now. By Pizarro's original reasoning blood should have been spilled long ago. He feared a diminution of courage in his men and sent word back to Atahualpa that he was deeply disappointed since he had prepared a great banquet for that evening. It was perfectly true. There would be only one guest, Atahualpa himself. The rest would be lying in the square outside, dead. Could not the emperor come, he asked, with just a few unarmed attendants, to share the feast, leaving his great army outside? Could he not pass the night at Caxamalca instead of in a tent?

Atahualpa accepted. He and his unarmed attendants (many hundreds of them) entered the town, singing what the Spaniards afterwards called 'songs of hell', though the only hell on that day was in their own hearts. First came hundreds of servants, then the noblemen with their maces of copper and silver, some of them dressed in pure white, others in chequered red-and-white cloaks. The guards had rich blue liveries, full of ornaments. As to Atahualpa's litter it was seen not to be coated with gold but to be one solid piece. That alone must have put the tense soldiers in good heart again. And the noblemen had massive pendants hanging from their ears, the lobes of which from childhood had been stretched by weights, so that they hung almost to their shoulders. The Spaniards saw not the nobility of these men but their ears. Hence their name for Indian noblemen: '*orejones*' or 'big-ears'. The royal litter was lined with the vivid plumes of tropical birds. Round Atahualpa's neck was a collar of immense emeralds. He had golden ornaments in his hair, and on his brow was the crimson *borla* or fringe down to his eyebrows. It was the Inca crown.

When he and his five or six thousand men had filled the square they waited. Not a Spaniard was to be seen. He turned to one of his attendants and was just about to ask him where the foreigners had got to when, the very image of unction, out came Friar Vicente de Valverde, a Dominican (afterwards bishop of Cuzco), with a Bible in one hand and a crucifix in another. He approached Atahualpa, and began to explain through the interpreter Felipillo the doctrine of the Trinity, of all things. He started at the Creation and worked his way (none too clearly, for he seemed not to be sure about the doctrine himself) to the redemption of mankind by Jesus Christ at Calvary. He then told the spellbound Atahualpa that Christ had left a St. Peter to rule the earth for him. That was a long time ago, and even St. Peter could not be expected to live for ever, despite the divine mandate. He had passed his office on to successors and these (luckily no other Christians were there who might have laughed) were called popes. They were the absolute spiritual rulers of the whole earth. Friar Vicente finished by saying that the present pope had authorised the Spaniards to subjugate Atahualpa's part of the world (a complete lie) and bring the people into the same religious system, mostly for their own good. Pizarro, the military commander, would now step forward and—if the Inca would be so kind as to accept his rule from now on—would do the job of subjugation. All Atahualpa had to do was to treat the commander nicely, apart from confessing the errors of his religion, and then declare himself the vassal of the emperor Charles V.

Atahualpa had probably never heard anything so confusing in all his life. This foreigner's God was One, and then He was Three. 'That makes four,' he said to little Philip the interpreter, and little Philip agreed.

Then the Inca exploded with rage. He told the friar that he would be no man's vassal, and that while he did not doubt that this other emperor was a great man—he must be, he added, if he had sent his soldiers so far across the seas—no one could make Atahualpa serve him. He would, however, become his 'brother'. As for the man the good friar called a pope, he must be mad to talk of giving away countries that did not belong to him! In any case, this God he had just heard about had apparently been put to death by the very people he had created! What sort of a religion was that? And what sort of people were they who had committed the murder? After all the Inca God was still there—Atahualpa pointed to the last rays of the sun—'and looks down upon all his children'. He then asked the friar on whose authority he said all these things about the Creation and the Trinity. The friar's answer was to hand him the Bible. Atahualpa took a long look at it, turning over the pages, and then suddenly threw it to the ground and asked the friar to tell him what his comrades were doing in his land. He added that he would not move from the spot until they had accounted for all the wrongs they had been doing to his people, stealing and making war. The friar picked up the Bible and hurried off to the hidden Pizarro. He was not as brutally stupid as he seemed. He had no doubt used the Christian story to confuse and anger the Indian king, and he had succeeded. He could now hand over to the secular arm. He went in to Pizarro and told him not to waste any more time talking to 'this dog' but to attack. 'I absolve you,' he added.

Pizarro went out and waved a white scarf, his signal for the gun to fire. It fired. And from every corner Spanish soldiers dashed out to their war-cry of 'St. Jago and at 'em!' They poured into the square on foot and on horseback. They fired their muskets, drove their horses into the terrified crowd, trampled them down and put them to the sword while smoke from the guns obscured everything. The Indians offered no resistance, except for those close to the Inca's litter. These massed together and tried to tear at the Spaniards with their fingers. They clung to the horses' legs. The rest were trying frantically to get away. But every escape route was closed. Their bodies piled up in the narrow exits of the square as they were cut down. The pressure of the fleeing crowd was so great that part of the town wall crashed down, and hundreds got away. They were pursued by horsemen, and most of them died in the fields outside. None of the army surrounding the town came forward to help. There had been no plan on the Inca side for such an emergency. That was the degree of so-called 'hell' in the Inca mind that day. Meanwhile the battle round the litter went on. Atahualpa was still held high above his attendants' shoulders, swinging about perilously and almost toppling down on to them. A soldier dashed forward to finish the job off his way by running a sword through the emperor but Pizarro screamed out at the top of his voice, *'Nadie hiera al Indio so pena de la Vida!'* ('no harm to the Indian on pain of death').

The litter was overturned at last and Atahualpa fell—straight into Pizarro's arms. The imperial band was snatched off his brow by a soldier, in an action curiously reminiscent of the crown of thorns at Calvary. It was suddenly all over. Not an Indian apart from Atahualpa was left alive in Caxamalca. It had taken no more than half an hour.

The army outside the city simply drifted away. A people that had been taught to depend on those above them—and essentially on one man, the Child of the Sun—had no resources in the face of the Child's disappearance. They scattered to their homes, and the story of the massacre began travelling all over the empire.

Pizarro's secretary recorded afterwards that 2,000 natives had been murdered that day. That was almost certainly an underestimate: no doubt it was designed to soften the wrath of Charles V when he heard about it. The figure may have been as high as 10,000, though no one can be sure about it.

That evening Pizarro kept his promise and entertained the king at a splendid banquet. They sat side by side and looked out on to the square, which was still littered with piles of the dead. Atahualpa had little appetite, and sat gazing in silent gloom across the town while Pizarro tried to jolly him out of his mood by telling him that he had lost the battle because Christ had not protected him. He had been 'punished' by God also for throwing down that Bible. So he should not take it too badly. The Spaniards, he added, were forgiving people, as long as you were careful not to make war on them.

According to Felipillo, who had already taken a dislike to his own emperor and was no doubt paraphrasing every remark he made freely, Atahualpa only spoke to say casually that the day's events were simply 'the fortune of war' and that he admired the way it had all been done. Another highly improbable speech put into his mouth was that he had intended to draw the Spaniards as far into his country and his confidence as possible to kill them off—those he did not need as servants. He had had his eye on their muskets and their horses too, he added (according to Felipillo).

The next day thirty Spanish horsemen rode over to the Inca palace and rounded up the wives and concubines, and those of the attendants who were still there. And they came away with all the gold, silver and emeralds they could lay their hands on. No one offered any resistance. It was not so much that the Inca sun had been eclipsed: it had undergone a sea-change which they could not yet understand. They obeyed the Christians and gazed at them with rapt awe not because they were conquerors but because they had the Child of the Sun in their possession. And they wanted to join the Child as soon as possible, even in captivity, even in death. To go with the Child on the last journey towards the Mansions of the Sun was the greatest privilege.

By this time there were a vast number of Indians, including soldiers who had not dispersed, entirely dependent on a tiny band of Spaniards who saw them as so much fodder. The most bloodthirsty of Pizarro's men wanted to kill them off, or at least cut off their hands to disable them for battle. Pizarro, whose massacre had been political, scorned this idea and gave out a directive that all Indians, apart from those serving the Inca or himself, must return to their homes. They would come to no harm if they lived peacefully.

His men were now supplied—for the time being—with most of the things they wanted in order to establish themselves as a garrison and await reinforcements. They had plenty of food, gold and women. They rounded up herds of llamas and slaughtered them. It was the Inca custom to round these animals up once a year in a great royal hunt. Only a few of them were slaughtered for meat. The rest were sheared and sent back to the heights, after being controlled for diseases. It meant that the breed had flourished. Within months of the Spanish influx the breed was in danger of extinction, so gluttonous was this handful of men. The massive stores of the Inca's palace—which included everything from the finest cloth to grain —were broken into and distributed, without care for where future supplies would come from.

Meanwhile Atahualpa was under heavy guard, but in spacious apartments together with his women and attendants. He was continually visited by noblemen from outside the town. They brought him gifts, and shed tears before him. Being an astute man, and perhaps more mature than his Christian guards, he began to watch

Pizarro and his officers in the hope of divining their real motives for turning his kingdom upside down. He clearly did not believe in their mumbo-jumbo about one God being three and then four. Having been groomed in a highly spiritual religious system he could certainly tell the difference between a saint and a savage. And these men were clearly savages. What, then, had brought them here?

It was not long before he saw that, like savages everywhere, they were most interested in what glittered. While being tutored daily on the Creation, the Fall and the Redemption (and showing much quickness as a pupil) he noticed that Spanish eyes quickened more when they looked at the gold pendant round his neck than when they looked up at the cross on the wall. And he quietly set out to blind them with gold.

He promised Pizarro and his men what was, for them, as near paradise as they could ever hope to get: gold enough to cover the floor of the room he stood in (about 22 ft. long and 17 ft. wide) to the height of his upstretched arm (about 9 ft.). Pizarro then drew a red line along the wall at this height. The deal was on. In return for the gold he promised to release Atahualpa (which he had no intention of doing). He also promised not to melt down any of the ornaments he received but to keep them in the state he found them. He had no intention of keeping to that either. But he gave his word. And a Christian's word was, as everybody knew, as good as his bond.

He then gave the Inca two months to fulfil his part of the bargain. Most of the gold was to come from the capital of the empire, Cuzco. According to Atahualpa, the roofs of the temples there were plated with gold, and this would be removed at his order. He also sent couriers to every other part of the empire, to strip the royal palaces and temples of their most easily detachable ornaments. The treasure then had to be hauled on the shoulders of his subjects across mountain and river. In this way Atahualpa hoped to regain his kingdom. Had the Spaniards been as simple as he thought, this might have happened. But their appetites were complicated by their nationalism, and this nationalism was identified with what they took to be the Christian religion. They required of the Inca not only his gold but his conversion. And conversion in their sense meant his total subservience. This he did not fully understand, even at the end when the faggots were being prepared (under the direction of the good friar) for his burning.

There was one argument which Pizarro continually pressed on him and to which, though it was the opposite of a Christian argument, Atahualpa always nodded in a solemn and thoughtful way; that his God had deserted him by giving the victory to such a small number of men. Here he may have understood something deeper than Pizarro intended or knew—that there was a certain destiny in events, and that this destiny was always prepared in some way by oneself. In the Indian religion there was a strong sense of human shortcomings, which accounted for the well-nigh obsessive propitiation that went on in every home; spitting out the half-chewed cocoa leaf, so as to leave something for the spiritual presences all around, was one such act of propitiation among hundreds. It was perhaps the weakest point in the religion, and one that led to too great a passiveness. It was this passiveness that had given the Spaniards their chance. And finally everything *was* the will of God, Atahualpa must have reflected; he had to bow to this will. It did not mean that the Christians were right, or that his own faith was wrong. It meant that a design was afoot which he did not understand, and which he had therefore failed to predict or prepare his people for. The brutal Spanish argument that God was tribal and supported the hardest heart and the hardest sword could not have had much influence on him, though Pizarro thought it had.

Meanwhile Huascar (who was by now also under Spanish arrest) sent word to Pizarro that Atahualpa, never having lived in Cuzco, could not know the degree of the treasure there, nor did he have the right to carry it away. He would offer a much bigger ransom. Pizarro's answer was that he would bring Huascar to Caxamalca to have the matter thrashed out between the two brothers, and then decide which of the two was telling the truth. Huascar was found drowned before this could happen, and it seems certain that Atahualpa gave secret orders for the murder to be carried out. Apparently his brother died screaming that Atahualpa would soon meet an equally violent death. When Pizarro accused Atahualpa of

originating the crime he denied it warmly, and claimed that he had
had no contact with Huascar's court since his arrest. It seemed most
unlikely, and Pizarro showed as much moral indignation as he could
manage.

A fabulous amount of gold plate began arriving in Caxamalca on
Indian shoulders. It was a slow business but hardly a day passed
without something glowing warmly on the horizon. The Spaniards
watched with astonishment. It all seemed too easy, and a curious
feeling arose among them that they were being duped in some way.
It could be a subtle royal ruse, whereby Atahualpa was using his
couriers to contact his provincial governors and alert them to the
present state of affairs, with a simultaneous national rising in view.
Like Macbeth the Spaniards saw plotting fingers everywhere, and
more so as the golden wages of murder came piling in. Again Pizarro
went to the Inca and accused him: was he not plotting rebellion?
Atahualpa's answer was to promise Pizarro a free conduct to Cuzco,
so that he could see for himself what was going on. Since Pizarro
wished to reconnoitre the country anyway, he agreed. He sent off
a number of his rougher types under Indian escort. Then he
ordered his brother Hernando to search for the famous temples
where Pachacamac and the Sun God were worshipped side by side,
and which were said to be about a hundred miles away on the coast.
They might yield more gold plate than all of Cuzco put together.

Hernando was treated with unqualified generosity wherever he
went. There was no sign of hostility, much less of rebellion. His
soldiers were given quarters and were well fed, and it was obvious
that Atahualpa had given orders that the white man must be shown
reverence. The officers who went to Cuzco had the same experience.
They rode all the way in litters, on Indian shoulders, and they were
served like kings. There were even public celebrations in Cuzco to
welcome them.

The city glittered with gold, just as Atahualpa had promised. As
to the temple, its main door was of turquoise and coral and crystal,
but the inner shrine, which the Spaniards had no hesitation in
violating, contained only a dumpy idol amid the foul stench of
sacrificed animals. It was removed and broken up, and a cross was

put in its place, after the stench had been removed. This was not all they violated. They broke into the convent of the Virgins of the Sun and treated themselves to the women inside. They complained that the work of dismantling the gold plate was not going fast enough. The temple should, to please them, have been reduced to rubble to make the job easier. But the Indians were taking their time. Priests had hidden much of the treasure. And they took care not to reveal to the Spaniards where the other temples of the city lay. The visitors had to content themselves with piling as much gold on Indian shoulders as they could carry—700 pieces of solid gold plate, each one about ten inches long. For all this they treated their bearers, the priests and the local noblemen who came out to welcome them like dogs.

Reinforcements arrived at Pizarro's headquarters from Panama under Diego de Almagro in February 1533. There were 150 foot and fifty horse, well-armed. At once rivalries began between the two chiefs, and it was whispered to Pizarro (by Almagro's own secretary) that Almagro had come to usurp him. On his side Almagro was told that Pizarro disliked and distrusted him. But for the moment the old comrades continued to co-operate with each other, and Almagro had his secretary hanged for treason. It was obviously to their mutual advantage—for the moment—to stand together.

Pizarro's brother, Hernando, was much less happy about Almagro's arrival. He refused to emerge from his quarters to greet him. It was partly this that decided Pizarro to send him to Spain to present Charles V with 100,000 ducats' worth of the most superb gold ornaments from Cuzco, and—when this sweetening had been done—to argue the case for the recognition of Pizarro as the conqueror of Peru. This gold (so as not to lose anything) was to be deducted from the 'royal fifth' later. Another reason for sending Hernando away was that he had taken a strong liking to Atahualpa, and might have interfered with Pizarro's plan to liquidate him at all costs.

The Spaniards then set about breaking up all the glittering objects from the golden pile and melting them down to ingots of a uniform standard in value, so that they could be divided among the men equally. The total value of the haul turned out to be something in the region of what would today be £35 millions-worth of gold, apart from a vast quantity of silver.

Here there was a hitch. Almagro's men demanded their portion on the rather spurious grounds that they too were guarding the royal person and the royal treasure, and that without them these might by now have been lost. Since wealth and greed often go together Pizarro's followers were unwilling to share a single nugget. Pizarro argued that Almagro's men should be satisfied for the moment with a token sum, in the hope of greater shared returns later, when every temple in the country, every Convent of the Sun, every royal palace had been smashed to pieces and the contents stolen. He and he alone had, after all, carved out the path to this treasure. And the next stop along the path was Cuzco itself.

That was finally agreed. The gold was divided with solemn and God-fearing justice by the commander himself, in a special ceremony. An hour later his entire army consisted of rich men. It might have been predicted that it would not make leadership any the easier. A small amount was set aside for the church that had just been built in Caxamalca. It was not very great considering the divine help received.

Now that all the gold was in and Atahualpa could serve no further purpose there was the problem of what to do with him. Everyone had had plenty of chance to see that he commanded absolute awed obedience among his people. Pizarro himself later wrote that any Indian would at once have thrown himself off the side of a mountain if the Inca had ordered it. He would have done it gladly, and as a privilege. It was clearly dangerous to set such a powerful man free.

And Atahualpa now had the effrontery to *ask* to be set free! It was really too much. Pizarro decided to again find traces of rebellion in the country. This time it was with the help of the little interpreter Felipillo who had had an affair with one of the royal concubines and would in normal circumstances have been put to death at once, together with his family. Felipillo piled up imaginary charges against the Inca, knowing that his king felt personally outraged and was after his blood. Once more Pizarro accused Atahualpa to his face and this time the Inca smiled. He asked the Spaniard not to 'jest' with him. But he understood well enough what the accusation meant: continued imprisonment. The fact was that the remarkable qualities the Spaniards found in him—courage, astuteness, refinement and utter reliability in his word, together with great friendliness towards his kidnappers—were the very things that made them fear him, and ensured his death.

Pizarro was under pressure too, principally from Almagro and his officers, to do away with Atahualpa as soon as possible. At least this is what he claimed. It may be that among his own men certain guilty apprehensions were stirring. They felt that enemy armies were assembling everywhere, and the Inca's pleasant calm seemed to make it all the more certain. They were afraid for their gold. Surely the Indians were itching to lay their hands on it, as their own hands had itched?

Atahualpa had another close friend in Hernando de Soto. Pizarro sent him away in charge of an expedition—to search out the imaginary traces of rebellion. The Inca now had no friends in high places. Then Pizarro 'agreed' to put him on trial; he let the pressure on him grow, and appeared to give way to it. Twelve charges were trumped up. One of them was that Atahualpa had ordered the murder of his own brother; another that he practised idolatry; also that he had too many wives, and had tried to organise a rebellion. Witnesses were called, and no doubt Felipillo slanted every remark they made against the man he feared more than any other on earth. The date was 29 August 1533. Atahualpa's sentence was a foregone conclusion. He was to be burned alive that same evening (otherwise the officers on reconnaissance might return and give the lie to the charge about rebellion). The only thing needed was the blessing of the Church. And the faithful friar, who no doubt still remembered his Bible being flung on the ground, gave it at once. A tiny minority in the camp argued against the sentence, on the grounds that only Charles V was fit to try a king. They were overruled, and the result was that they lodged an official protest in writing.

Atahualpa wept for the first time when he was told of the sentence. Pizarro too shed tears of a sentimental kind. Officially he could not deny the men under him—the rich men under him—their prey. Atahualpa, recovering after a few moments, begged him to show pity at least towards his children, and also to have his remains taken to Quito, his birthplace.

Then the good friar Valverde set hard to work to save his soul before his death, urging him to abandon superstitions that would surely cause him to end up in hell. As to the manner of the execution, there was some obscurity about its nature as far as the Church, in the person of the friar, was concerned. For Atahualpa was being given the death of a heretic, having been tried for treason. But the Inquisition did not reside in the person of the friar, nor had the Inquisition put the Inca to the question. Nor had the trial been legal, since Charles V did not even know about it, or even acknowledge the right of Pizarro or any of his men to administer his law. The execution was, in fact, by trying to look like a heretic's death, covering up for the illegality of the trial. In proper inquisitorial style Atahulapa was offered strangulation instead of burning if only he would accept baptism. He did accept, since a few drops of water sprinkled on his person (no superstitition, this?) was little to pay for so much. He must by now have begun to see the men round him as madmen rather than the rogues they had seemed before; for weeks they had been telling him about a divine creature who had suffered little children to come unto Him and admonished unforgiving behaviour wherever He found it. Surely they were mad to strangle him in the name of that creature? Had Atahualpa known anything about events in Europe at the time he might have felt that the madness was general.

That evening he was strangled to death, with the gentle friar still murmuring prayers for the salvation of his soul. Like Christ's before him, his body was left all night where it fell. In the morning he was given full funeral honours in the newly consecrated church. News of the murder travelled quickly to the local population, and the Mass was suddenly interrupted by wailing women who rushed to the altar to embrace the Child of the Sun and offer themselves to him for the last journey. They were removed from the church, and later some of them committed suicide in the traditional manner.

Pizarro even dishonoured his promise to have the Inca's remains transported to Quito. Atahualpa was entombed in the church. Later Indians secretly removed his body and took it to his birthplace. And, later, another Christian generation broke his Quito tomb open, having heard that it contained treasure.

On his return from reconnaissance Hernando de Soto reported that the country was quiet. He had seen nothing to suggest rebellion. He was told of Atahualpa's execution—or rather, Pizarro was ostentatiously walking about in deep mourning, and making sure that he was seen. De Soto was shocked and angry. Pizarro had no right, he said, to put Atahualpa to death without a proper trial, for which the Inca should have been sent to Castile. He had been most 'rash'. Pizarro admitted this. He claimed that several of his officers—including the gentle friar—had 'misled' him about Atahualpa and given false evidence. Later, when these men heard about their commander's accusations, they claimed just as loudly that he and he alone had been responsible for the Inca's execution.

The empire was thus without either leadership or, from its own deeply religious point of view, any reason for existing. The Child of the Sun had been snuffed out and there was no one to take his place. Many Indians, released from the duties as well as the ecstasies of their worship, imitated their new rulers and seized whatever gold or silver they could find, as if a special secret hitherto unknown to them might be hidden in it. Private armies started up. Pizarro saw that a successor to Atahualpa must be named if the revolution was not to go against him. He himself could not maintain order over a foreign people (especially as he was unable to read or write even in his own language) but a captive Inca could. The heir to the throne was Atahualpa's younger brother Manco, and he happened to be still alive. But Pizarro—for whom Manco was an unknown quantity —preferred another brother called Toparca. A coronation was arranged, and there was once again a Child of the Sun in the Spanish camp, this time a puppet whose commands to the people were

Spanish commands. The *borla* was put round his brow by Pizarro himself.

The Spaniards now advanced to the capital, in September 1533, taking the Inca and his court with them. On the way there were definite signs of hostility. It was bitterly cold, and the horses soon wore out their shoes on the rough paths. They had to be re-shod with silver. Food supplies were low. No one attacked them yet, but villages where they expected to find hospitality had inexplicably been burned to the ground before their arrival. A bridge or two had been removed. The Spanish column had a feeling that it was being watched from the heights. And just before Xauxa, on the other side of the river over which there was no bridge, a small Indian army was waiting for them. The Spaniards with their usual unhesitating courage plunged into the water to reach the other side whatever the result. This movement, quite unexpected, disconcerted the Indians, who turned to run away. The Spaniards landed and gave chase and cut most of the Indians down. That was how 500 men could dominate an empire, by means of a boldness which the other side simply could not visualise. The Indians were no less reckless. They simply had other expectations of what an enemy would do. Time and again they expected the Spaniards to prefer taking their commander-in-chief alive rather than dead, and so lost the battle when he was unexpectedly cut down on the spot.

Hernando de Soto, sent forward to reconnoitre the land beyond Xauxa with sixty horsemen, reported that the worst trouble still lay ahead. Many of the bridges had been destroyed, villages burned to the ground, supplies removed from the storage points, huge trees felled across the path. Some Indians caught his men in a defile and there was a brisk exchange in which, for the first time, a number of Spaniards were killed. It shook Spanish morale as it bolstered that of the Indians. Ahead there were even more Indians, and the defile was narrower. Also the Spaniards were now exhausted, and weak with hunger. The Indians suddenly poured down on them from in front, as they were climbing. De Soto's answer was to spur his horse, screaming out the battle cry, and simply crash through them, hoping his men were close behind. They were. It succeeded. But a good number were killed, and this time several horses were lost too. Nearly everyone had a wound of some kind. After resting a while and watering the horses de Soto put in an attack, but without denting the Indian lines. Night fell. Both sides were waiting for dawn, within earshot of each other. The Indians numbered thousands; the Spaniards fewer than fifty. Luck was on their side. Pizarro, anxious not to lose touch with de Soto, had sent Almagro forward with all the available horses in the company. Almagro arrived in the night and, feeling that de Soto was in trouble, sounded his bugles along the defile until the trapped Spaniards woke and answered with theirs. Contact was made while it was still dark, and at dawn the Indians saw that the enemy had more than doubled, and withdrew without offering battle.

When they had reached open country again the two Spanish commanders decided to sit and wait for Pizarro. Meanwhile Pizarro was accusing another prisoner of his, the Indian general Challcuchima, of organising rebellion, precisely as he had accused Atahualpa, and with the same idea of liquidating him before he proved too powerful. Atahualpa's highly competent general Quizquiz was clearly leading the revolt against the Spaniards, and Pizarro accused his prisoner of communicating with Quizquiz secretly. The general denied the charge, and was put in chains. Then the young Inca, Toparca, died—of natural causes. It was a splendid chance to accuse Challcuchima of his murder. He was quickly brought to trial and condemned to be burned to death. Unlike Atahualpa, who had accepted baptism and strangulation, Challcuchima replied to Father Valverde's urgent pleas to change his mind that he did not understand the religion of the white man and that was that.

The heir to the throne, Manco, now paid Pizarro an unexpected visit in great pomp, and asked for his 'protection', showing that he had in all probability cut himself off from the bulk of his followers. Thus the invader had created internal feuds, which secured his hold on the country all the better. Pizarro answered the young prince cleverly—that he had been sent to Peru to vindicate the rights of the Huascar house, and to 'remove the usurper' (meaning Atahualpa) from Quito. So nothing could be more welcome than having a genuine Huascar on the throne again. The march went on, and so did the fighting. It made no difference to the Indians on the other side that there was a future Inca in the Spanish midst. Pizarro managed to gain open country and meet up with de Soto and Almagro, and with this force confronting them the Indians fell back.

The Cuzco which came into sight, on 14 November 1533, shining silver in the distance, was not quite the magical city they had been nursing in their hearts. Still, it was magnificent, with a clear stream running through the middle of the city, its buildings rather like those in Caxamalca, low-lying, with spacious halls for banqueting, around a vast central square. The streets were long and narrow, in a regular pattern remarkably reminiscent of ancient Roman towns. The walls of the houses were sometimes painted in vivid primary colours. The newcomers gazed at it all with awe, but the inhabitants (who had after all seen white men and horses before) returned to their normal lives. The Spaniards could hear them singing and dancing all night in their houses, and assumed naturally enough that they did this as a matter of habit. In fact they did it when a great misfortune had befallen them. It was another ceremony of propitiation.

Tents were set up in the square, with the horses tethered close by, in case of trouble from the inhabitants. One glance at the Temple of the Sun and the surrounding convents showed that there was still plenty of booty left. Despite Pizarro's orders his soldiers did some unofficial plundering. Tombs were violated for treasure. The local inhabitants were tortured when suspected of hiding gold. The stores of food and clothing were broken into. Again most of the gold and silver was melted down to standard sizes, and then divided up. The new Inca was crowned with the usual festivities. The Spaniards took up more permanent quarters in the buildings round the square. But stability was not the result.

The rest of the story looks very much like one of retribution for the adventurers. The Inca escaped from Cuzco and was captured again. Indian forces gathered outside the city, and once more the Inca got away, this time for good. The Indians began besieging the city. They rained burning arrows and red-hot stones on to the thatched roofs and a great fire started. There was terrible fighting in the streets. Gold and silver would not feed hungry men. The stores were low, and the fields outside the city remained un-cultivated. The officer who had pursued the Inca and failed to catch him, Juan Pizarro, lost his life in a skirmish. There was no longer a unified command. Francisco Pizarro managed to get out of the city with a detachment, to set up headquarters in Xauxa, leaving behind two other Pizarros to run the Cuzco garrison. Almagro went off to conquer Chile, in a campaign full of physical torment for his men. He returned to Cuzco in April 1537 and clapped the Pizarro brothers into gaol. It was now civil war between the Spaniards. But again a real division was prevented by Francisco, who signed a treaty with Almagro by which his brothers were released. But this peace did not last. Again there was war, and after some bitter fighting Almagro was taken prisoner.

Hernando Pizarro returned to Spain, a very rich man, but was received coldly by Charles V. He was then thrown into prison, where he spent many years.

Meanwhile his brother Francisco was giving vent more and more to his cruel nature. In a dispute with the Inca (there was now official peace between the Spaniards and the Indians) he had one of the king's attractive young wives, whom he had taken prisoner (and almost certainly made love to), strapped to a tree and beaten almost to death, before she was killed slowly with arrows in every part of her body. She did not plead for mercy or utter a word of complaint.

A group of young Spaniards under Juan de Rada organised a plot against Pizarro and, on Sunday, 26 June 1541, screaming 'Death to the tyrant!', they entered his house and cut down most of his attendants (the others having deserted their chief). Old as he was Pizarro put up a good fight, and killed three of the conspirators before he received a wound in his throat and fell to the ground. He is said to have made the sign of the cross on the floor with his own blood and then kissed it reverently before he died.

It took some years of constant war and conspiracy for another Pizarro—Gonzalo—to enter Cuzco in triumph in October 1547, and become its rebel president against Charles V's colonial government. Within twelve months he had been captured by the legitimate governor, Pedro de la Gasca, a wiser and more peaceful man than any of the Pizarros. Then he was beheaded. The charge against him was that he had murdered the viceroy and usurped the government on the grounds that 'his brother had won Peru'. This time the charge was true.

In 1589, when the dust had settled, an officer called Mancio Sierra de Lequizamo dictated a will to his confessor in which he addressed Philip II: 'His Catholic Majesty must know that we found these countries in such a condition that there were no thieves, no vicious men, no idlers, no adulterous or evil-living women. All these kinds of behaviour were forbidden; immoral people could not find a living, and the Inca's subjects all had honest and profitable occupations. Cultivated land, mountains, mines, pastures, hunting, woods and everything else were organised and shared in such a way that each one knew and owned his heritage; no one else could occupy or seize it, and there was no need to go to law. Wars, although numerous, did not hinder trade, tilling of the soil, culture and other activities. Everything, from the most important to the smallest detail, was organised and co-ordinated with the greatest wisdom. The Incas were feared, obeyed, respected, and venerated by their subjects, who considered them to be extremely capable rulers. Their governors and captains had the same qualities, and as they had at their disposal power, authority, and the desire to resist, it was necessary to deprive them completely of power and possessions by force of arms. In this way we subdued them and compelled them to serve God our Father, depriving them of their lands and placing them under the Crown, thanks to which, and because God our Father has permitted it, we have been able to consolidate our domination of this realm, which was composed of many peoples and quantities of riches; and we have made the rulers who submitted to us into slaves, as the world knows. We were a very small band of Spaniards when we undertook this conquest, and I desire His Catholic Majesty to understand why I draft this account. It is to unburden my conscience and to acknowledge my fault. For we have changed these natives, who had so much wisdom and committed so few crimes, so few excesses and extravagances, so that the possessor of 10,000 gold and silver pesos could leave his door open, and by fixing a broom to a small piece of wood across the door, show that he was away or absent. This sign, conforming with custom, was enough to prevent anyone from entering and taking anything away. Also they despised us when they saw amongst us thieves and men who incited their wives and daughters to sin.'

The idea of 'treasure' gleamed bright in the Christian mind at this time. Heaps of gold and silver were increasingly seen as wealth itself. Ever since the eleventh century, when trade had first begun to break across the feudal domain, something more fluid than hard landed possession had become the mark of power. It was natural that the symbols and measures of exchange should in time come to seem wealth itself.

The Spanish penetration of the Americas was a search for bullion rather than for trade. And 'bullionism' inevitably became an end in itself, as money (the symbol of healthy trade) grew in importance. Gold began to look like a real possession, though in itself it could produce nothing consumable. But, more than this, bullion had become necessary because of the increasing use of the money-loan in politics. It was needed to pay the interest, and to float further loans. 'Empire' in the modern sense came about.

This influx of gold and silver into the mother country, while it looked like the arrival of bounty, and entirely beneficial, was in fact the thing that gradually sapped Spain's strength over a period of a century and a half. Today such bullion would be 'sterilised' by a government so that it would not drastically disturb the price-system. But in the sixteenth century it was used at once as spending power, with the result that while the productive capacities of the country remained the same, an increased demand sent up the prices beyond the spending power of most of the people. This meant a gradual drift of labour into the deceptively rich cities, and a resultant abandonment of the land. Thus the real wealth of the land became less as the apparent wealth—and the increasingly extravagant imperial designs—grew out of all proportion. In the end the bullion served to pay only the vast interest that had piled up on the loans, and gradually it failed even to do that.

Thus the Spanish Empire dwindled in the end because of the zeal which had brought it into being, and the new trading countries— Holland, England and France, which saw that real as opposed to symbolic wealth lay in trade—stole all the fruits in time. This does not mean that more sophisticated mercantilist theories displaced primitive 'bullionistic' ones, through growing experience. Trade was simply seen to be a way to the bullion. The concept of treasure as wealth remained, for the simple reason that it was the basis of the whole trading psychology, as opposed to the feudal and rural psychology. The moment the new trading countries got *their* wealth, and began applying themselves to empire, they too followed their bullionistic appetites, and created debts they could not pay. Spain simply provided the first example of 'money-empire'. It was as different from the Hapsburg concept of empire as anything could be. But for the time being it saved the Hapsburg power.

Chapter 7

Wars Holy and Unholy

In the Netherlands Charles could deal with the protestants more firmly than he could in Germany. The country belonged to him. He sent his spies and agents through the land to smell out heretical opinion. He did not—because he could not—stop the heretics from meeting secretly. He left it to his spies to mingle among them and denounce them. There were horrible executions everywhere. The effect was simply to make the movement bolder. He turned the protestants into willing martyrs. Between 1521 and 1550 he published eleven edicts against heresy, and at least 50,000 people—earlier estimates said 100,000—perished by the axe, fire, hanging or burial alive. In 1523 he had sanctioned the burning of two Augustinian monks for Lutheranism, and this had had much to do with the spread of the Anabaptist movement. Its doctrine of shared property appealed to the poorest—the ones most shaken by the financial crises which continually hit Antwerp and other banking centres. It was easy for any great prince to get a loan in Antwerp. But it was not always easy for Antwerp to get him to pay up. Later, in 1561, England, France and Spain refused to honour their signatures, all of which involved vast sums. A setback of this kind, which looked from the outside like a simple paper transaction gone wrong, ricocheted down society until it hit the most humble. Banks and Anabaptism were closely connected.

In fact, the whole protestant revolution might have settled down or found a *modus vivendi* with Rome had it not been for extraneous forces on which it fed. The Spanish Inquisition was perhaps the greatest single cause of the spread of the heresy it set out to abolish. This had little to do with the Church as a whole, much less with the papacy. The Spanish Inquisition had a special character which provoked the northern temperament to an equally special type of almost joyful rebellion, reminiscent of Alexandria under the Decian persecutions.

At the same time Charles needed the Netherlands badly. He needed the crippling taxes paid by her merchants and traders. He needed her ports to go on thriving. But he wanted to suppress the very movement that free commerce had brought into being—and the boldness that went together with free commerce everywhere. It could not be done without a terrible struggle. The struggle was inherited by his son but never resolved.

A series of bad floods and bad harvests only helped the protestant leaders to show how disastrous it was to have one's conscience decided in Rome. It gave to their sermons an apocalyptic note. And it was not long before cruelties began among the protestants themselves.

The Anabaptist movement was the most deeply popular movement of them all, and in some ways the purest. To the powerful on both the protestant and the catholic side it was the most dangerous too, being a social as well as religious movement. Hence the special attention given to it by the Inquisition in the Netherlands. It came into being between 1523 and 1525 in Zürich to reform Roman baptism, hence its name. In Anabaptist eyes the Roman baptismal form had no Biblical basis. They urged citizens to refuse to have their children baptised in this way. They began rebaptising according to their own rite, which involved a declaration of faith in Christ. They required their members to leave public affairs. They must never use force because force was unChristian. Anabaptists could never go to law. The movement's doctrine of free will had a lot in common with Pelagian teaching—Pelagius having been St. Augustine's greatest opponent in the matter of original sin—and was naturally rejected by those of Augustinian background, most of course by Luther. Some Anabaptists practised sex-rites and polygamy. Balthasar Hübmaier was put to torture by the Zürich protestants and then banished. The protestants also decided to drown another leader, Felix Monty, in the element he loved most, water (1527), while a third was beaten through the city before being banished.

This failed to stop the spread of Anabaptism among the peasants not only of the country around Zürich but in Germany and Austria too. And Luther's support of the princes in the Peasants' Revolt helped the movement to establish more of a hold than it would otherwise have done. Hans Huth, a kind of wandering prophet, who died of burns after being tortured in Augsburg (where his fellow-Anabaptist Hübmaier opposed him), helped the process too by the legend he created among the peasants everywhere from Stein am Rhein to eastern Bohemia. Hübmaier was burned at the stake in Vienna, while his wife was thrown into the Danube with a stone round her neck. Jakob Hutter, the Anabaptist leader of numerous Bohemian settlements (which were more or less communist), was burned too, and his followers were hounded from place to place. They were wanted by neither protestants nor catholics. But Anabaptism continued to increase its hold on simple people everywhere just because of the degree of cruelty meted out to it by both sides. Some of these groups emigrated to America.

Melchior Hoffmann, the Anabaptist leader in Strasburg, had worked at one time as a Lutheran missionary. But he quarrelled with Zwingli and tended more and more to pooh-pooh Luther. He had been banished from Denmark. In 1533 he announced that Strasburg was to be the New Jerusalem from which the 144,000 heralds mentioned in *Revelation* ('And I looked, and, lo, a Lamb stood on the Mount Sion, and with him an hundred forty and four thousand, having his Father's name written in their foreheads') would go out and convert the entire world. At the same time the Anabaptist movement was declining in the city, and the council decided that it was powerful enough to clap Hoffmann into gaol, where he spent the last ten years of his life. It was this failure that brought the whole Anabaptist movement down.

But in Münster it dominated even the Lutherans for a time. When the Dutch Anabaptists heard that even the catholic prince of Münster was powerless against them they began a mass emigration to the city. But they were turned back with some cruelty at the frontier. In Münster the movement was led by Bernhard Rothmann, and well financed by the cloth merchant Bernhard Knipperdolling.

The Anabaptists got control of the city in January 1534, and the Dutch leader Jan Matthys (Hoffmann's second-in-command) joined them from the Netherlands with a few of his own people.

The Lutherans and catholics fled from the city, and the catholic prince began to prepare his counter attack. Matthys was killed in a skirmish. Anabaptist defences were hopeless—they were so convinced of God's support that they thought organisation unnecessary. John of Leyden took over the Anabaptist leadership and brought in a state of holy emergency, under twelve elders. The smallest sins were punishable by death—swearing, gossiping and complaining. Polygamy was legalised because there were too few men. The leaders hoped not only for more babies but for braver men this way—since monogamous marriage tended to give the woman the upper hand. John of Leyden had sixteen wives. When one of them was rude to him, divine guidance moved him to cut off her head and stamp on her body in front of the others. He made himself king, and then may even have gone mad. Meanwhile the city was under siege. It lasted until the summer of 1535—when a massacre of the Anabaptist army took place. John of Leyden was tortured to death. The Münster horror brought down great cruelty on Anabaptists everywhere. They were drowned, or scorched to death slowly.

It took the protestant-catholic struggle one step further to implacable extremism. Each side seemed to the other a desperately dangerous movement to subvert European order. When subversion begins to be talked of, the moderates cease to be heard. In London fourteen people were burned for Anabaptist teachings (1535), all of them immigrants from the Netherlands. The Baptist Church in England owed much (through its leader John Smyth) to the Netherlands Anabaptist, Menno Simmons, who had travelled around Germany and his own country for the past twenty-five years comforting the persecuted and preaching absolute peace.

Charles had another religious quarrel to look to—one more immediately dangerous, especially to Spain. His persecution of the *moriscos* had stirred the sympathies of fellow Muslims in North

Africa. In 1526 he had charged the Inquisition to define heretics as those who did not look or speak like the men around them. Failure to eat pork or drink wine could be taken as evidence against a man. An old *morisco* was hunted down and tortured for preferring water to wine, and beef to pork. Certain *moriscos* were exempted from Charles's mandate on the payment of a heavy fine. But thousands fled from the city of Granada. In 1529 they were forced to leave their own quarters of the city and take up residence among the 'old' Christians so that any concerted retaliation on their part would be difficult. Charles also got a Bull out of the pope absolving him from an accession oath which he had taken at Saragossa, promising not to interfere with the religion of the remaining Moors in Aragón.

The result was a series of bloodthirsty Arab raids on the Spanish coasts—Málaga, Valencia, Murcia, Cadiz. From their stations in Morocco the Spaniards tried to cope. Charles sent Andrea Doria, the Genoese admiral, to attack the pirates at their hold-out at Cherchal near Algiers (1530). But he avoided Barbarossa, the fierce commander of the Turkish fleet, already responsible for carrying off thousands of Spaniards, Sicilians and Neapolitans into slavery.

The Turks were in fact being so successful that it was necessary to bargain with them. Francis I, dreaming of attacking Genoa while Doria was elsewhere, began treating with the Sultan. Even Ferdinand was beginning to see that perhaps one should open discussions with him. He put out feelers, and ended with an agreement about the Hungarian frontier (22 June 1533). Charles had a hand in this. Cornelius Schapper, Ferdinand's official ambassador to the Porte, was in fact Charles's emissary. The Sultan intimated that he was prepared to make some kind of treaty with Ferdinand but not with Charles. Thus to say that Charles was now the focal point of European politics is far from saying that developments worked to his advantage; he was invariably the centre referred to in anything new, but invariably the loser thereby. Ironically, the agreement between Francis I and the Porte in the previous year had been largely arranged by a Spaniard who had gone over to Paris. A formal French embassy had been sent to Constantinople and a full-scale treaty was signed in 1535. And two years later a Turkish

embassy was received in Paris. The Sultan had thus fought his way
to recognition as an equal power in Europe. And he regarded his
greatest enemy—to be brought down at all costs—as the Hapsburg
family.

Hapsburg attempts to make an agreement with the Shah of Persia,
hoping for an attack on the Turks from behind, failed. It was found
that the Shah was making a separate treaty with the Sultan at the
same time. Charles, meanwhile, was impatient to lead an expedition
against the Turks, partly to cripple Islam and partly to captivate the
imagination of all Europe. Also it was the one expedition abroad that
the Spaniards would accept with enthusiasm. When Barbarossa
took control of Tunis, Charles began making secret preparations
for this expedition. To his closest advisers he never revealed that
he himself would be taking part. His idea was to attack Tunis. He
pushed his naval preparations ahead under cover of a series of ban-
quets and hunting parties at various places—Toledo, Valencia,
Madrid—to which the court moved.

At this time he did as little as possible to aggravate the situation
in Germany, in case he should lose the support of the German
princes and have to use his stretched resources among them. This
helped Henry VIII. For Charles instructed his ambassador at the
court of St. James's not to sound a note of blame over the recent
divorce affair. He again needed friends. On the other hand, he did
tell his sister Mary, now governing the Netherlands, to prepare
secretly for a defensive war against Francis I, should that become
inevitable—if 'the most shameless and unreliable of all opponents'
(as his chancellor Granvelle called the French king) were to overstep
even his extravagant mark, with his endless claims to the ownership
of Milan and Genoa and other places. To camouflage this second
secret plan Charles sent Francis messages of goodwill through the
newly married Count Palatine Frederick, to whom Charles had just
given his own fourteen-year-old niece Dorothea in marriage (the
count was fifty-three). Frederick happened to be in Paris on his way
to the Netherlands. Charles also tried to stop Francis interfering
diplomatically in Germany but without effect. He did his best to
blacken Francis's name among the German princes. He let them

Titian's portrait of Philip II,
Charles V's son and successor to the throne of Spain

*The Hall of the
Ambassadors in the
Alhambra Palace, Granada*

The Escorial, Madrid

know through his emissary, Adrian de Croy, count of Roeulx, that Francis had told the Sultan that he would 'welcome' a Turkish attack on the Empire. He also intimated that Francis I had persuaded the Sultan to put the Turkish fleet at the pirate Barbarossa's disposal, simply to embarrass Spain. All this was partly meant to engage the French and Germans in an argument that would drown any talk about Charles's own secret preparations for a crusade.

His councillors were not in a crusading mood. Don Juan de Tavera, archbishop of Toledo, was openly against the plan. It would not benefit Castile and he thought Francis would tip off Barbarossa anyway. The idea was that Charles and his brother-in-law, the Infante Luis of Portugal, were to head a fleet of Spanish and Portuguese warships. Andrea Doria was to join it. The Castilian grandees showed themselves warm in support. German mercenaries were brought down to Spain, together with Italian and Maltese troops. In June 1535 the fleet set sail for Africa. Within five days it lay off Carthage. The troops disembarked in good order, and the stronghold called La Goletta, where Barbarossa had massed his men, was put under siege. After three weeks a combined sea and land attack was made, with the Spaniards and Germans coming in from one side and the Italians from the other, while the Knights of St. John attacked from the sea under cover of simultaneous rounds of fire from all the ships. The stronghold collapsed, and Barbarossa's entire fleet of eighty-two galleys fell into Charles's hands. Some of Barbarossa's artillery was found to be embossed with the French lily.

Instead of cutting back to a Spanish port for refitting (water was short, and most of his horses had died) Charles decided to push on to Tunis, to deal with Barbarossa himself. The imperial troops advanced but were harassed all the way. In the absence of horses, men dragged the guns along. Then some remarkable news came. Christian slaves in Tunis had seized arms and forced Barbarossa to flee. He got away with the flimsy remnants of the Turkish fleet to Algiers. This meant that nothing of more than prestige-value accrued to Charles's victory, since Barbarossa was still free. But Charles needed prestige at this moment. As planned he then crossed

6

to Italy and made a triumphal entry into Naples, where he stayed for three months, with the usual noisy celebrations. From there he went to see the pope in Rome (to his relief Clement VII had died the previous year and the Farnese Paul III had taken his place). It seemed that all that Gattinara had hoped for was now realised.

Meanwhile Francis was determined to conquer Milan, especially as Charles had his hands full in the Mediterranean. Charles tried to sever Henry VIII's friendship with Francis by suggesting that a husband should be found for Princess Mary, the daughter of Catherine of Aragón and therefore Charles's cousin. Cromwell, Henry's new chancellor, was sympathetic, Henry dead against. Catherine of Aragón had in the meantime died (on 8 January 1536), which cleared the air between Charles and Henry; but there was no chance of bringing Henry back into the Church, and therefore no chance that he would want to strengthen Charles's hand in the Empire, or that he would give up using a spasmodic friendship with France for its immense nuisance value everywhere in Europe. He seemed to be proved right by the fact that Francis I suddenly rushed down into Savoy (to which, through his mother, he had a claim) and occupied Turin on 3 April 1536. The duke of Savoy fled.

Francis's descent into Italy infuriated Charles, but he did not show it to the French ambassador at Naples. He was anxious to divert attention from his own secret plans. But it was not for nothing that the speech he delivered at the pope's side before the College of Cardinals and the French and Venetian ambassadors was in Spanish. He attacked Francis for going back on his word, and said that while he himself had always wanted peace he was not afraid to fight. He was again prepared to save the blood of his subjects by fighting Francis himself in a duel—the duchy of Burgundy for himself if he won, and Milan for Francis if he lost. At this point the pope, thinking it was the end of the speech (and no doubt happy that he himself had not been mentioned) broke into applause. But Charles cut him off sharply by adding that he looked to the pope to decide which side the Church was on. Paul's answer was procrastinatory. He said that since Francis had made peace offers, these should at least be heard. And he was against a duel of any kind. Meanwhile he himself would stay neutral.

That was the most Charles could expect—and it seems that he was happy with it. The ugly dream of a papal understanding with France, which had happened under Leo, was at least laid. And he got Paul to agree to a council. It was scheduled for May of the following year, at Mantua.

Now he decided to attack both the French forces in Savoy and France itself. He planned a two-fold action, one from the south via Provence, and the other from the Netherlands on to Paris. The Tunisian victory seems to have persuaded him to this large-scale enterprise. His army crossed into Savoy on 25 July 1536, but they found no one there. The French commander had not only withdrawn his men but scorched the earth. He also refused to be provoked at his new defences at Avignon. After six weeks, the imperial army had to retreat. As for the attack from the Netherlands, under Nassau, it petered out even more quickly, and at great cost to the country. Ghent had refused to subscribe to the war at all, or even to be considered part of Mary's defence system. The French army—in not much better condition than the imperial army—now pushed back into Savoy, as far as Turin but without retaking it.

Charles's speech was thus made ridiculous. The prestige he had carefully built up in Africa had shrivelled. He returned to Spain in Andrea Doria's fleet in February 1537.

Francis suddenly announced that in view of the fact that Charles had 'violated the Madrid and Cambrai settlements' by attacking him, he would now seize Flanders, Artois and Charolais as his own. This gave Mary in the Netherlands a chance to appeal for more funds from the Estates General. They gave her what she wanted, and a new force was raised under Nassau and Roeulx. They plunged into some fierce fighting. The French massacred the townspeople of St. Venant. An armistice was signed at Bomy on 30 June 1537 for ten months' mutual recuperation.

It was clear that the Empire was plunging into a disastrous war that might finally split it in two. Only Francis's financial exhaustion had made him stop the war, much to Mary's relief.

All Charles had left was his diplomatic juggling skill (like every other power in Europe, from Venice to the Vatican). He used it now to make an alliance between the pope, Venice (whose ships had lately been attacked by the Turks) and his brother Ferdinand against the Sultan. Francis I was bitterly annoyed at this since it robbed him of two allies against Charles. A personal meeting was now arranged between Francis, the pope and the emperor, to take place at Nice. The pope and Charles arrived on 9 May 1538. Then the French king came. But he negotiated with Charles through the pope and his own queen Eleonore. It took over a month to reach an agreement, and then it was worth practically nothing. They would not fight each other for ten years. The territorial *status quo* was to remain as it was. When the treaty had been signed and the pope had gone back to Rome. Francis invited Charles on to his galley, and then returned the honour by visiting imperial headquarters in the town itself. Charles's tendency to indulge a dream of undivided Empire was encouraged by this meeting. He and Francis spent many warm hours together, eating and drinking and talking over the many relatives they had in common. But the dream hardly lasted longer than the meeting.

Charles had often shown that he had no wish to use force on the protestants. He had after all no objection to attacks on the pope's moral authority as long as they strengthened his own. But many people in Germany were now saying that he would use force soon, once he had dealt with the Turks and the French. One thing he could not stand: a state of schism that cut the Empire down the middle. And protestantism was provoking this.

Duke William of Bavaria urged him to make a surprise attack on the protestants under cover of preparing another Italian war. At the same time the duke (a warmer catholic than he was a Hapsburg) was having secret talks with the protestant 'Schmalkaldic League'. As to the proposed Council of the Church, the protestant league disliked Mantua as a meeting-place and proposed Germany. They added that the pope (who had denounced Lutheranism vigorously in a Bull of 2 June 1536) should not be president of the council, since he was an interested party. By now Charles's imperial vice-chancellor, Held, had managed to get a catholic league going, led by Louis of Bavaria and Henry of Brunswick.

Charles decided to hit the Turks again. His sister Mary's letter imploring him to think of the poor finances of the Empire, and the troubles in the Netherlands, and especially the fact that he had not the strength to pursue an attack right into the heart of Turkey, came too late. He got another fleet together under Andrea Doria, together with Venice. The attack came to nothing (September 1538). Just before it started Barbarossa had been thinking of going over to the imperial side. Now he stayed with the Sultan. Charles was forced to turn his attention back to Europe, for fear that its divisions would make a further attack on the Turks impossible. His queen Isabella died after an unsuccessful delivery in May 1539. And partly to forget his bereavement he planned to make a visit to the Netherlands, the first in eight years. He would leave Spain in the hands of his son Philip, who was only twelve years old at the time.

Francis invited Charles to pass through France, and he accepted. They met at Loches on the Indre, and Francis tried to persuade him to marry his daughter Margaret. The emperor refused. Charles went on to meet his sister at Valenciennes. Ferdinand was to meet him in Brussels, to confer about the religious state of the Empire. But the Holy Roman Empire seemed barely to exist. Charles was exhausted.

There was new trouble in the Netherlands. The war with Francis two years before, when Ghent and Flanders had refused to contribute anything towards the Artois campaign under Nassau, had left a situation which Mary had not yet been able to clear up. The justices of Ghent had wanted to go in with her, while the guilds and the radical party had been against her. Civil war had broken out, and spread to nearby villages. Commercially Ghent was in decline, a major cause of the unrest. Antwerp was now the great new centre of prosperity. Mary had failed to bring peace. Instead, a civil war between two opposing parties—one of bureaucrats (suspected of filching public funds) and one of radicals—now began to look like revolution. The town even asked Francis I for help. Mobs took over

and venerable burghers were led from their houses for slaughter.
One of these, an old man of seventy-five, had his beard shaved off
like a witch before being put to the rack and then executed. Evil
spirits were thought to linger in hair and give the victim courage.

The revolution was against Mary, not Charles. It was hoped even
by the mob leaders that he would settle matters to their advantage.
By the autumn of 1538 the whole of Flanders was in a similar state
of seething rebellion with no very clear objective except the destruction of the chief citizens. In February of the following year Charles
entered Ghent in state with Mary, the papal legate and various
ambassadors and princes. Five thousand *landsknechts* of the kind
that had made so many Italians tremble followed him, and began
murdering and pillaging right and left while he himself took up
residence in the palace of his birth.

Meanwhile Ghent's rebel leaders were executed. The soldiers
were given more or less full pillaging rights, even after the armistice.
A whole district was demolished to make way for a new fortress.
Ghent was stripped of its public treasure and all its arms, and of its
independence. Charles insisted on a public apology. Justices and
burghers came to the palace and knelt before him, in procession.

It was the classical way to crush a revolt, but not a way to settle
the Netherlands. He put the Inquisition at the disposal of the
bishops.

Protestantism had by now spread to Scandinavia and the eastern
Baltic states via the German communities there. The Danes were
now virtually cut off from Rome. King Christian II had refused to
persecute the Lutherans, while the present Christian III continued
the work of de-Romanising the country's legal and taxation system.
In 1536 Sweden came under the Danish crown, and adopted the
same national church, as did Finland (which belonged to Sweden).

Antwerp, too, had a powerful German community—this and the
town's prosperity gave it a key-position in the coming struggle. It
had helped English protestantism before Henry's rupture with
Rome. In fact, protestant ideas had entered England via Antwerp–
London trade, and had first established itself among Germans
resident in London. Tyndale's New Testament was printed in

Antwerp and distributed in London between 1526 and 1536. Tyndale, Coverdale and England's chief Lutheran, an Augustinian monk called Robert Barnes, had been forced to go into exile. When Henry cut himself off from Rome and confiscated the monasteries he adopted the Bible in its Tyndale and Coverdale translations. His execution of Ann Boleyn and his marriage to Anne of Cleves in 1540 showed that he had severed himself not only from Rome but from the Empire, and all but identified himself with France.

Meanwhile—first at Speyer, then (when the plague suddenly struck Speyer) at Hagenau—Charles worked hard with Ferdinand to make a Church Council possible, though neither side in the struggle seemed anxious for a settlement (a point Charles tended to hide from himself). The Bavarians did their best to make even the talks at Hagenau difficult. They felt that a council would only encourage the protestants to take themselves seriously. But Charles persisted. Protestant delegates (including the Zwinglian Myconius and John Calvin himself) came to Hagenau.

The Zürich reformation had been handled rather urbanely by Huldreich Zwingli. It had been little more than a discussion inside the town council, which controlled a county population of 50,000 people and two nearby towns (Winterthur and Stein am Rhein). There had been nothing like Luther's call to freedom, for the practical reason that freedom had already been there. Switzerland was outside the Empire, except as a pool of mercenary soldiers for the emperor. Also Zwingli tried to differentiate his work from Luther's. He emphasised that his basic ideas had been inspired by his teacher at Basle long before Luther came out into the open. Mass was abolished in Zürich in 1525 and replaced by his own quite un-Lutheran communion service—little more than a formal rite, without symbolic overtones and designed simply to remind the communicant of the manner of Christ's death. Three years before, a group of Zürichers had eaten smoked sausages in a special ceremony during the Lenten feast, to show defiance of Roman practice. Marriage of priests was also allowed here (concubinage among catholic priests was admitted to be general at this time). Finally they denied papal authority, and the monasteries were dissolved.

But Zwingli was not without troubles of his own—from the Anabaptists, against whom he helped decree the death penalty, though they had started as his followers. In the same way, when the peasants of the Bernese Oberland rebelled against the abolition of the Mass some years later, the Zwinglians used force. And what had started as reform quickly became simply a new *status quo*, with no more freedom than before. Far more than Lutheranism Zwinglianism became identified with current respectability, so that in the end the movement began to look to some of its supporters like a social one, concentrating on sound public morals. But the movement succeeded.

In 1528 reform had been adopted in Berne too—everything from Zwingli's communion service to the dissolution of the monasteries. This had immediate political disadvantages for Charles V, in that Berne made an alliance with France against Charles of Savoy, who was now—since Francis's invasion—a close protégé of the imperial government. On the other hand, certain other Swiss towns clung to the Church and burned their protestants, in the cantons of Lucerne, Unterwalden, Schwyz, Uri, Zug. And in 1529 they countered Berne's move by making a so-called Christian Union with Ferdinand the Hapsburg though they decided to withdraw from it when a Zwinglian army attacked them.

Meanwhile there developed a struggle between Lutheranism and Zwinglianism, despite Philip of Hesse's efforts to bring them together. A meeting between Luther and Zwingli was arranged at Marburg, but they failed to resolve the matter of the new form of communion service. There were arguments about the Mass and transubstantiation. Zwingli took a rationalist line, while Luther chalked on the table Christ's words 'This is my body', and would not budge from his doctrine that while the Mass was not a sacrifice or a good work, as many saw it, it was not a totally empty form either, and *some* presence was in the bread and the wine, and not a vague spiritual presence at that. Above all he was against the idea of the bread and the wine as symbols. On this the two sides separated, Luther having proved that he was a far better catholic than most people now thought.

Religious war started in Switzerland, which at least shows that it was not Charles who plunged Europe into war later, and that the will to fight was quite as strong in the protestants as in the catholics. Zwingli's idea was to persuade the catholic cantons to adopt protestant doctrine by blockading them. The blockade failed, because supplies continued to come in from the Common Lordships or what is now the Ticinese or 'Italian' Switzerland. The catholics then decided to declare war (1531) on Zürich, which was found to be in no position to defend itself. Zwingli died on the battlefield at Kappel. The war left the situation more or less as it had been before, except that both sides agreed to stay as they were, with regard to doctrine.

These differences of doctrine were often differences about definition, even terminology. The Roman doctrine that the bread and wine of the Host become the flesh and blood of Christ at the moment of consecration had been declared *de fide* in 1215. The various protestant attitudes in this doctrine of transubstantiation were attempts to revise mediaeval thinking in the light of the rationalism that the Renaissance had rediscovered in its study of the ancient world. Hence the view that the bread and the wine were 'symbols' of Christ's presence. More extreme was the Zwinglian attitude that they were not even symbols but 'reminders'—and therefore all that much more rational. Hence too the identification of Zwinglianism with social respectability (or good business), since a rational religion (which for Luther, as for the Church, was a contradiction in terms) never created dangerous enthusiasms. Luther, on the other hand, wanted to re-establish the 'primitive' Church, as it had been at the time of the apostles. But his movement was swallowed up in the more general protestant movement—to rationalise religion, that is to secularise it.

Really, to think of the Reformation as a quarrel about religion—to call the vast process of the sixteenth century the Reformation at all, as if it effected a great change in the Church, or created a new church, or sprang from any need for a new one—is to make a mistake about the whole nature of the time. So quickly was the religious question brushed aside that in three centuries the words 'God' and 'Christ' had become for masses of people even less than symbolic. What 'reformation' did this represent? What 'catholic restoration'?

It was a process of secularisation that happened not outside the Church but inside it, and not in spite of the Church but because of it and through it alone.

Those men who thought about religion—and there were very few of them, though they did form an élite with the maximum influence on courts and princes—mostly agreed that the Christianity of the time was little better than crude superstitition. Luther actually did say that you were lucky to find two real Christians together in one place.

And the fact that Charles was unable to prevent a religious war seems to indicate that something like a philosophy of war had come into being by the sixteenth century. At least, every new doctrine was engulfed at once and turned into fuel for bloodshed. A few men seemed aware of this, and frightened by it—catholics like Archbishop de Talavera in Granada; some Anabaptists, lonely thinkers like Denck (called 'the Anabaptist pope' and author of a book called *Of True Love*), and Caspar Schwenkfeld (a Silesian aristocrat under Denck's influence, whom Luther called an idiot and 'possessed by the devil'). Indeed, the need felt by princes for 'expansion' in every direction was a haunting sense that something infinite was now missing. This is why Charles V at one end and Luther at the other were powerless to stop religious matters becoming matters of war, though neither of them wanted it that way.

This 'secularisation' of life was the most spectacular change of the sixteenth century. Almost no one recognised that the total destruction of the idea of a Church, even the banishment of religious feeling from all public areas, might be involved. The cruelty of the time indicates the tremendous involvement of people in this process. The religious doctrines were simply standards by which a man was judged to be socially safe on the one hand or subversive on the other. War and murder (at the stake or the scaffold) were changing into an almost detached activity. This was what made the sixteenth century the first century of modern war, modern espionage, modern terror.

Again and again—at the burning of a heretic, at a massacre, at a battle of persecution—there was an atmosphere of distaste for the human creature himself, which made the actual wars of the time, in Italy and Provence and Savoy, seem comparatively old-world. According to Luther, God shared the distaste. Here is where the militant protestants met the militant catholics—in a fervent revival of the doctrine of original sin, first expounded in its modern form in barbarian times.

John Calvin's reformation in Geneva in the 1540s simply meant an acute moral vigilance over the life of the city. Twelve elders worked closely with pastors of the new church. There was the death penalty for sexual promiscuity. A youth was beheaded for hitting his parents. Calvin's system even included garbage-disposal. Two or three witches were burned annually.

Calvin rejected Lutheran 'consubstantiation' (the doctrine that Christ was present 'with' the Host) on the grounds that Christ could not descend to elements as 'corruptible' as bread and wine.

Charles failed to bring the two sides together in their conference at Regensburg (1541) where he moved from Speyer. All the German princes were invited, and he passed a month in jousting and hunting while waiting for them to assemble. The catholic side was no more united than it ever had been, and no more willing to come to terms. If anything the protestants were closer to the emperor, in their willingness to make some solution possible. At first, on the purely doctrinal side, it looked hopeful. The way had been prepared by Gropper and Gerhard Veltwyk (a converted Jew) on the catholic side, and Bucer and Capito for the protestants. The latter were fascinated by the work of their opponent Veltwyk, probably the best Hebrew scholar of his time. He had written a book, in Hebrew, to be read by Jews, called *Wanderings in the Wilderness*. It described his conversion to Christianity.

There seemed every chance of reaching a settlement, in this kind of atmosphere. But the princes had their politics. The Bavarians, when they arrived at Regensburg, advocated what later became the counter-reformation policy. Dogma must be armed. Duke Louis, Duke Henry of Brunswick and Duke William argued with Charles that a council would only end in talk, and that the best plan was to

reach a temporary agreement under cover of which the Empire
would prepare for an anti-protestant war. On the other hand, the
protestant landgrave of Hesse, Philip, promised Charles all the
support he could give him from the start, to avoid a rupture. This
looked like a lucky stroke for Charles. He hoped to win the attention
of the protestant princes through Hesse and, in part, this happened. On his side, the Landgrave Philip needed some powerful
protector, after his bigamous marriage had put his whole authority
in question.

The theological arguing went on for a month—between Gropper,
Julius Pflug and Eck for the catholics, and Bucer, Melanchthon and
Pistorius for the protestants. A papal legate turned up unexpectedly, and was unexpectedly mild, for the good reason that
he intended to make agreement impossible, should a chance of
agreement appear to offer itself.

There was very nearly agreement on certain vital issues like
marriage for priests, the doctrine of 'justification' and communion
'in both kinds' (bread and wine) for the laity. Charles seemed ready
to endorse a compromise. But on the deeper matters of transubstantiation and papal primacy the conference ran into rough water.
Even here there could have been agreement, had both sides been
determined to compromise. Bucer refused to budge on the matter
of the sacraments, and as good as said that there could be no discussion on it. Charles complained that the catholics spent their time
quibbling about the word transubstantiation itself. Gasparo Contarini, the Venetian papal legate, seemed to think at one point that
the doctrine of justification had been settled—at least he wrote to the
pope that it had. But both sides showed more willingness than they
really felt. When the conference, a complete failure, was winding up
(the twenty-three articles of the 'Book of Regensburg' were rejected
by both sides), Paul III announced through his legate that he would
like to call a Council of the Church at once. Having made sure of the
impossibility of such a thing, he felt free to urge it with all enthusiasm. The war-party was the only one left with anything
practical to suggest.

Chapter 8

Abdication

Gradually Charles V gave more ear to the Bavarian school of war. The only reason why he did not attack the protestants at once was that he needed their help against the Sultan Suleiman, who was about to invade Hungary in person (Zapolya having recently died). The Diet gave him 10,000 foot and 2,000 cavalry to fight this war, but only for three months. In return for this gift the protestants got a proclamation guaranteeing imperial protection for their priests—even in catholic lands—and the reform of the monasteries.

But Charles had a secret agreement with the catholics which the protestants did not know about, guaranteeing all the old dues and taxes and privileges.

His finances were in a mess—which took him hurrying back to Spain. He was even unable to pay his own courtiers. Naples and Sicily financed a brief and unsuccessful second attack on the Turks in Africa. The Austrian inheritance could hardly keep its own lands in decent administration, let alone help to finance the Empire. The Netherlands were rich, but squeezed dry, and the recent war had cost a lot of money. More would have to be spent on war in that area, if the squeezing—and the proportionate discontent—went on. The French king's attack on the Netherlands, in the summer of 1542, with the help of Denmark, Sweden and the terrible Martin von Rossen of Gelderland ('burning is the magnificat of war'), relied very much on Dutch discontent. When the Spanish harvest failed in 1543 Charles needed the Netherlands even more.

Naples, Sicily (with its corn trade) and Milan (with its salt monopoly) were reasonable sources of royal revenue, but the chief remained Spain, with its direct taxes (the Castilian *alcabala* was a capital levy of 10 per cent), church grants, special grants from the pope (mostly used against the Sultan), money from indulgences and revenues from the three knightly orders. Gold from the West Indies poured into the royal exchequer in rapidly increasing amounts. Between 1503 and 1505 the bullion imports of gold and silver had amounted to £213,800, in the equivalent English currency of that time, while in the 1540s it was approaching the million mark (a few years later, between 1556 and 1560, it was £4,599,000). But Charles continued to go to the banks for loans, and much of the royal property in Spain was mortgaged. At least a third of his expenses could not be covered by income. The simple fact was that he was having to fight too many people.

He maintained that the protestant question was being exploited by the French king. In the Netherlands and Germany protestantism could easily become Francis's fifth column. Charles therefore determined to defend the Netherlands by squashing France (once again). England was to attack the French coast; Henry VIII, scenting war (and victory for the Empire), quickly tacked round to Charles's side.

Charles left Spain in the hands of his son Philip, who was now sixteen. He sent Spanish troops to the Netherlands by sea, and he himself went to Genoa with his commander-in-chief, Ferrante Gonzaga, and the Marquis del Vasto, together with 3,000 Spanish and 4,000 Italian troops. The reliable orthodoxy of Spanish troops was his mainstay; the *tercio* was already the terror of Europe. Eighteen thousand other troops were to await him in Speyer, on his way from Italy to the Netherlands.

Charles was never to return to Spain as its king. He took this trip ostensibly to settle the Netherlands and to break the French, but in fact to decide the religious question by war. In his secret instructions to his son he spoke of 'important matters which are so dark and full of doubt'. He was too uncertain of them himself to give clear advice about them. They were to be the dominant problem of his reign—and of Philip's too.

As a first move in the religious war Charles had Martin Bucer banished from Bonn by the elector of Cologne, then his armies more or less razed the town of Vlaten to the ground. He took Jülich, and was then across the Gelderland frontier. He forced the duke of Cleves to give up the province and return to catholicism, but gave him Ferdinand's daughter (after his obligatory divorce from his French wife). He had thus entered Germany as a conqueror. Yet had the duke's allies (France, Denmark and the German princes) stood by him the victory would not have been possible. This taught Charles a great deal. He saw how much he could gain, with Spanish troops and Spanish money, from the divided state of the protestant camp. The landgrave of Hesse told the elector of Saxony a little story about the mouse and the boy who fought each other and were both gobbled up by the kite.

Charles's policy, frankly aggressive after 1541 (despite renewed friendship with the protestants at Speyer in 1543, and Luther's congratulations and the pope's horror at this) was not implemented by himself. The Spanish territories were becoming richer, and the implementation of his policy of aggression fell to the man who inherited the riches at their maximum point, his son. Philip II was the outcome of Charles's political thinking; by the time of his reign it was Spain and not the Empire that was doing the work. But now Charles's character changed visibly. He became for the first time bitter and scornful. He was suffering from gout—made worse by consuming vast amounts of meat and beer which his doctors every-where tried to discourage.

He advanced into France, making for Paris, where there was panic. The old pattern was renewed; weeks of negotiations produced a treaty very like those of Madrid and Cambrai. But now there was a difference—a secret treaty of Crepy which has remained unknown until this century. It stipulated that Francis would provide Charles with troops against the protestants if all other alternatives but force should fail—the same number that he had pledged to give against the Turks: 10,000 infantry and 600 heavy cavalry. Francis promised to help restore Geneva to the duke of Savoy. He was to fight the other protestant, Henry VIII, should he cease to be what he was at present, Charles's closest ally (in a war against France!). It was in fact the capitulation of Boulogne to the English on 18 September 1543 that persuaded Francis to sign these treaties. The pope tacked round to the emperor's side, and when Francis wrote to him asking for a Council of the Church—as the treaty obliged him to do— Paul III fixed one at Trent for 15 March 1545. Yet when Charles and the papal legate, a member of the Farnese family, met at Worms they talked not about the council but about the war on the protestants. It began by Charles saying that he 'feared' a protestant attack. Rumours of fresh war began to circulate in the city. A Sicilian monk caused an uproar by challenging Charles in a public sermon to declare war on the 'heretics'. The papal legate left Worms hurriedly and in disguise, during a thunderstorm. He was back in Rome in ten days. This time Paul III was ready to part with both money and troops. He was even generous: 12,000 infantry and 500 cavalry, and 100,000 ducats, plus half a million ducats on Church lands in Spain. To his annoyance, Charles kept him to his promise of the council, perhaps aware that its almost certain failure would give his war a double justification.

Charles was also anxious that any reform of the Church should come from the council and not from the pope, so as to render it more palatable to the 'heretics' when the time came to make a united Church again. Behind the official policy his confessor Pedro de Soto was trying to persuade him to cut the council and go to war. He argued that the protestants were still quarrelling among themselves. He said that it was a sin to doubt whether the war would be successful. It was unimaginable, he added, that Paul III would desert him in such a war (Paul did).

The Landgrave Philip of Hesse got wind of this. He intercepted a letter from Charles to the king of Poland asking him for help against the protestants— and advised the Schmalkaldic League to prepare for war at once. He and the emperor went hunting together when they met in Speyer (1546). Charles was on his way to meet his brother Ferdinand again—or rather to join forces with him. Philip of Hesse happened to make a reference to the wealth of the Empire, to which Charles's minister, Granvelle, said that it wasn't worth a penny—'only anxiety and vexation'. When Charles got to Regensburg, where another religious conference (rival to that at Worms) had just failed, the world got wind of a murder which caused an ominous stir. Juan Diaz, a young Spanish protestant, had gone to the conference with Martin Bucer. He had returned to his home on the Danube afterwards, and had been tortured by his brother Alfonso, a catholic who had also been at the conference. Alfonso then hired assassins to murder him in his bed. It was the first atrocity-story of the war.

Recruiting went on everywhere in Germany, on both sides. The protestant princes and electors refused to attend the Diet which Charles called. Charles wrote to his sister Mary that if he and Ferdinand did not take action at once all of Germany and eventually the Netherlands might turn protestant. He ordered her to mobilise the Netherlands. His object was to attack Saxony, and eventually he persuaded Ferdinand to join with him in this.

The war with the Schmalkaldic League began in a series of skirmishes and lengthy outflanking movements which came to no conclusion, even by the end of 1546. The league tried to get money out of France, unsuccessfully. Charles became master of southern Germany almost without firing a shot.

As for Trent, troops marched through on their way north constantly, and the papal legate was beginning to argue that the council had become unnecessary. Only about forty bishops attended it—and the majority were Spaniards and Italians. The three Jesuits were Laynex, Salmaron and Convillon, and their function was really—by presenting an exhaustive definition of what being a catholic meant, and insisting on the primacy of the pope—to block any real compromise. Saxony was attacked. It was now that the pope chose to withdraw his troops from Charles—who screamed abuse at the papal nuncio, to the effect that 'the French pox' (which the pope was supposed to have) was excusable in the young but not in the old. He moved camp from Nuremberg to join up with Ferdinand in Bohemia. When it came to a fight, on the Elbe, he was among his own Spanish troops, shouting encouragement. This battle developed into a chase. The elector of Saxony was captured and put under Spanish guard (24 April 1547). Later in Wittenberg Charles put the Landgrave Philip of Hesse under house arrest, and with these two leaders of the Schmalkaldic League in the bag he felt he had scotched

German protestantism. He intended to use Philip of Hesse as a hostage to secure the fulfilment of good peace terms.

In the early part of 1547 both Henry VIII and Francis I died, and it looked as if a safe catholic empire was once again possible. The pope even began to hope that England could now be forced back into the Church. He asked for the council to be moved to Bologna. Then when the move had started he denied having made any such suggestion. The papal legate (he was raging too now) advised the pope to have the council returned to Trent, but Paul refused. Charles threatened to call a new council. Paul tried to renew his old friendship with France (where the young king Henry II looked like becoming a good replica of his father) in an anti-imperial league, together with Venice. This made Charles think of invading Italy again and scooping up the papal states as he had done just over twenty years before. He then formally declared that the council must move back to Trent, which it did on 1 May 1551.

The war had in fact settled nothing of the actual religious question, and it began to look as if religious differences were simply expressions of differences in power. Charles, belonging to the old world, went on struggling for a settlement at the Diet of Augsburg which he now summoned (Titian painted his portrait there). He knew that the protestants would never again accept the catholic Church—its sacraments, its saints and its Mass. He devised—with the catholic Germans bitterly against him—'alternative' forms of worship, in an attempt to legalise the present schism, and in total opposition to anything that the pope, especially with the bright young Jesuit movement behind him, would think of. Luckily for the pope, the elector of Saxony, though a prisoner, rejected Charles's suggestions too.

But Charles hoped to make this German war the basis of a future imperial society through his son Philip, whom he had already declared the heir to his Spanish dominions, including the Netherlands. By a long-standing previous arrangement Ferdinand, Charles's brother, was to have become emperor on his death or retirement. But now Charles insisted on Philip, not Ferdinand's son Maximilian, succeeding to the Empire on Ferdinand's death.

Distribution of the Protestants
in the middle of the 16th century

BALTIC

NORTH SEA

NETHERLANDS

POLAND

SILESIA

Bremen

Munster

Wittenberg

Antwerp

Brussels

Cologne

Marburg

Erfurt

Anabaptists

Anabaptists

Mainz

Frankfurt
am Main

Wurzburg

Prague

BOHEMIA

Worms

Anabaptists

MORAVIA

Strasburg

B A V A R I A

Augsburg

AUSTRIA

Vienna

FRANCE

Anabaptists

Munich

Salzburg

Anabaptists

Basle

Zurich

Innsbruck

Anabaptists

Berne

SWITZERLAND

TYROL

Anabaptists

HUNGARY

Geneva

ADRIATIC

Lutheran territory

Calvinist and
Zwinglian territory

In most of the obvious ways the young Philip was a disappointment. He disliked wine and tournaments (he fainted while watching
one of them). His nature was the opposite of gay. But he was devout.
He loved religious ceremonies above all others. There lay the basis
of Charles's hopes of him; with Spain at his disposal Philip would
bring about a united Church again, by persuasion or by war. It was
this that made Charles see him as the future emperor too. But
Ferdinand's side of the family disagreed.

Then, as if to emphasise that whatever was done to knit the
Empire closer only served to divide it in the end, something happened that Charles had been dreading since his youth; the German
princes made a treaty with the French. It was negotiated (October
1551) by Maurice of Saxony, who had just been fighting for Charles
and had suddenly identified himself with his father-in-law, the
landgrave of Hesse. For a subsidy of 70,000 crowns a month for the
raising of troops, France was to take those parts of the Empire not
yet German-speaking—Metz, Verdun and so on. The idea was to
cut Charles off from the Netherlands—that is, to bring the Empire
as an effective strategic unit to an end. The presence of Spanish
troops in Germany had stung everyone. And Charles had again, by
his success, become almost everyone's enemy. Germany seethed
with rebellion. His presence in Hesse was described as a 'bestial,
unbearable and constant slavery, like that of Spain'. In a way he had
decided on a war for the whole century. The battles he fought were
only the mild beginning of something that nearly reduced European
society to barbarism in the Thirty Years War of the next century.

German troops approached Augsburg, meaning to attack the
imperial troops. Charles tried to get away to the Netherlands but
found his way blocked in the rear by the French. He was forced to
retreat south to Innsbruck. He wrote to his brother Ferdinand
urging him to use his influence with the princes to get them to
abandon their French alliance and make peace. But he could not
even be sure that Ferdinand himself was not in contact with his
enemies! More and more the Spanish support had become a source
of isolation.

The Spanish presence in Germany had produced an image of

Spain as reactionary, and of Charles as irrevocably in the Spanish camp. And just as Europe saw France as her only guarantee of independence against the Hapsburg domination, now France was her only guarantee against the Spanish too. The fact was that Charles's plan—a dream, really—of uniting Germany and Spain had become impossible. Spain was too powerful. She was the equivalent of Hapsburg power and perhaps more. Charles's sister Mary had recently scored some victories in the duchy of Burgundy, which meant that Spanish power was planted there too for the first time. It secured French hatred for Philip in advance of his reign.

The duke of Alva was once more called from Spain to command his troops, and Charles was again at war with France. Henry II occupied Metz, very largely by means of a trick, and appointed the duke of Guise as its governor.

Luckily for Charles all the German princes had already come to terms with him when he marched on Metz. He failed to take it. In the bitter cold there was mutiny among his troops, and he abandoned the attempt in January 1553. From now on he left the conduct of German affairs to Ferdinand. He was forced to recognise that the adherents of the Augsburg Confession had equal rights with catholics; he signed the document himself (the Treaty of Passau, August 1555) only because his brother persuaded him not to abdicate before a religious settlement was complete. It hurt him to do this, since he was more of an orthodox catholic even than a Hapsburg.

To make things worse for him the new pope Paul IV (Pietro Caraffa, a Neapolitan in his eighties) turned out to be wildly pro-French and anti-Spanish (he called the Spaniards 'the spawn of Jews and Moors'). He held Spain responsible for the present state of Italy—divided and subservient compared with its freedom in the previous century. He had been in Rome during Charles's sack of 1527. He had been *nuncio* in Spain and had disliked its 'vile' people. He took extraordinary steps to cripple Spanish influence. These were dangerously disproportionate to his power. He even started talks with the German protestants. He suggested to the Sultan Suleiman I that he should leave Hungary and concentrate his attention on the Two Sicilies. That was the degree to which religious differences had become policy-differences, adjustable to the needs of the moment. Paul wanted to free Italy from Spain—by means of France—and he signed a treaty with the French king by which Naples was to be given to one of the king's sons (December 1555). Sicily was to be given to Venice. In answer to this Charles sent the duke of Alva down into Italy, and it looked as if there might be a second sack of Rome.

In the same year Charles abdicated. He saw that none of his schemes as emperor, on any front, could possibly succeed, and his abdication was a recognition of the fact that power now lay with Philip, his son, as the king of Spain, and with Ferdinand his brother in his separate conduct of German affairs. His health was all but broken. Mary of the Netherlands, his sister, gave up her throne with his. Charles's court settled close to the monastery of San Jeronimo, in Spain, where he withdrew. He remained there for the last three years of his life in more or less peace and quiet, always consulted during a crisis by Philip or Juana his daughter (who later acted as regent during Philip's absence from Spain). The country was now tranquil, a sanctuary after the world north of the Alps. Philip became its king officially in the first month of 1556. Charles died two years later, in September 1558.

Chapter 9

'God must have turned Spanish'

Philip felt out of place in Germany and the Netherlands. For one thing, the hearty drinking made him sick. He enjoyed women no less than his father, but there was something more introspectively voluptuous in his tastes. He was a suspicious and reticent man. As a child he had shown a distaste for exercise. His father, on the other hand, had broken many lances and had always accompanied his armies on horseback: during his first voyage to Spain he had whiled away his time on board joking with his fool, Jan Bobin. He had played chess or cards in the evening with the other passengers. He had promised wine to the sailor who caught the first glimpse of land, and had watched a man swimming from boat to boat during a dead calm with a bottle of wine tied round his neck, for a wager. It is difficult to imagine Philip with a fool. There seemed no time for that sort of thing. He governed from his desk. He spoke Spanish and no Flemish. Loved by the Spanish since childhood, austere in an essentially Spanish way, he was still the fruit of Charles's grooming. The festivities for his birth had gone on during the sack of Rome. When news of the sack reached Charles he did not at once suspend the festivities. Only when he felt the disapproval of the people—and of great churchmen like the archbishop of Toledo—did he do so. He learned, then, that Spaniards did not necessarily joust and dance while their fellow-countrymen chased the pope from his apartments to Castel Sant'Angelo and—at first acting under orders—sacked and raped until they were almost senseless. Fools and pleasant wagers no longer belonged in this world.

Philip felt that he was Spanish through and through. He hated to be away from Castile, and made sure that he was absent as little as possible. He could barely understand present happenings in Germany. The treaty his father had signed at Passau was simply a document for the toleration of heretics in his eyes. Burning them was simpler and purer. In this too he was characteristically Spanish. This did not mean that Spaniards were crueller than anyone else but that they felt catholicism to be complete—a system of thought which explained all experience and could satisfy any amount of zeal. Philip had seen his mother at prayer for hours at a time. He had been told by his father again and again to give his first thoughts to God, his second to men.

He had been brought up by dignitaries of the Church. (His lenient tutor, Juan Martinez Siliceo, became archbishop of Toledo and primate of Spain.) His upbringing had been mild but hemmed in with etiquette. This gave him a solemn look. As a child he had hardly laughed. He preferred—at a time when the first books were producing a new introspective temperament in masses of people— to write down his thoughts rather than to speak them. Audiences wore him out. While he took little exercise he was nevertheless erect and fine-looking, with blue eyes and light hair and a fair complexion, not typically Spanish at first glance. He was pale. His eyes were often red from excessive reading and writing. He even read in his carriage. He was as unwise as his father in his eating habits. But he did eat less extravagantly, and he never drank. He slept a great deal all his life, perhaps because he took so little air. There was nothing rash in his temperament, unless it was in his sexuality, which wore out one wife after another.

Reading and writing were in fact the key to his system. He insisted on knowing the smallest particulars about the provinces under his control. He trusted discussion with others less than their written memoranda before him on the table. For almost forty years he lived on the reports he received from every part of his empire, annotating them in the margins. To his advisers he appeared to have no other life. After his return to Spain in 1559 he never again left the peninsula. His habits became more and more simple, until by the end of his life he was working in a room furnished no better than a monk's at the Escorial Palace. He disliked delegating authority. His justice was administered by a small number of *corregidores* who could mete out punishment freely to high and low alike. In his time their terms of office went far beyond the legally permitted two years—to five and six, for the simple reason that this allowed him a more direct and personal hold on the country. It was more effective to make his wishes known to a few powerful men, directly responsible to him, than to numberless officials who got in each other's way. The *corregidor* was virtually a ruler of his department or county, and saw that all royal decrees were rigorously applied. Gradually under Philip the other local officials dwindled in importance next to this virtual dictator. But while he loved to have a local despotism exercised in his name, he required it to be exercised strictly according to law. That too was characteristically Spanish. To ensure this he used a watch-and-ward in the form of the so-called *residencia* or prolonged residency of an official (usually an ex-viceroy or ex-*corregidor*) after he had retired from office. This experienced and respected man sent secret reports to Madrid on the officials round him (including the new viceroy or *corregidor*) and heard appeals and complaints. Philip used this system in the Indies as he did in Naples and Sicily and Spain itself—it caused endless domestic troubles. Only in Naples was the *residencia* not taken up, because there was no likelihood of appeals or complaints being voiced, so powerful was the viceroy there: almost a Philip in his local stature.

It was a modern system for which the communications at the time were simply out of place. It meant that while Philip's policy was felt everywhere it transpired it so slowly that new events often overtook its effectiveness. He needed the radio and the telegraph system. His mind would have adapted perfectly to these techniques. On the other hand, he did not run a dictatorship. That system of government, being over-centralised, rarely lasts more than a few decades. Instead, he took advice exhaustively. But only computerised information and the urgent telephone conversation could have made his system work as he wanted it to. One type of advice that he always lacked was financial. Like many of the men round him he failed to understand why it was important. Yet he depended on it as none of his predecessors, Hapsburg or Spanish, had done. In this too he was a characteristic Spaniard. In 1548 the Cortes of Castile had proposed that the export of cloth and silk to the Americas should be stopped because the gold that came back often went into the hands of foreign merchants resident in Spain. The deputies could not understand why they themselves must be the losers thereby.

Philip was scrupulously just, perhaps more so even than his father. The law was there to be interpreted. He chose his judges with great care. If sometimes his government was coldly severe it was because the law was followed to the letter—to the point where it was no longer justice. A system like his lent itself in the end to terror-methods. His government proved that there is no contradiction between the use of these methods and the scrupulous observance of the letter of the law.

Philip's first wife, Maria of Portugal, had died when he was eighteen (1530) soon after bearing him a son, Don Carlos. In 1553, three years before he came to the throne, he had heard of the death of Edward VI of England, who had not only been strongly protestant but had traded Boulogne (which Henry VIII had occupied) for a closer understanding with the French. The new queen of England was catholic. Would it not be a good idea for Philip to marry her? It would bring England back into the Church and keep her there for good. Mary Tudor was Charles V's cousin, and at the age of six had been thought of as his wife. She was the only issue of Catherine of Aragón by Henry VIII. Spain was perhaps the dream of her life, and not only because of her mother; much was due to Juan Luis Vives, her tutor for a number of years. Vives had been brought over to England by Queen Catherine after he had sent a copy of his edition of Augustine's *City of God* to Henry VIII. He was already well known on the Continent as a humanist, and a close friend of Erasmus. He became the first Professor of Humanity at Corpus Christi in Oxford. The entire court was present at his inaugural lecture. He advanced distinctly modern ideas on education, one of them being that a child's needs should be studied, and that the needs of one child varied from those of another, so that higher learning was therefore not for everyone. He wrote a little book called *Instruction of a Christian Woman* for Mary. In 1528 he had returned to the Netherlands because of Henry VIII's divorce plans and the consequent eclipse of Catherine's life. At her typically Renaissance court men like himself had counted. He left on the young Mary an impression of balance and grace. It made her look for Spanish advisers as soon as she ascended the throne.

She turned to her 'family'—namely the Emperor Charles and his son. Charles's representative at the English court, Simon Renard, from the Franche Comté, began to negotiate her marriage with Philip. From England's point of view there were clear advantages in having a close relationship with the greatest continental power. On the other hand, Mary always tried from her vulnerable position on the edge of Europe not to be absorbed by any one power, and to play skilfully the game of changing sides. Henry VIII had played it to an obsessive degree, and had thereby all but played away his influence. But during his reign neither Spain nor France (the latter closely related, through the Guise family, to catholic Scotland) had got a foothold in England.

Mary's interest in Spain was more than a catholic one, though it was mostly that. Spain was the only effective counterweight to France, and thus the only hope of securing a powerful throne in England. This applied as much under protestant Elizabeth later on as it did under catholic Mary. Spain held the key to England's fortunes. Charles's concern to have the friendship of a country whose trade with the Netherlands was a potent factor in imperial finances, and whose ships could make trouble in Dutch waters whenever they wanted to, had kept England independent of France. And Philip's reluctance to allow England—even protestant England—to be swallowed up by the Guise family was the key to Elizabeth's later survival as England's queen. At any time Spain could have crushed the tiny island. If, when Philip later decided to try to do this, Elizabeth was already strong enough to turn his boats away, she was so only by virtue of his policies. Above all the Spanish discovery of the Americas, and the beginnings of an Atlantic trade, changed England's position from that of an island on the edge of a powerful continent—largely an outsider to continental issues, and rather puzzling in its always changing affiliations—into that of a rich trading power.

A bargain was struck in Mary's marriage negotiations. England could perhaps be brought back into the Church, but nothing would convince the barons whom Henry VIII had made rich with Church lands to hand them back again. They would much rather get rid of Mary. Luckily Charles understood this. His representative Simon Renard was advised to approach the problem with great caution. Accordingly he arranged with Mary that ecclesiastical lands already distributed by her father would not be restored to the Church. This immediately won over parliament (whose members owned the land) and they were ready to accept the country's reunion with Rome. In this they were not even unrepresentative, since England was still predominantly catholic in feeling. On the other hand, very powerful elements, particularly in the City, were protestant. Mary's need of a strong husband followed not only from this (naturally the danger of civil war had to be kept in mind) but from the fact that a woman was not looked on as fit to govern a country. Her marriage with Philip was a purely political matter from the beginning. She had never felt inclined to marry (so she told Simon Renard). On Philip's side he found in her a not very attractive aunt eleven years older than himself. There was some talk of her marrying the emperor after all, but Charles was by this time trying to disentangle himself from state affairs.

Marriage negotiations went forward, with Mary making sure that England lost none of her independence in the deal despite her love of Spain. Philip II had to promise that he would not employ foreigners in English public offices or drag England into any war between his father and the French, or lay a claim to English armaments or ships. At Mary's death Philip was to have no further rights in England. Any son they might have would inherit Franche Comté and the Netherlands jointly with the English crown, while the rest of the Spanish inheritance would go to Don Carlos. In the event of Don Carlos's death everything was to go to the English king. It was an extraordinary agreement. To the protestants it looked like a Spanish plot. Even to the catholics, overjoyed at the thought of getting the Spanish empire, it must have looked as if Spain would necessarily and inevitably take England over. The French were frightened at any close relationship between England and Spain, and did their best to provoke alarm about the agreement in London. This was easy. It could be shown that Simon Renard was much closer to Mary than any English councillor. Was he not already shaping England's future?

But more than this the idea had taken root outside the court that England could expect 'outlandish' men to land at Plymouth after Mary's marriage to one of them. The feeling against Rome in England was political and social more than religious. And this feeling now extended to Spain. Catholic foreigners were becoming for increasing numbers of Englishmen (though they were as yet a minority) a clear menace. The protestant movement in England was more strictly nationalistic and social (hence it had come from the top) than any other in Europe.

The celebration of Mass in the city churches caused the first riots of Mary's reign. Both Charles and Philip, in urging Mary to caution when dealing with her enemies, seemed to understand that in England religious feelings ran less deep than social ones, and that they could be dealt with by a clever distribution of land (apart from a few executions for high treason). Philip's intercession saved many Englishmen from the flames. Foreigners in London were horrified at 'Bloody' Mary's zeal in getting rid of her political enemies. Philip even had his confessor Friar Alonso de Castro preach in London against the religious persecution.

But both Philip and his father thought that Mary's sister, Elizabeth, being of pure English stock and obviously protestant (despite her assurances to Mary of the opposite), should be locked up in the Tower together with Edward Courtenay, earl of Devon, a noted 'rebel'. Simon Renard overheard her saying to the French ambassador at Mary's coronation that the crown was 'heavy' to which the ambassador replied, 'Have patience, it will soon produce a better.'

Imperial courtiers were pelted with snowballs in the London streets. Londoners lowered their heads when the ambassadors themselves passed by. There were risings in the Midlands, in Devon, in Wales, though none of them came to anything. Sir Thomas Wyatt's rebellion nearly succeeded. Courtenay, earl of Devon, was mixed up in it, which meant that Elizabeth at least knew something about it.

Mary began trying and executing protestants with what was for England unprecedented fury. Nothing like the continental persecutions had taken place in England, and Mary's short reign left an indelible horror of Spain behind it. Sir Thomas Wyatt was brought to trial, and examined again and again for evidence of Elizabeth's complicity. Nothing concrete could be brought against her, but she was taken to the Tower—it is said with Simon Renard's encouragement, as he was anxious for London to be a safe place for Philip when he arrived. Leaflets were distributed in the streets. They read, 'Hold fast, keep together, and we shall prevent the Prince of Spain from entering this realm!' Thousands of Londoners poured to an echoing wall which on receiving the shout 'God save the queen' replied nothing, but on hearing 'God save the Lady Elizabeth!' echoed 'So be it!' Wyatt was executed. His head was mysteriously stolen from the Tower. Elizabeth, her record clear, was released. But she was placed under house-arrest at Woodstock near Oxford. It was dangerous to imprison her for too long, and dangerous to set her free. When her barge passed down the river on its way to Woodstock the city merchants had three salvoes of artillery fired.

On 25 July 1554 Philip and Mary were married at Winchester Cathedral. It was the Feast of St. James, Spain's patron saint. Philip was dressed in a white doublet and hose, with a cloth-of-gold cloak studded with pearls. He and his court were remarkably elegant. In London the gallows were taken down and free drink was distributed. Philip did his best not to give the impression either to his own courtiers or to Mary that he wished to interfere in English life in any way. He kept a stern hold on his retinue. They had very proud ways, and a great distaste for England. Kissing on the mouth was always an accepted form of greeting in England, but the duchess of Alva found the earl of Derby's kiss hard to bear, never having clapped eyes on him before. The Spaniards thought English women badly dressed, English manners uncouth. There were some bloody encounters in the streets and Londoners had the impression that there were four times as many Spaniards as themselves. There were rumours that the archbishopric of Canterbury, vacant since the protestant Cranmer had been burned at the stake, was to be given to a Spaniard, and that 12,000 Spaniards were about to land in England to lay hands on the crown. On St. Andrew's Day, 30 November 1554, the papal legate, Reginald Pole, an Englishman who but for French voting would by now have been pope, entered the kingdom and solemnly absolved the English nation for its schismatic notions. England was received back into the Church. But Pole had lingered in the Channel for some days, to make sure that the English were not in a mood for revolution.

With England once more catholic, everything must have looked marvellous to Charles V. There were disappointments ahead. The first was that Mary produced no heir. For a time she was thought to be pregnant. A *Te Deum* was sung and the bells rang out all over London. But weeks passed without any sign of a child. Philip was impatient to get away. He had no love either for Mary or her people. The pregnancy turned out to be the swelling of dropsy. For years she had been unwell, and suffered from fearful headaches. Philip left England for Flanders on 29 August 1555.

He made a second visit two years later to win England over to his war against France. After that he never came back. To Mary he said that he would be returning within a month. To his own court he said that if he set foot in Spain again he would never leave it, especially for so 'poor' a matter as his English marriage.

Mary's reign lasted hardly five years. She died childless at the age of forty-two. By this time Spain had become the name of everything undesirable in English ears. Her persecutions had left a nasty taste. She had lost Calais to the French. The loss was blamed conveniently but quite wrongly on Philip. In fact the English had rejected a Spanish offer of help and the Calais defences had been in a state of rot.

Peace was made with France twenty days after Philip became king, which left him free to deal with Paul IV. The duke of Alva had been made Viceroy of Naples in 1557, and was now ordered to prepare to move with his Spanish battalions towards Rome. Being of a truculent and proud turn of mind Alva had started preparing long before he got the order.

In the first months of the new reign Charles's influence on Philip —towards peace and caution—was great, but only because Philip was not yet his own master. Imperial policy was now in Ferdinand's hands. It took some time for dynastic dreams to roll away and for Philip to find his own strength. The Hapsburgs still counted for something. In fact, the 'loss' of the Empire to Philip was only an advantage. He was now on an equal footing with France. He was not obliged to fight on several fronts at once. Above all he had the compact strength of Spain behind him, and no doubt he would call on the energies available in Castile for a new Holy War as his Spanish predecessors, Ferdinand and Isabella, had done. If he did, it would be the Holy War of all time.

Paul IV's hatred of the Hapsburgs was the basis of what foreign policy he had. He all but insulted Charles's ambassadors. He locked up Alva's emissary. In September 1566 the duke of Alva marched across the border between the Two Sicilies and the papal lands with 12,000 men. The Spanish Church supported Philip against the pope. Spanish theologians had been called together and asked if it would be 'legal' for Philip to put an embargo on all Church revenues in Spain, and stop all moneys going to Rome. And the answer had been yes. This was surely the smoothest act of protestantism so far. A council was even suggested—to investigate the circumstances of Pietro Caraffa's election to the papal throne. By 18 November Alva was in Ostia.

So far the French king, Henry II, had not moved to help the pope. But suddenly, in the last days of 1566, the duke of Guise crossed the Alps with 13,000 soldiers. He reached Rome in March. The pope told him that he would like to go out right away and fight the duke of Alva's army of 'Jews, Moors and Lutherans'. Guise humoured him and continued his march south. Here he was checked. His siege of Civitella near Naples was unsuccessful, so much so that he is supposed to have remarked, 'God must have turned Spanish'.

In the meantime Philip took advantage of Guise's absence from

The Duke of Alba

*Antonio Perez,
Philip II's secretary*

Catherine de' Medici

Prince William of Orange

France to put in an attack from the Netherlands. He captured St. Quentin on the Somme, and Guise was at once ordered back to France to defend Paris. He left Rome and Alva advanced to the gates of the city, where he met three cardinals to discuss peace. He had very strict instructions from Philip not to sack Rome. The bargain he struck with the three cardinals was that he would clear out of the papal lands if the pope kept his nose out of Franco-Spanish quarrels in the future. This Paul IV learned to do. The experience of seeing an army at the gates of his city, capable of sacking it a second time, infused caution into his policy. That is to say, he found it wiser to acquiesce in the total subjugation of Italy to Spain. To cover his position, he was allowed to give absolution to the duke of Alva and the Spanish people for having recently attacked the Church. At the ceremony of absolution Alva went on his knees before Paul. Clearly it was to Philip's advantage to have an acquiescent Rome rather than a sacked Rome seething with hatred. This way, the pope was shown the red light without a shot having been fired.

Philip had approached Mary Tudor to help him in his war with France. She obliged by declaring war on Henry II, thus running the risk of seeming to her people to be fighting for Spanish interests (even against papal ones). There was a tremendous Spanish victory at St. Quentin in August 1557. Seven thousand Frenchmen were captured, including the constable of France himself. The rest were killed or put to flight, out of a force of nearly 20,000. But Philip failed to follow this up—to his father's horror. He did not march on Paris. This would have reduced Henry II's prestige to nothing.

The truth was that Philip was nervous of taking bold steps. He preferred piecemeal and methodical attacks. None of his later bold actions—notably against Portugal and England—came off. In this particular case his hesitation was based on considered policy. He simply did not believe he could win Paris. Two English kings had tried before him and failed. But his hesitation had much the same effect as a sack of Paris. St. Quentin was mercilessly sacked instead, by the Spanish and German troops. Women and children were massacred. A great part of the town was razed. Philip did his best to control matters when he arrived, but blood-lust had taken over.

7

Unpaid soldiers were inevitably undisciplined. And also perhaps a taste for violence was beginning to grip more and more people, in low places and high. It took months to occupy the town.

Peace negotiations went on for six months, between October 1558 and April of the following year. The duke of Alva, the prince of Orange and the minister Granvelle represented Spain, while the French delegates were the constable of France and the duke of Guise's brother, cardinal of Lorraine.

During those months Mary Tudor died and Elizabeth, on whom Philip knew he could not rely, became queen. He proposed marriage to her, as the most effective guarantee of continued English support. His ambassador, the duke of Feria, got no definite refusal from her. She was much too fine a diplomat ever to say a categorical yes or no when not absolutely necessary. One thing was clear—that she had no wish to incur her sister's unpopularity by following the same policies, even apart from her own protestant inclinations. She also knew how far she could go in displeasing the strongest prince in Europe. She knew that the English pirates (actually her own seamen) were continually setting out from the southern ports to worry Spanish galleons in American waters, and to threaten as far as possible the flow of gold back to Spain. She knew her value to Philip as a counterweight to the Guise family. By the marriage between Francis, Henry II's son, and Mary Queen of Scots (who regarded herself as the rightful queen of England) the powerful Guise family already had a foothold in Scotland. Philip, through the duke of Feria, put it to Elizabeth that she could either follow the late Mary Tudor's policies and support him with armies, or else lose Calais for good. She chose to lose Calais. It was better than losing her identity as England's new hope.

In the treaty that was signed at Cateau-Cambresis the French kept Calais but lost all the territories taken from the duke of Savoy over twenty years before. This gave Spain control of Italy. It was now virtually a Spanish colony. The centre of catholicism seemed to be shifting from Rome to Madrid, precisely as Philip had wanted it. The treaty with the French also stipulated that he should take Elizabeth of Valois, the daughter of Henry II and Catherine de'

Medici, as his wife. This time Philip struck lucky. Their betrothal was celebrated in France while he was negotiating peace-terms. Their life together was intensely happy—perhaps the happiest period of Philip's whole life. The Spanish people called her *Reina de la paz* or 'the queen of peace'. Henry II of France was pledged not to make war in Italy again.

There seems to have been a secret agreement between Philip and Henry II about the need to root out 'heresy'. During a stag-hunt in the Bois de Vincennes Henry told the prince of Orange (who later turned against the Spanish in the Netherlands, perhaps because Philip did not make him the governor there) that he and the duke of Alva had discussed together an important plan. This was no less than the systematic removal, by burning or imprisonment or intimidation, of protestants in every country where Spanish troops could be used. The plan was Alva's, rather predictably. Henry was apparently already worried by the great numbers of protestants in his own country—the 'vermin', as he called them. The danger, to his mind, lay in the fact that many influential Frenchmen were protestants, which meant the danger at any time of a *coup d'état*. Protestantism was now clearly subversion. It had become for its enemies a political movement. And the approach of catholic kings and princes to the whole religious question accordingly became a defensive or what we would now call reactionary one.

Philip was in general agreement with the plan. He had only one proviso. 'Heresy' must not be rooted out in England or Scotland. He preferred caution in this area. Above all, he preferred to do the rooting-out himself, and not in French company. When the time came, he would like to get rid of both the protestants in England and the French catholics in Scotland. Alva had too military a mind to perceive these important subtleties but he went along with Philip's policy. It probably never occurred to him that Philip felt English protestantism to be a useful protection against the mighty Guise and Valois families, rather than a threat to himself.

Elizabeth's value to Philip increased in a dramatic way when Henry II was accidentally killed in a tournament celebrating the betrothal of Elizabeth of Valois to Philip. Montgomery ran a lance through him. It meant that Mary Queen of Scots was now the wife of France's new king, Francis II, though for the time being this threat to English and Spanish interests was only potential, as Francis was under sixteen and a rather weak creature at that. It was still a victory for Elizabeth of England, in that it gave Philip a reason to be more tolerant of her activities in American waters than he had been hitherto. It also meant that she could build up England's strength until such time as Philip's tolerance was exhausted. She knew that Philip would then attack her. She knew too that Spain was exhausted by its war with the French, and that Philip was as much interested in a long period of peace as she was.

An attack on her sooner or later was inevitable, unless she repeated Mary Tudor's satellite policy. Philip meant to re-establish the catholic faith everywhere. He returned to Spain, after stunning France and clearing her out of Italy, to put this deepest of all his programmes into practice. An *auto-da-fé* was held in his presence at Valladolid (Sunday, 8 October 1559). The royal gallery was placed opposite the scaffold. A procession left the Inquisition prison at sunrise and entered the square to the sound of bells. On that day, until two in the afternoon, no one was allowed to travel by coach or sedan-chair or on horseback through the streets where the procession was to pass. The prisoners had their heads shaved. The penitents were dressed in a *sanbenito* or penitential sack of yellow cloth marked with a red St. Andrew's cross, and they wore no shoes or stockings. Those to be burned wore a sheepskin sack called a *zamarra*, with a tall conical cap of paper on their heads called a *coroza*. Both costumes had devils and flames painted on them, and sometimes a portrait of the 'heretic' himself, with flames underneath him. Anyone whose sentence had been commuted from burning had the flames inverted. The lesser penitents simply wore coarse black cloaks and trousers. That morning both the inquisitors and the condemned had an enormous breakfast.

The Inquisition prisons were not the damp, dark and terrible places they are often supposed to have been. They were invariably private houses. On the whole the inmates were well fed. They were looked on as victims of their own darkness, and not as felons. It sometimes occurred that in one of the royal prisons, where conditions were really bad, a prisoner tried to get examined by the Inquisition so as to be transferred to one of its prisons.

Before the procession started the condemned were exhorted again and again to repent. Those who did so got the milder 'Spanish' death by the *garrotte* or strangulation, and the quite unrepentant were burned at the *quemadero* or stake. The Dominicans were always given the privilege of leading the procession. They carried the banner of the Inquisition: a rough green cross on a black background, between an olive branch and a sword, with the words *Exsurge, Domine, et judice causam Tuam* ('Rise, Lord, and judge your cause'). At the end of the procession there were porters carrying boxes of corpses which had been disinterred from their burial places, having been judged posthumously. Only the ceremony took place in the city itself. The burning was done outside on the place of the *quemadero*, which literally means 'hearth' or strip of pavement kept for the purpose.

There was a vast crowd. The king solemnly swore to the inquisitor-general, Hernando de Valdés, that he would give all necessary support to the Holy Office of the Inquisition against heretics and apostates. The sentences were then read. On this particular day, the Florentine godson of Charles the emperor, Carlo de Sesa, was one of the condemned who had chosen the *quemadero*. Passing Philip he asked him how he could possibly tolerate such performances, and Philip replied that in the case of a man as evil as Sesa (Sesa was a protestant) he would happily 'build a fire' for him.

Wrath was now the dominant emotion of the protestant-catholic struggle. Both sides felt it increasingly. On 27 September 1540 a special Bull had been issued declaring the Society of Jesus official. A new monastic order had been created by the Spaniard, Ignatius Loyola, at a time when the Curia had decided that too many monastic orders existed and that they must be reformed or even in some cases abolished, apart from the fact that the Church had twice laid it down, in 1215 and 1274, that no more orders were to be created.

The highly crusading if not aggressive nature of this new order had appealed to the pope and his cardinals as a sort of special force that would re-establish papal authority everywhere. It was the pope's own 'army'. The Bull was called *Regimini militantis ecclesias*.

The order was not exactly new in ideas. St. Dominic many centuries before had taken a journey to Rome similar to Loyola's and, like him, had won the protection of the powerful. Loyola's black cloak was in fact reminiscent of the Dominican 'black friar'. Also St. Dominic's lay order had been called the 'Militia' of Christ. The war idea had already been stated.

The 1540 Bull talked only of the order's role in 'propagating the faith', and not until twenty years later were the words 'and defend' added. The society was never intended by its founders as a papal force, whatever it may have become. It sought to 'open the eyes of the mind'. The society established first-class schools where fresh air and exercise were made part of the curriculum, and pupils were expected to be well mannered. This was no departure from earlier orders. But the society was thoroughly sixteenth century in its strict schedules, its rigorous programmes of behaviour, its grooming of the mind. The actual word 'Jesuit' was first used in Germany, to describe these 'black horsemen of the pope', and it meant 'severe'. And in 1640, a century later, according to the *Oxford English Dictionary*, the word 'Jesuit' was first used to mean 'treacherous'.

The Jesuits became the teaching arm of the Church. They opened colleges of their own—Padua (1542), Rome (1551). Above all, they became the teachers of monarchs, chancellors, bishops. They were soon to be found at every court where the prince was faithful to the Church. 'Consummate prudence, allied with moderate saintliness, is better than greater saintliness and mere prudence,' wrote Loyola.

They were soon caught up in the struggle against protestantism. The catholic bishops in Germany called on them to start work in southern Germany, and the university of Ingolstadt became their base. The Bavarian princes were quick to see the value of this rather military approach to the mind. The order's most bitter enemies were inside the Church—notably the Franciscans and the Dominicans, who had nothing like the same freedom of action. At least one Dominican crossed himself every time he saw a Jesuit. And a Franciscan of Ingolstadt called the order 'the scourge of the monks'.

Loyola had written the first sketch of his *Spiritual Exercises* as a young man in Manresa, in the 1520s, and he perfected them over the years until their final form in 1541. They were printed in a Latin translation seven years later. They had nothing meditative about them. They were the plain description of a method. The devotee was told to live in a solitary cell for a month, observing complete silence unless at Mass or talking to his confessor. He was to direct his thoughts to the filth of his own condition, and to imagine the horrors of hell, to feel with the utmost vividness the flames licking his body. From this he must turn to the story of Christ. In this way he would feel the mercy that poured from Christ, its marvellous contrast to the flames. He would now feel peace. This peace was only possible by means of an absolute obedience to Christ, which meant an absolute obedience to his Church. The devotee was to surrender his own thoughts. Loyola's exercises ended with 'Rules for thinking with the Church'. Among the rules was one stating that if according to the Church a white thing was black, then it had to be proclaimed black immediately.

Loyola was not a fine theologian or even a good thinker. It was his will that counted. It made the Jesuit success astonishingly greater than even Pope Paul had hoped. Jesuits began to get the reputation for moving mountains. In Spain the Jesuit delegate Aroz persuaded the former viceroy of Catalonia, Francesco Borgia, duke of Candia, to found the first purely Jesuit college in Europe, and endow a new university. To Charles V's great displeasure the duke later became a fully professed member of the order. Charles wanted him raised to the rank of cardinal (the pope was willing enough) but Loyola's influence blocked it. Jesuit schools for Christianised Jews were established in Rome. Members of the order were sent to every part of Europe. Francis Xavier went to the Indies. The papal delegates at the Council of Trent were both Jesuits. They acted as the watchdogs of doctrine.

The order was very much the child of Castilian zeal. Loyola had

once been a page at the court of Ferdinand and Isabella, and fought
the French in Navarre under Charles V. He was now the 'General'
of a monastic order. Its holy war on the heretical mind was conceived
down to the finest details of strategy. Within two years of recognising
the order Paul III saw that the sixty members he had laid down as
the maximum were far too few, and by a Bull of 14 March 1543 he
allowed Loyola to increase the membership to any number he
wished. In the same document he conceded the general 'and his
successors' an unprecedented right—to alter any of the statutes of
the society as they thought fit. Even the pope need not know of these
new rules. It meant in effect that the pope could claim ignorance of
things he wanted done but must officially disapprove of. The society
was expected to be worldly for unworldly ends. In the case of
Andreas Lippoman's bequest of a large estate to the Jesuits in
Venice for the establishment of a college (1542), Laynez (a Jesuit
leader) is said to have bribed the doge's mistress, with Loyola's
approval.

By a further decree, hardly more than two months later, the pope
gave the Jesuits the right to preach from whatever church they
wished, to set up schools wherever they wished, to establish pro-
fessorships wherever they could, to hear confessions from the highest
men of state and to give absolution wherever they happened to be;
and to confirm, to celebrate Mass, baptism, marriage without the
approval of the local priest or even bishop. It was tantamount to
electing the order a papal *corps d'élite*.

Two or three years later, on 5 June 1546, Loyola asked that the
number of his army be increased, without extending the order
itself, by making a third order apart from the 'professed members'
and the novices. They were to be called 'coadjutors', and were
divided into 'spiritual' and 'secular' arms. They had none of the
powers of the members themselves; they were purely administrators
of Jesuit law. Being a 'spiritual' coadjutor meant having been
through all the severe tests and penances and confessions laid down
for the novice, without attaining the higher level of membership
proper. It was a name applied to the professors, rectors, confessors
and preachers of the order. The 'secular' coadjutor or 'short-coat',

as he was often called, was not a priest, and therefore never taught in schools or colleges; he simply took over some of the burdens of secular organisation. Many kings and princes were 'short-coats'. When Jacob Miron was reluctant to become John III of Portugal's father-confessor on the grounds that Jesuits were out of place at royal courts, Loyola reprimanded him vigorously: 'On the contrary, kings require good priests for their guidance all the more from the circumstance that they have many more allurements to sin than ordinary mortals.'

By that time the Jesuits had achieved an astonishing influence in Portugal. Almost the whole court had Jesuit confessors. Queen Catherine, Charles V's sister, was confessed by Father Michael de Torres, which had important consequences when the king died and she became regent of the country in 1557. On the other hand Loyola was careful never to allow the society to become an instrument in royal hands. When the Archduke Ferdinand wanted the Jesuit Lejay, whom Loyola had sent to him, made bishop of Trieste (1546) he opposed it as an infringement of the society's statutes. He himself turned down the offer of a cardinal's hat.

The extraordinary process by which the pope seemed to be ceding his own power to the Jesuits was completed by the Bull of 18 October 1549. This not only laid down that no member of the order could accept a bishopric, archbishopric or other high church office, but that the general could disregard any recommendations that came direct from the pope about the movements of his members. No dignitary of the Church had the power to claim the services of a Jesuit, and in the case of a member's services being lent, that member was still entirely under the general's discretion. The general also had the power to absolve his members from every kind of sin, and every kind of stricture that came from inside or outside the Church. Members must never confess to anyone but the general or one nominated by the general. If a member was released from his vows by the general he was forbidden to join another order unless it was the Carthusian (perhaps the strictest of the orders at the time, and the one least likely to show curiosity about other friars, or act on inside knowledge of them).

Jesuits were outside the jurisdiction of the ecclesiastical courts, and answerable only to the pope. When a city or republic was under papal interdict or excommunication only the Jesuits could celebrate Mass, behind locked doors, and those local people who were their servants or helpers were excluded from the excommunication. Naturally no dignitary of the Church could excommunicate a member of the order. Jesuits were to be exempted from all taxes and dues. Any lands or buildings or moneys bequeathed to them were to be considered as automatically ratified by the pope, without the need to consult him. Any man or woman who visited a church or holy place nominated by the general on a certain day was to receive dispensation from sins—and a visit outside that day secured dispensation for seven years or 'seven times forty fast days'. The general could send a delegate to any university he wished in order to deliver lectures, without consulting anyone beforehand. Anyone who interfered with Jesuit operations ran the risk of excommunication.

The order was thus rendered an entirely self-sufficient secret society. The Bull hinted strongly that favour from the Jesuits was of a higher degree than that obtained from Church dignitaries or other monastic orders. The baffled anger and envy all this would cause, especially inside the Church, must have been foreseen since the Bull came several years after the earlier decrees—and they had caused resentment enough. But the anger was part of the operation, designed as a spur to zeal.

Above all, the Jesuits more than anyone denounced 'heresy' as synonymous with subversion of the state. This was perhaps their chief appeal to monarchs, when the monarchs were catholic.

Philip was perfectly prepared to burn heretics when they did not repent, and conduct a holy war on men whose doctrine of the Eucharist differed from his own. Yet he was far from being a cruel man, or even very bigoted. He read books and manuscripts avidly. He sent to every part of Europe for new acquisitions for his vast library. He collected pictures, befriended Titian and supported El Greco (though he did dislike his altar in the Escorial). He prayed

long and fervently, and held back from social life. He took a special
interest in flowers—yellow jonquil and roses and orange blossom.
He enjoyed clingstone peaches, and listened to the nightingales, and
wrote to his little daughter about birds.

He did inspire fear in many people. At court it was said that 'his
smile and his knife were close together'. But he was certainly not a
bloodthirsty man. It was his extreme mystical disposition that
isolated him and made him seem mysterious. And this, while it
supplied him with the energy to follow one policy and one alone (the
defence of the Church) throughout his life, gave his decisions a
seeming ruthlessness. That is to say, he was enough of a mystic to see
the body simply as a vehicle, and therefore not to recoil too much
at the thought of death or physical mortification. He regretted the
need for persecution, he regretted executing people. But the alternative, for him, was the collapse of the only faith, followed by a
liquidation of Christian civilisation at the hands of the Turks. He
saw himself (and he was perfectly right) as the only prince left in
Europe strong enough to defend Christendom against the heretic
within and the infidel without. He was prepared to give up his own
body in the fight. And he was prepared to give up other people's.
This was precisely his feeling when he later imprisoned his own son
Don Carlos, whose nature he could not educate or tame. 'At last,'
he wrote to his sister, the Empress Maria, who had interceded for
Don Carlos, 'I have chosen to make a sacrifice to God of my own
flesh and blood, and to place His service and the universal welfare
and happiness before all other human considerations.'

The irony is that without the mystical devotion he might have
saved more of the Church than he did, and been able to face the
Turks with a united Christian army. As it was, his concessions to
heresy (and he certainly made them in the Netherlands, though they
were brief and perhaps not sincere) were seized on by the protestants
as signs of weakness, while his harshness simply provoked them to
greater courage. For they were mystics too—in the same way that
he was; that is, not enclosed and silent in a monastery but in the
thick of public affairs. And perhaps there is no more dangerous
mixture than the desire to be a monk and the desire to succeed in

life. The result of the bad mixture on both sides was a society that had no time for mysticism at all.

A great change was coming about in the sixteenth century. Imperceptibly the mind was taking the place of what had hitherto been the spirit. The mind and not the spirit was now the illuminator. Religion began to deteriorate into 'beliefs' as opposed to experience. The mind wanted to be clear about what it believed. The last Council of Trent laid down the Roman 'dogmas' for all to see; there could be no mistake in future as to what constituted 'heresy' and what did not. In 1557 the Roman Inquisition was reorganised on the basis of the Spanish Inquisition, and the first index of banned books came into being.

Religious discussion was now rational discussion. The catholics and protestants at their councils argued not only with each other, for days and weeks, but among themselves; and most of the discussion hinged on definition to such a point that outsiders (Charles V had been one of them) began to wonder where the spiritual experience itself had gone. The whole protestant-catholic struggle can indeed be seen as little more than a symptom of this transference of religious experience to the mind, ending in the eighteenth-century sanctification of the mind above all other faculties. And the word 'spiritual' began its long journey of deterioration, until it came to mean little more than bloodless.

On behalf of strict dogma, outside of which lay the devil, devout men like Philip could perpetrate the most unthinkable cruelties and repressions. The burning of a 'heretic' was rather like a surgical operation. You might feel a certain physical horror but a disease was being cut out and therefore the operation was to the good. In the same way the torture of animals in laboratories is justified by later, secular generations; it is for the 'good' of mankind. The 'heretic' was seen as having as little right to life as the 'experimental animal' today.

Men were afraid of contamination. Both the reformer and the counter-reformer considered himself as working in the interests of hygiene. Burning disinfects in the fastest way. The air was so full of uncertainties that it seemed best to do the job of disinfecting boldly and coldly. Panic was in the air. Jesuits had once run through the streets of Gaetà in Italy bleeding from thorns and half-naked, shrieking 'Do penance! Hell is for sinners, heaven for the chosen!' and the terrified local population had immediately rushed to church.

Precisely as the inner experience waned, so outer conduct became more important, until it was thought that at the end of life this conduct was weighed up and either punished with hell or rewarded with heaven. Men were now angry, and it was perhaps natural that they should impute anger to God as well. Lutherans were said to leave their churches tight-faced with righteous anger, not bright with illumination.

Much had changed. Until the middle of the sixteenth century there had seemed nothing unusual about a man experiencing religious ecstasy. Isabella of Castile, her daughter Juana, Charles V —they had all known the experience. Charles V had, all his life, been torn between the most desperate anguish and the wildest transports of ecstasy. The same was true of his grandson Don Carlos. But by Don Carlos's time such an experience seemed out of joint. And in the strangest way it *was* out of joint in his case, perhaps because of the way he was treated by those round him.

Increasingly the leading catholics were suspicious of such an experience, while the leading protestants poured scorn on it. The distrustful treatment of the *alumbrados* by the Spanish Church is proof of that. So is the protestant treatment of the Anabaptists and the so-called 'spiritualist' thinkers like Denck and Schwenkfeld. Enthusiasm of any kind, however lonely and quiet, seemed too disturbing a force for the two opposed orders trying to establish themselves as the only right and true one. More than this; the faculty of religious experience seemed to have fallen away from the mass of the people at this time, like an unused faculty of the organism, until it became customary for millions to live and die without the smallest inkling of what it could mean to be religious. In the most paradoxical way the period of maximum religious discussion ostracised the basis of religion. The Christian became the lay creature he is today.

The voyages of discovery were a search for paradise and gold.

Apparently the paradise was no longer felt inside. There was something frantic about that search. The search for 'knowledge' too was much like an effort to fill the gap left by the absence of the deepest knowledge of all, which no number of books could elicit. And the orthodoxy—was that a frantic effort to put up something strong and unchangeable in place of an experience that had really collapsed?

Anyone could become a heretic by saying the wrong thing. It could happen in a moment. A Spanish constable at the Mexican court trying an English servant, Robert Tomson, for heresy in 1559 repeated Tomson's chance remark that the saints 'being of wood and stone' should not have prayers offered to them. The witness had replied that the prayers were addressed not to 'these here but those above', to which Tomson said that prayers should be offered only to God, 'who stood with open arms in heaven'. Whereupon the witness made Tomson a comparison, saying that when a poor man wished to ask a favour from the king, he was only too glad to commend himself to some 'favourite courtier'. But Tomson stood his ground. 'For that very object,' he said, 'the king stationed himself at a window so that great and small might address him, and in like fashion God stood at a window when Mass was being said.' At this the witness accused him of heresy—Lutheran heresy. Tomson was condemned to a term of imprisonment. It was a way of teaching people to leave all ideas alone, in case they touched flames.

In Spain the ownership of a book was now enough to incriminate a man. A neighbour could be denounced for not having fasted on the right day. It was during Philip's reign that the *alumbrados* or 'illuminated ones'—a mystical body which emphasised the inner light to the exclusion of any outside authority—came under the suspicious eye of the Holy Office. Under Charles V there had been only sporadic individual trials of these people. Thus religious intensity was now suspect.

Philip II kept the Inquisition under close and unremitting personal control. He chose its officers with the greatest care, and threw them out without ceremony when he thought fit to do so. He knew its secrets. It was therefore an instrument of terror in his hands—

since outside the law. And because of this shared role as catholic élites, the Spanish Inquisition and the Jesuit movement hated each other. All his life Philip tried to cripple the Jesuits in some way, but always unsuccessfully. Any striking manifestation of faith aroused his suspicious scrutiny. Under Philip the safest way for men high and low was always the middle one, with a minimum display of imagination. Mediocrity necessarily thrives where men are frightened. Philip came to admire St. Theresa of Avila and may even have received her. But she was examined and kept under strict scrutiny for a time, in case her plan to clean out the top-heavy ecclesiastical stables of Spain might have subversive motives. At this time Spain had 400,000 monks and 300,000 priests. By 1570 a quarter of Spain's adult population was clerical, not to mention an army of clerical hangers-on.

For Philip the work of the Inquisition was important political work, since heresy anywhere in his dominions was *ipso facto* rebellion against himself. He tried to introduce Spanish methods into Milan and Naples but without success. The popes were on the whole horrified by them. And ordinary Italians simply shrugged them off. But everyone was frightened just the same. Spanish embassies were always the ones most closely watched.

Philip even used the Inquisition in politics, since he (the state) was identified with the faith. In 1578 he found that his customs officers had no legal way of stopping a horse-dealer in Saragossa from exporting horses to enemy-France. His answer was to claim that these horses were clearly destined to be used by the Huguenots, once on the other side of the border. The Inquisition tried the dealer, and he got 200 lashes, with a fine and five years in the galleys.

This was all part of exercising an 'authority which is so necessary and becoming for the service of God and for the good government of what He has entrusted to me' (a letter from Philip to Granvelle). Later in the century Pope Sixtus V (elected against Philip's will) stated categorically that 'the preservation of the catholic religion' was 'only a pretext for the Spanish king, whose principal aim is the security and aggrandisement of his dominions' (in a letter of instruction to his legate in Paris). This was not a truthful valuation of

Philip, but it was how Philip's actions looked outside Spain. After all, he had more control of the Church in his own country than any other ruler in Europe. Charles V too had been granted the right to appoint bishops himself. This became an endless source of trouble between Spain and the popes. Philip could people the Church with dignitaries whose faces fitted his interests. And sometimes his need of money played a part in the choice. He saw his position as precisely contrary to the way Sixtus V saw it. Philip once wrote to Granvelle that people tolerated heresy in his foreign dominions simply because they were *his* dominions, and in order to undermine *his* authority. This was truer than Sixtus V's appraisal of him. France would never have encouraged protestantism in Germany and the Netherlands, or made treaties with the Sultan, except to undermine the Spanish empire. Even the pope was to treat with the Turks with the same end in mind.

Rome was rapidly ceasing to be the legal centre of the catholic world. By a decree of 1572 Philip's council of state invalidated papal briefs on Spaniards under trial in a foreign court. It was a declaration of independence, another example of the smooth protestantism that went on in high places. It meant that the pope had no real authority in the Spanish empire, and that the Spanish Inquisition could take his place, under Philip's guidance. On the other hand Philip could not go too far because of Church revenues, some of which, like the *cruzada*, were retractable by the pope at any time. And the pope learned to stand up to Philip when he looked like winning. In the case of Bartolomé Carranza, once Mary Tudor's confessor and now accused of Lutheranism after he had become primate of Spain, Philip insisted on his own Inquisition trying him. But he lost the case. Eventually, in 1566, the man was sent to Rome, where he was given a cosy imprisonment in an apartment of Castel Sant'Angelo for the next nine years. The pope thus succeeded in snatching one of his best lambs from the wolf.

Carranza (a Dominican) had been denounced several times in his life—first at the age of twenty-seven, for having defended Erasmus. He had survived the examination to become not only a Regent of Theology but an examiner for the Inquisition. Pope Paul III had conferred on him the right to read prohibited books, and he had censored many books himself for the Holy Office. Indeed, the first Index of Spain had been placed in Carranza's hands, at the burning of the first Lutheran in Valladolid in 1544. It is said that the utter fearlessness of the victim made a deep impression on him; the man had looked into his eyes for a moment and asked him, 'Do you envy me my happiness?'

Carranza had also been at the Council of Trent. As Mary Tudor's confessor he had supported the burning of the archbishop of Canterbury, Thomas Cranmer. But in London he had preached on St. Paul's *Letter to the Galatians*. This was dangerous ground because the *Letter* had been the starting point of Luther's doctrine. His enemies had begun to watch him closely. What sounded good catholic doctrine in London could sound heretical in Spain. Jealous men pinned an indictment on him for voicing 'Lutheran ideas'. And he was a fervent man. That perhaps was the chief mark against him. The Inquisition got to work on him secretly. It interrogated people who had heard him preach in England and Germany. A witness claimed that Carranza had denied the existence of purgatory in the scriptures. Another said he had advocated 'mercy to converted heretics'. Some of the witnesses were put to torture. Although nothing of a clearly heretical nature could be pinned on Carranza, the inquisitor wrote to the pope asking for permission to arrest him, and got it. Yet it was Carranza's boast that he had brought back 2,000,000 Englishmen to the Church, and had dealt with 30,000 English heretics by burning or banishment.

The papal indictment against him listed a collection of his Lutheran sayings: that faith was the only valid basis of works; that works without faith could not obtain grace; that grace could not come to one who had lost faith; that 'justification' was possible only through faith. Indeed, it was difficult to read St. Paul's *Letter* without deriving something like the Lutheran interpretation from it. But Roman doctrine had become something one did not discuss at all unless one wanted to court danger. It was now much like a political dogma. Men began to talk to each other with caution as a result, and to open their thoughts only at home. That this has become a deep feature of the Italian psychology may be due to the Spanish presence over a long period in that land.

Philip found it a very expensive business running a catholic empire that would eventually eclipse Rome. In 1558 he did what his father had never quite managed to bring himself to do—he extended the *alcabala* to New Castile and to the Spanish colonies. He also placed a heavy duty on the export of Castilian wool. In 1559 free trade with Portugal was stopped, and customs houses were set up on the border. All the gold, silver and quicksilver mines of Spain were nationalised. Philip did the same with the salt pits later. In the first fifteen years of his reign he doubled the royal income. He increased the *encabezamiento*, by which the cities of Castile paid an annual subsidy into the royal exchequer. Spain was now being bled for world commitments by a Spaniard—not a Hapsburg. It made no murmur of complaint.

Chapter 10

The Council of Blood

Philip's war on heresy delivered him into the hands of the enemy more surely than if he had left things alone. He could never resist putting down a protestant, and because this would not work in the Netherlands it was the Netherlands that brought about the failure of his design, as German protestantism had brought about the failure of his father's.

Now that the Netherlands were the Spanish Netherlands he felt he could do there what his predecessors had done in Naples and Milan, namely Castilianise the population. But the Netherlands, with their affiliations to England, their sense of independence derived from sea-trade, their protestantism backed by prosperity, their closeness to France, were a different world from catholic Italy. They were the freest and most prosperous element in the empire. The country was flat and excellent for agriculture. The sea yielded a rich supply of fish. Communications were quick. The Scheldt, the Meuse and the Rhine joined one town to another, and made the transport of supplies not only fast but reliable. The Netherlands soon became the commercial crossroads of northern Europe after the Mediterranean gave place to the Atlantic in importance. Cities like Bruges, Antwerp, Ghent, Ypres were some of the richest in Europe. The Antwerp *bourse* was the most important in existence. Philip II owed 12,000,000 ducats to one Antwerp banker alone, a man called Tucker. Elizabeth, like her father, kept a permanent agent there, Sir Thomas Gresham.

The two languages spoken were Flemish and Walloon, and the country consisted of seventeen more or less autonomous provinces. The dukes of Burgundy had for long tried to bring these under the control of a strong central government. It was not easy. Each province had its own type of administration and its own parliament which voted supplies to the duke. Charles the Bold had instituted a central parliament at Malines, to which all the seventeen provinces had to refer. And finally Charles V had brought in three councils to govern centrally on his behalf—the Privy Council, the Council of Finance and the Council of State. It was the last that did the actual governing, consisting of nobles nominated by the emperor. Not that these men gave any of their freedom away. They were jealously aware of every attempt to trim local claws—and Philip's later difficulties were first and foremost due to his slighting their authority. They were popular men. The count of Egmont, the Montmorencys, Henry de Brederode and above all William of Orange (descended from the younger branch of the house of Nassau, which had vast properties in Germany) were the leading lights of Burgundy's twenty-two proud, vigorous, brave and often dissolute noble families.

Philip omitted to make William, prince of Orange, the regent of the Netherlands. Instead he chose his own none too competent sister, Margaret of Parma, an illegitimate daughter of Charles. But she was dependable, conscientious and above all (being a Hapsburg) loyal.

The appointment turned William into both a rebel and a protestant. He became a champion of independence from the 'Spanish vermin', as he called them, twenty years later. The fact was that Philip did not trust him. After the death of his wife Anne of Egmont, William had married the niece of Maurice of Saxony—who had played Charles V so many tricks. She had been brought up a Lutheran. And the marriage had been carried through without Philip's consent or even knowledge. Margaret of Parma called William a 'fox' in her letters to Philip. When William spoke of 'my country' it was difficult to know whether he meant the Netherlands or Germany. His catholicism had always been cool. In Spain his apostasy was put down to the influence of his new wife. On the other hand she was a dwarf and of little sexual interest to William. The marriage also went badly and they were both extravagantly unfaithful from the beginning. But there was much concern in Spain over the fact that Anne was a close friend of Marcus Pérez, a Spanish Jew who had become a Calvinist, and was now one of Antwerp's leading

The Netherlands
1579-98

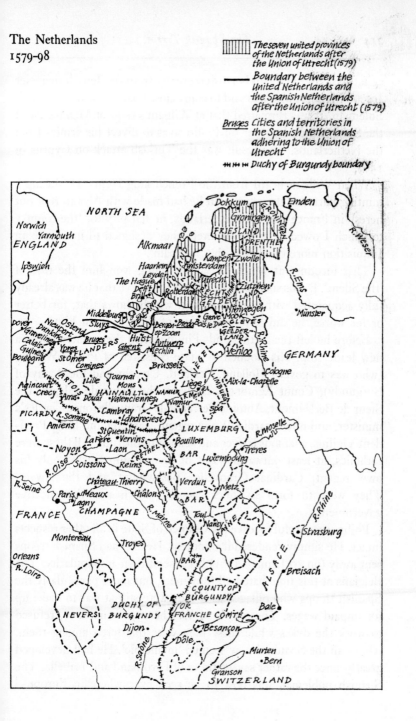

The seven united provinces of the Netherlands after the Union of Utrecht (1579)

Boundary between the United Netherlands and the Spanish Netherlands after the Union of Utrecht (1579)

Bruges Cities and territories in the Spanish Netherlands adhering to the Union of Utrecht

⊦⊦⊦⊦⊦⊦ Duchy of Burgundy boundary

NORTH SEA

Norwich
Yarmouth
ENGLAND
Ipswich

Emden
R. Weser

Dokkum
Groningen
FRIESLAND
DRENTHE

Alkmaar

Haarlem
Leyden
The Hague
Delft
Briel
Middelburg
Rotterdam
HOLLAND
ZEALAND

Amsterdam
Utrecht
OVERIJSSEL
Kampen Zwolle
GELDER-LAND
Zutphen
Wervichem

R. Ems
R. Weser

Münster

Dover
Nieuport
Ostend
Sluys
Gravelines
Dunkirk
Calais
Guines
Boulogne

Bruges
Ypres
FLANDERS
St Omer
Comines
ARTOIS
Lille

Hulst
Ghent
Mechlin

Antwerp
Bergen op Zoom
Breda
Bois le Duc
Grave Mook
GELDER-LAND
CLEVES
R. Rhine
Venloo

GERMANY

Cologne
Aix-la-Chapelle

Agincourt
Crecy
Arras Douai
PICARDY R. Somme
Amiens

Tournai
Mons
HAINAULT
Valenciennes
Cambray
Landrecies

Brussels
LIÈGE
Liège
NAMUR
Namur R. Meuse
Spa
LIMBURG

St Quentin
La Fère
Noyon
R. Oise
Soissons
Laon
RETHEL
Vervins

Reims

LUXEMBURG
Bouillon
BAR
Luxembourg

R. Moselle

Treves
Metz

R. Rhine

Château-Thierry
Meaux
Lagny
Paris
FRANCE
CHAMPAGNE
Châlons
R. Marne

Verdun
BAR

Toul
Nancy
LORRAINE

Montereau
Troyes

R. Seine
Orleans
R. Loire

BAR

Strasburg

ALSACE
Breisach

COUNTY OF
BURGUNDY
OR
FRANCHE COMTÉ

Bale

NEVERS
DUCHY OF
BURGUNDY
Dijon
R. Saône
Dôle

Besançon

Murten
Bern

Granson
SWITZERLAND

agitators. Later William borrowed greatly from the Jewish financier Joseph Mendes, who was said to enjoy close relations with the Sultan Suleiman. It was rumoured that at William's request Mendes asked the Sultan to declare war on Philip so as to divert his armies from the Netherlands. The result was the Turkish attack on Cyprus in 1569.

When William heard from the French king Henry II, during a hunting party, of the agreement he had made with Alva to root out heresy in France and the Netherlands, he felt pity for 'the country to which I owed so much, wherein they designed to introduce an Inquisition more cruel than that in Spain'.

That meeting, at which he said nothing, won him the title of 'the Silent'. By his silence he led Henry to believe that he was already fully acquainted with the agreement, which shows that, for better or for worse, he did have something of the fox about him.

Before he left the Netherlands Philip settled the country under a new leadership. His Council of State consisted of Prince William (who was to govern Holland, Zeeland, Utrecht and the duchy of Burgundy), Count Egmont (Flanders), the Sieur de Glajon, the Sieur de Berlaymont, Antoine Perrenot de Granvelle (once Charles's minister, and now a cardinal), the regent Margaret and lastly President Vigilius, a famous lawyer and scholar of the time. All these were catholics, at least outwardly. But of them Philip trusted only his own regent, Cardinal Granvelle, Berlaymont and the lawyer. They were to form an inner *consulta* which was the effective government.

Philip was careful to leave the Council of State in all other respects intact. He simply rendered it impotent. He also had Spanish troops sent away (on 10 January 1561) because of their unpopularity. The Belgians at this time hated all foreigners, but more particularly the Spanish troops who pillaged as if they were still at war to make up for unpaid wages. The people of Walcheren, for instance, refused to work the dykes while these men were quartered among them. Above all the Spaniard now seemed 'invincible'. He had developed greatly since the rather savage times of Ferdinand and Isabella. The Spanish nobleman was now to be seen everywhere in Europe—

austerely elegant, self-assured, proud of belonging to the finest country in the world and unable to believe that foreigners did not agree. Nothing united the world against him more than this self-assurance. He became feared and hated precisely where he was admired, and proportionately to the admiration. Where Italy's Renaissance seemed mostly a matter of taste and imagination, Spain's was one of power and know-how. There was already an entire Spanish literature on all the 'new' studies from navigation to botany, written by settlers in the Americas.

Cardinal Granvelle too had become unpopular. Even the ex-minister Simon Renard, who felt that he had not been sufficiently rewarded for his part in Philip's marriage negotiations in England, turned against him. Philip recalled the cardinal to Spain. The Netherlanders hoped that Margaret would be less inclined to turn them into imitation Spaniards if she governed alone. In other words they feared Granvelle's Spanish tendencies and knew that Margaret was susceptible to flattery. But the decrees against heresy increased. The definition of 'heretic' became more severe. In 1559 Philip made fourteen new bishops—men he could rely on. They had seats in the Estates-General and even took precedence over the nobles. It was a dangerous game turning noblemen into rebels. The nobles had succeeded in getting Cardinal Granvelle recalled—but the bishops stayed. And Philip saw to it that patronage was in the hands of the *consulta*, not the Council of State.

Meanwhile Calvinism was spreading. Charles had found it the most sympathetic of the heretical sects, and had left it relatively unhindered. It was in fact much more radical than Lutheranism, in its doctrine of original sin and the hopelessness of the human condition, as well as in its rejection of catholic practices. John Calvin, a French theologian and humanist, had been driven from his country by persecution and had settled in Geneva, where he re-formed Church and State under 'pure Gospel' principles.

A small Calvinist rising in 1561 was put down by troops. Many Lutherans had become Calvinists, after the movement had spread from England and France. Geneva was the home of its Church, and by now the focal point in Europe of anti-catholicism. The Calvinist appeal was a fervently rationalist one—against pomp and super-stition and even imagery, on behalf of a pure reading of the Gospel as truth that needed no gilding. Five years later Margaret received a noble deputation of 'beggars' as they came to be called, because they begged her to modify her decrees against heresy. Their petition, the so-called 'Compromise of the Nobles' (which they never showed her), begged Philip not to establish the Spanish Inquisition in the Netherlands. It also threatened force, in ripe mediaeval language. The leaders were Viscount de Brederode and Louis of Nassau (William of Orange's brother). William himself veered this way and that, and continued to profess the greatest loyalty in his letters to Philip. However, Granvelle had advised Philip to remove 'this dangerous man' to a glorious job away from Flanders. He maintained that William only wanted mob-approval, and would play Calvinist, Lutheran or catholic according to the advantage of the moment. William of Orange was certainly a serious enemy from Philip's point of view, being by far the best politician among the Netherlands leaders. He declared in Council of State that he 'could not with a clear conscience approve the excessive power which kings and princes arrogated to themselves of control-ling their subjects in their consciences and giving them such a form of worship as seemed good to them'.

In the end he persuaded the excitable Brederode to present a more sober document to Margaret. And Philip agreed to issue a General Pardon. But there were rumours that he was raising levies in Ger-many for use in the Netherlands. And secretly, in the presence of Alva and a notary, Philip declared that he had agreed to the General Pardon 'under compulsion' and reserved the right to punish anyone he considered a rebel against himself or the Church. In other words he meant to go back on his promise.

And he did. It happened after an outbreak of Calvinist iconoclasm in Flanders. More than 400 churches were desecrated, in two weeks. Antwerp Cathedral was sacked. The crowds screamed, 'Long live the Beggars!' They left the cathedral stripped of its mediaeval marvels. The operation—the *beeldstorm* as it was called—was astonishingly sudden, a burst of anger that could not have been premeditated. Naturally it looked to the catholic side like the most premeditated work of the devil. And it did prove that among protestants as among catholics a taste for violence could pass for religious fervour.

Margaret at once collected troops from various parts of the Empire and put them under the governor of Brussels. She managed to stamp the iconoclasm out (1567) without much difficulty, as it was the work of surprisingly small groups. Egmont and Philip de Montmorency, Count de Hoornes, supported her rather than the rebels, as sacking churches was not on their programme. William of Orange had a few of the ring-leaders executed in Antwerp but lost much of his popularity by not taking a bold stand sooner.

Margaret now advised Philip to show a lenient hand, wisely enough. He refused. He told her that the Pardon was no longer valid. She must levy taxes without consulting the Estates, confiscate property if necessary and—this was final proof that he meant to do without her in the future—disband her own forces. He had already ordered the duke of Alva to take his Spanish troops back to the Netherlands. They made an orderly march through Burgundy, under the strictest orders to keep the peace everywhere. These companies had been drawn from Milan and the Two Sicilies, and were used for peace-time occupation. Still, in the Franche-Comté, in Luxembourg and France, wherever they passed, there was the greatest anxiety. Catherine de' Medici feared a few reprisals for her suspected protestant sympathies and took care to keep the army well-fed on its way. There was no major incident, and the troops arrived at the gates of Brussels in good order. According to Count de Hoornes' secretary there were 24,000 souls encamped outside the city, including 2,000 whores.

It was a clear and unashamed military occupation. The duke of Alva was the new government. Margaret, still the wife of Ottavio Farnese (though they were separated), returned to Italy. Everyone knew that the days of relative leniency were over. Alva already had experience of governing a foreign population. He had been viceroy of Naples for a brief period. There was every reason to expect the worst from him.

During the first month he did nothing. Then on 8 September 1567 two members of the Council of State, Egmont and Count de Hoornes, were arrested. Alva wrote to Philip that he had arrested 'as few men as possible' from these councillors' retinues; after all, he added, he and Philip were agreed in not wishing to cause unnecessary bloodshed. But there was some difficulty about the legality of trying two Knights of the Golden Fleece. Alva advised the king to strip the two men of their collars. But Philip, a stickler for legality, could not bring himself to do this. He simply ordered the trial to go on. After all, being himself the fount of all legal authority in his kingdoms, it was up to him to decide who should be tried and who should not. Thus he killed stone dead the Burgundian traditions which had occupied much of his father's energies.

Simultaneously the Netherlands representative in Spain, Baron de Montigny (Hoornes' brother), was flung into gaol, accused of plotting with William of Orange to bring German troops into the Netherlands and dislodge Philip's government. Montigny was also dangerously close to Philip's son, Don Carlos. He was strangled a few months later in his cell, and a report was put out that he had fallen ill and, despite immediate medical attention (Spanish doctors were possibly the worst in Europe at the time), had quickly 'declined'.

The duke of Alva now replaced the Council of State with a new council of seven men. He called it 'the council of troubles'. The people called it 'the council of blood'. Three of the councillors were Spaniards. Their deliberations, which were entirely secret, overruled those of the national assembly. Their justice was above that of the courts. They could arrest, indict, sentence at will.

On 4 January 1568 eighty-four people were executed. On 20 February one hundred and eight. On 20 March fifty-five. Egmont (once described by Granvelle as a 'good, honest catholic led astray by his friends') and Count de Hoornes were put to death for high treason in June 1568. As Knights of the Golden Fleece they had been 'disloyal to their sovereign'. The duke of Alva tried to get a pardon for Egmont but failed. A platform for the double execution was put up in the market place opposite the town hall, and a whole Spanish regiment or *tercio* of twenty-two companies surrounded it to keep the crowds back. Even the Spaniards present felt sympathy for Egmont, who had barely uttered a protestant sentiment in his life. The two men were beheaded. The crowd rushed forward and dipped their handkerchiefs in the blood. The heads were exposed for hours afterwards. Egmont left eleven children.

William of Orange had managed to get out of the city and was forming an army with the help of Lutherans and Calvinists. He engaged Spanish troops when he was not yet strong enough and was defeated twice, in April and July. He then had to escape the country as best he could, without an army.

Meanwhile Alva ordered Philip's chosen bishops to get to work on the heretics in their areas. He gradually filled government posts, as they fell vacant, with his own men. He tried to fix a tax (a 5 per cent levy on real-estate sales and 10 per cent on personal estate sales) which would be the equivalent of the Spanish *alcabala*. The Estates refused to consent to this, despite threats to their persons, and managed to persuade Alva that such a tax would cripple the Netherlands economy. He accepted a lump sum instead—2,000,000 florins a year for two years. Later he dishonoured his agreement. At the end of the two years (1571) he imposed the *alcabala* just the same. This single act, taken against the advice of the Spanish ambassador in Paris, put the Netherlands into a state of open war. There was a slump. Merchants left the country in hordes. Rents decreased to less than 20 per cent of their former value. The textile industry all but collapsed.

The only man who supported Alva was his own son, Don Fadrique. Not even Philip was on his side. The fact was that he was too old and embittered to yield to the friendliest advice. In Paris there were already 400 prominent merchants in exile from Brussels, Antwerp, Lille, Douai, Arras. Philip wrote Alva a letter of consternation in which he advised him not to impose a tax that struck directly at 'the nervous system and substance of the country'. But he left Alva in charge. The result was the capture of Brielle by rebels on 1 April 1572. Also 'sea-beggars' under the leadership of Lancelot de Brederode roamed up and down the Channel looking for Spanish ships, from their hideouts in English ports.

Of all the places to which a Spanish soldier could be posted, the Netherlands was the lowest on his list. It was cold and always seemed to be raining. He was battered and stung by the only sure armament left to an occupied people—ridicule. They sang songs about him which he could not understand but which made them laugh. He himself rarely sang in the Netherlands. His officers were gagged and bound with red tape. In fact a new word for this entered the Spanish language—*balduque*, from the Dutch town Bois-le-duc. And on the other side too a new word developed: *dukdalf* (from the 'Duke of Alva'), the name in Dutch of a mooring post.

Yet Alva sincerely thought that the Netherlands had been settled, and wrote to Philip to say so. For an army commander the absence of rebellion on the home front or hostile armies on the battle front meant peace. There was one small problem left. English seamen were still giving trouble in 'Spanish' waters—on the other side of the Atlantic. Their successes were a dangerous example to the Dutch. There was only one thing to do with Englishmen—arrest them. He could hardly arrest the whole English nation but he could arrest all the Englishmen in the Netherlands. And this is what he did.

Philip was not at all convinced that the Netherlands had been settled, or that Alva was the man to settle anything but a battle. He argued for a General Pardon. Eventually he forced Alva to grant this, though Alva made sure that it was done as slowly as possible. But however the two men differed on details of policy, they were together in wanting absolute control of the Netherlands, at whatever cost to human life.

At least 1,700 people were executed. Some put the figure at more like 8,000. Philip's attitude (expressed in a letter) was this: 'Why talk about 1,700 put to death—and many of them vile animals, such as the Anabaptists—and not about the thousands who would die in the Netherlands if they succeeded in transplanting the Huguenot wars there from France, as they wish to do?' The Inquisition in the Netherlands was particularly horrible. Victims who tried to speak at the stake had their tongues screwed down—or the tips scorched so that the whole tongue swelled and protruded from their mouths. The tortures imposed were panic-stricken in their subtlety.

Philip saw the Netherlands as a menace not only to his economy (if it should go protestant and anti-Spanish) but to his whole strategy in the north, particularly where it concerned France and England. Those two countries might easily form a 'bridge' with a protestant Netherlands to keep Spain out of northern Europe for good. Yet Egmont and Hoornes had died catholics. The fact was that Philip feared Flemish catholics along with the protestants. For they were not Spanish. It was clearly desirable to make the Netherlands a kind of Spanish bastion by means of which he could control England, France and Germany too. His pretext was the need to master heresy there. Therefore the duke of Alva seemed the right man. No one else could have frightened the Flemish as he did.

Francis II of France died of an abscess on the brain. He had reigned only one year and five months. During that time Philip had been terrified that the duke of Guise and his brother the cardinal of Lorraine would, with the queen, Mary Queen of Scots, unite Scotland with France. If Elizabeth of England were also to die Mary might become queen of Scotland, France and England together— given her claim to the English throne. For this reason he did not sponsor a movement to dethrone Elizabeth as part of his general counter-reformation policy, despite the fact that Elizabeth was not only a heretic (and therefore unfit to govern) but, in the eyes of the Church, illegitimate and not a true heir to the English throne.

Philip feared that the Guise family might create too powerful a catholic state, and thus rival his own leadership of the catholic world. And Paris was perilously close to Brussels. The Guises were not above helping the protestants there, just to embarrass him. There was already a complicated espionage system working in Paris. Spanish agents had their ears open for every new policy move at court. The network had been organised by the duke of Alva at the time of Philip's betrothal to Elizabeth of Valois, when Philip had sent him to Paris as his own representative. Alva had left it in the hands of Cardinal Granvelle's brother, a Burgundian called Thomas

Perrenot de Chantonnay, now Spanish ambassador in Paris. Charles V's Burgundian connections were very useful when it came to talking fluent French and knowing the French background like one's own. Franche Comté was the path that Spanish troops always took on their way north to the Netherlands. It was a bridge to the Spanish throne diplomatically as well as territorially.

Philip's horror of a Scottish-French union made him hope secretly that the Scottish heretics—John Knox and the Lords of the Congregation—would seize power there. It was a ridiculous situation, especially as John Knox had been the author of a fierce attack on his English queen, called *Blast against the Monstrous Regiment of Women*. But the Treaty of Edinburgh on 6 July 1560 between England and France, which guaranteed Elizabeth's right to the English throne and Scottish independence from France, relieved him of his worst fears (and the sin of wishing heretics success).

Suddenly the situation changed in France too. The child-king Francis II died (December 1560), bringing the queen mother Catherine de' Medici ('Madame la Serpente', her son the new king called her) back into prominence. She was Elizabeth of Valois' mother, and with her the Valois family returned to power. The duke of Guise and his brother were now in eclipse, which was good in that they had been anti-Spanish but bad in that Catherine tolerated protestants more than Philip liked. Her shrewd competence could become a menace equal to the Guise one. The Guises were fiercely catholic, which frightened Philip. Catherine's party was moderately and tolerantly so, and this also frightened him.

Bribery was the long arm of Spanish foreign policy. Catherine asked Philip to consider giving Spanish Navarre to Anthony de Bourbon, on the valid grounds that its acquisition in the reign of Charles V by Spain had been illegal. Philip did not give a categorical 'no'. Instead, he played with Bourbon, making him believe that he would be given Navarre or other territory if he proved a good catholic (Philip knew he was secretly a protestant). He was so far successful in this game that Bourbon accepted instructions in the faith by a teacher recommended by the Jesuits, who were now well-established in Paris. He even expelled the Huguenots from Paris.

Philip was later saved the embarrassment of putting his promises into effect by Bourbon's death in 1563 at the siege of Rouen.

A man prominent on the list of foreigners receiving Spanish gold was an old French soldier called Blaise de Monluc. He had played a great part in remodelling the French infantry and felt he had been insufficiently rewarded by the king. His was precisely the kind of resentment that Philip delighted to use. The occasion came to him via a Spaniard in France called Felipe de Bardaxi, a captain who had been accused of heresy by the Spanish Inquisition but who had managed to escape to France. He had joined the French army under Monluc's command. It was he who proposed to Monluc that he should approach Philip II with the offer of delivering the province of Guienne into his hands. The Spaniard hoped in this way to mend his own reputation in Spain, and Philip went along with him. Bardaxi's cousin Juan, already a spy in France, was given charge of the whole operation. Philip revealed nothing of this even to his own ambassador in Paris. Monluc wrote to him and he replied. But Catherine de' Medici's secret agents intercepted the correspondence, and Monluc was asked to come to Paris to face trial. He refused. Catherine thought it safer to drop the case and even go through a feint trial of his accusers. The letters between him and Philip continued.

Monluc tried to organise a meeting between Catherine and Philip to discuss a joint programme for the suppression of heresy. Catherine was, after all, Philip's mother-in-law. She had hoped that her daughter would have greater influence in Spain than in fact she had. Elizabeth of Valois was certainly most popular in Spain, but an attack of smallpox had kept her away from Philip in the first months of their marriage, and after that she had never achieved real political influence over him. But now Philip was happy enough to send her to Paris, in the duke of Alva's company, to talk with her mother. He was reluctant to go himself, because he knew that Catherine was also having talks with the Sultan.

Elizabeth and Alva met Catherine at Bayonne (14 June to 4 July 1565) but all that resulted from a fortnight of talks was mutual distrust. Philip failed to get more than general statements about heresy out of Catherine. It convinced him that his espionage network in Paris was doubly necessary. A new ambassador, Francisco de Alava, had succeeded Chantonnay the previous year, and the bulk of his work consisted in being chief of a secret service operated from Madrid. Catherine issued a series of decrees in Paris against the publication of protestant literature, but this was as far as she went. She had her own power to look to. There had already been a civil war in France (1562–3) between the catholics and the protestants, whose influence was spread unevenly over the country, and the peace she had made was by no means secure (a second war came in 1567, a third in 1570).

In September of 1565 some French protestants in Florida were massacred by the order of Pedro Menendez de Aviles. At that time Florida meant all the land north and north-east of the Gulf of Mexico, since there had so far been no penetrations into Louisiana. The viceroy of Mexico, Luis de Velasco, had urged Philip to explore Florida, and had won his case not because anything by way of wealth could accrue from it (the last probe had found a land 'full of bogs and poisonous fruits') but because the French might get there first. For twenty years or more now the French presence in American waters had been growing. There had been many French attacks on posts round the Gulf of Mexico and the Caribbean islands. The Spanish expedition (June 1559) was a failure. There was almost a mutiny. Philip ordered that the idea was to be abandoned, since the new country appeared to be uninhabitable.

This was what gave the French (most of them Calvinists) their chance. They landed at the mouth of the St. John river in May 1562, and set up a colony. Philip knew every detail of the operation as it happened, through his spies in France. The leader of the expedition, Jean Ribaut, went to England to try to get help for the reinforcement of the colony, having failed in France, and the Spanish ambassador in London, Alvaro de la Quadra, bishop of Avila, passed on all the details of this attempt to Philip. In Philip's eyes the French and English were pirates on a par with the Turks, since the Spanish occupation of all the American lands save Brazil had been endorsed by a Bull of Alexander VI.

When Francisco de Alava, the Spanish ambassador in Paris, heard about the French colony he gave immediate orders to the governor of Cuba to go and wipe it out (May 1564). He made no bones about his mistrust of Catherine. He insulted her to her face whenever an occasion offered itself, and showed great friendliness towards the Guise family. He made Catherine feel that she was at the mercy of his spy-system—which was not far from the truth (she later asked Philip to recall him, which he did).

But the colony had left Florida of its own accord. A new French colony arrived a week later, but the Spanish missed them too. The French then began raiding Spanish posts. In March of the following year Philip authorised Pedro Menendez de Aviles to try a second time to settle Florida, with 500 colonists. The actual expedition, due to Aviles' private spending, was three times as big as that authorised when it sailed from Cadiz in June. But early in May Jean Ribaut had sailed from Dieppe. He arrived a week before the Spaniards. While Ribaut was out at sea again, trying to engage the Spanish fleet, the Spaniards on land made a surprise attack on his little colony at night, and 132 Frenchmen were murdered in their beds. Fifty women and children were taken prisoner. A group of 140 Frenchmen was reported stranded on an island. They offered to give themselves up, being unarmed, in return for a safe conduct, but Aviles refused. They were all murdered in front of him. When Ribaut himself and seventy of his men were found, the same happened to them. Aviles made it clear to his victims that he did not look on protestants as citizens with rights; he had Philip's orders to 'purge his dominions of all heretics'. Philip supported Aviles in this action against the *corsarios Luteranos* as he called these Calvinists, and his court treated the massacre as a victory of war.

The French retaliated by seizing the island of Madeira, then in Portuguese hands, in an expedition by Blaise de Monluc's son (who was at least a catholic). He had arranged that sixteen English ships should join him. When they landed he and his men butchered the inhabitants on Spanish lines, though his colony did not settle there, but only remained for a few weeks. Philip protested to Catherine just as if Madeira were a Spanish colony. And the idea may already

8

have formed in his mind of taking over Portuguese possessions in the Americas. He did not actually try until about twelve years later.

All this amounted to a state of war which no one wished to declare openly. In the case of the English pirates Philip brought his punishment of them almost to open war in 1564, when he ordered all English ships in Spanish harbours to be placed under arrest. But he could not afford—economically or strategically—to make war on England before he had settled the Netherlands.

As early as 1560 all crown revenues had been mortgaged to make more ready money available, and Philip's deficit for the end of 1571 was calculated at 9,000,000 ducats. Like everyone else in Europe at this time he wanted a period of peace in which to build up his strength. Elizabeth had refused to marry him. She had made her country protestant. She was obviously a friend of the protestant movement in Scotland, though she was playing a safe hand there too. She went far enough to offend but not outrage Philip. She knew precisely what kind of whip-hand she had over him. She could do his economy a lot of harm by cutting down on her trade with the Netherlands. There were other markets for English wool, should he retaliate by blocking her goods. When Philip suggested a conference to discuss this matter she agreed that it was necessary and then did nothing about it. Her ships went on interfering with Spanish trade between Cadiz and Antwerp, along the Channel. Quadra, Philip's ambassador in London, urged him to attack England while the going was good. There was also some talk of sending a Spanish army into Scotland with the excuse of stamping out heresy there. Having elbowed out the French, Philip would incite the English catholics south of the border to rebellion. But Philip rejected all rash plans— and Quadra was a rash man. Without the Netherlands under Spanish control the situation was such that one false move would bring out the whole of the northern world against him, by joining together the heretic and the catholic in a common detestation of Spain. France could cut the road across Franche Comté by which Spanish troops reached the Netherlands. Philip withdrew Quadra from London, and left the embassy vacant for six months. Then he sent the milder, though more stupid, Diego Guzmán de Silva, who in his despatches to Philip called Cecil 'a great heretic and clownish Englishman', Leicester a 'light and greedy man', and Bacon 'an obstinate and most malignant heretic'. But at least he did not storm for war. Instead he advised Philip to form an economic blockade against England when the Netherlands were settled. But Philip still had hopes that England would make a useful ally against France, once she was catholic again.

So he played tit-for-tat. When Sir John Hawkins coolly took ship-loads of West African slaves across to New Spain and sold them there, Philip had two of Hawkins' vessels impounded in Seville harbour, and Hawkins never saw them again. A youth called William de Orlando, who had once been one of Queen Elizabeth's pages, was taken from Hawkins as a hostage in Mexico. He proudly told the Spaniards in the viceroy's palace that, though a devout catholic, he would die for his queen. He was sent to Seville to be tried by the regular Inquisition (only the episcopal Inquisition operated in Mexico before 1571) and was then executed for his patriotism. English seamen who managed to escape the clutches of the Spanish Inquisition almost never spoke about the experience afterwards, from fear of reprisal. Philip also seized a number of English ships in Gibraltar harbour in 1563, and threw the 240 men of the crew into prison as heretics. This was done by the Spanish Inquisition on his personal order. Only eighty of them came out alive and returned to England.

In 1567 seven Spanish ships suddenly entered Plymouth harbour where Hawkins was fitting out a fleet for a second expedition to the Indies. He fired on them, and obliged them to lower their flags. No one could say what they had come to do. The Spanish ambassador had protested against Hawkins' preparations, and Philip may have intended this silent visit as a warning. The ambassador again protested at Spanish ships being fired on, and Elizabeth reprimanded Hawkins but allowed him to go on with his preparations.

The following year, in December, she allowed some Spanish bullion intended for the duke of Alva's exchequer to be seized on its way from Genoa to Antwerp. She may have made a secret deal with the Genoese shipping agent who was in charge of the ships. She certainly knew that the bullion belonged to Genoese merchant

banks until such time as it was received by the Spaniards in Antwerp
She thus neatly transferred a loan to herself.

The Spanish ambassador (now Guerau de Spes, who was as
aggressive as Quadra and more childish in his intrigues) protested so
loudly that Elizabeth had him put briefly under house-arrest, just
as Philip had done the last English ambassador to Madrid, Dr. Man,
for being not only a heretic (he had asked for the right to hold
Anglican services in his house) but a married priest as well. As
Elizabeth became more defiant (her raids brought in as big a revenue
as Philip was losing in the Netherlands) war began to seem inevitable. But the duke of Alva decided that no soldiers could be spared
to fight Elizabeth (which she knew) and that the Spanish ambassador
in London should be reprimanded. So she had won, for the time
being. Also she was relieved of the embarrassment of a catholic
queen on the Scottish throne; on 13 May 1568 Mary's army was
routed and she crossed the Solway into England as Elizabeth's
prisoner.

Philip still hoped that Elizabeth would be swept away without
much effort on his part. His ambassadors in London were always
intriguing and plotting to that end, not foolishly either, since there
was seething discontent among the English catholics. They could
do practically nothing without being accused of high treason. Saying
or hearing Mass and admitting the supremacy of the pope now led
to the gallows. Also a great many Englishmen were worried at the
country's bad relations with Spain and France.

A plan to marry Mary Queen of Scots to the duke of Norfolk
stirred Spanish agents in London to a new flurry of activity to get
rid of Elizabeth. A plot was hatched. The earl of Northumberland
and the earl of Westmorland joined it for the north of England,
and the earl of Arundel for the south. The Spanish ambassador was
in close contact with both. In November 1569 catholic rebels tore
down the communion table in Durham Cathedral and restored the
Mass there. Protestant books were burned. A detachment of
catholic troops took Hartlepool in the north on the Spanish ambassador's promise that they would get help from the duke of Alva. A
rumour went round London that Alva had vowed to make Elizabeth

hear Mass in St. Paul's Cathedral on Candlemas Day in the following February, and to pay his soldiers their wages on Cheapside. But by the end of 1569 the rebellion had fizzled out, and the remnants of the catholic force fled over the border to Scotland. However, the Spaniards had reason to believe that this first outbreak would lead to more effective ones.

Philip had settled for plots against Elizabeth's person, instead of the war which he could not afford. In this he was more enthusiastic than Alva who, apart from being a soldier and believing in pitched battles, also wanted to negotiate for the safe arrival of his bullion, before dealing a death-blow with his armies. His lack of enthusiasm for plots may account for the fact that none of them came off, and that English catholics began to burn with resentment against the Spanish for letting them down.

On 25 February 1570 Pope Pius V excommunicated Elizabeth and released her subjects from allegiance to her. He also urged Philip to support the northern earls, and put Mary on the throne with their help. Guerau de Spes added his persuasions, with the English catholics at his elbow. But, apart from the fact that Philip disliked following a pope's lead in anything (he had already blocked two previous attempts to excommunicate Elizabeth, in 1561 and 1563), he saw no evidence that Elizabeth would not one day make a good catholic and an even better enemy of France (she had not married a French king after all) than Mary. Europe was learning not to take English religion too seriously, and to realise that it was mostly a cloak for political interests, whether protestant or catholic. Catherine de' Medici refused to publish the excommunication Bull in France, which had been designed to follow up the revolt in northern England (it was at least two months too late).

Even at home in Spain Philip's policy, always turning on an obsessive concern with heretics, produced what could have become a civil war, and was actually a rebellion. The question of the Moors in Spain had been more or less settled, or so it seemed. His father had accepted a bribe from the *moriscos* not to apply the edict of 1525 to

the letter, which meant relaxing the atmosphere of Christian persecution. Philip characteristically revived this. He had begun posi-
tively enough: he intensified the doctrinal instruction of converted
Moors, and even sanctioned the publication of the catechism in
Arabic. The Inquisition was as little help as possible in this, and
called Arabic—as most Christian Spaniards did—a profane language,
tainting anything translated into it. *Moriscos* and Christians lived
side by side in the same towns, but no real society had grown up
between them. Here too the Inquisition was of little help. The
moriscos tended to collect into ghettoes, as an inevitable result of the
atmosphere of segregation, and then, when the ghettoes looked
strong, their walls were torn down. The *moriscos* had a reputation
for wealth. It was therefore useful to keep them in an unprivileged
condition so that fines and confiscations could at any time be applied.

It was one of Philip's most influential (and hardest) ministers,
Diego de Espinosa, president of the council of Castile and one-time
inquisitor-general, who persuaded him that the *moriscos* had in fact
not been fully converted, and that the black spots of heresy in Castile
must be cauterised. The 1525 edict was revived and enforced. The
Arabic language was banned. In future all Christian Moors were
to be educated in Castilian. Moorish baths were banned. Moorish
names and dress were banned. All births that took place in *morisco*
homes were to be attended by a Christian midwife, in case a
Moorish ceremony took place. On Christian holidays the doors of
morisco houses had to stand open so that passers-by could look in.
The new edict was published on 1 January 1567.

The traditional right of sanctuary in churches and on manor
lands was withdrawn. It meant that no Moor could hide from
authority. It meant too the end of the mediaeval concept of a certain
human inviolability. The Church that Philip purported to be
defending was hereby rendered incapable of offering its faithful a
last protection against the state. Yet he was urged to do all this by
the churchmen of Castile as well as by his ministers.

Moorish baths were then dismantled. All *moriscos* were to speak
and write Castilian within three years (though nothing was done to
teach them). The discontent this caused was slow to become rebel-

lion only because the edict was slow to take effect. The *moriscos* in Granada began collecting arms. They prepared hideouts in the mountains. Their first rising on 15 April 1568 was squashed. The second at the end of the year was more successful. Christian churches in the surrounding countryside were desecrated, Christians murdered and tortured. The captain-general of Granada, the marquis of Mondéjar, who would certainly have been against the edict had he been consulted, was ordered to put the rebellion down. In two months he had succeeded. His soldiers pillaged as if they were in a foreign country. The Moors tasted the same rather precipitate conversion to Christ which the Mexican Indians had tasted. Mondéjar—who had authorised only one massacre, because the *moriscos* had refused to give themselves up—could not hold his own men. His promise that Moors would be treated well if they surrendered was dishonoured. The remaining *moriscos* became desperate. Their leader, Aben Humeja, collected an army of 4,000 men. Don John of Austria (Philip's illegitimate half-brother) now took over the command of the Christian side. It looked like a full-scale civil war, and Don John was soon playing the role of a crusader-knight. On the other hand Philip forbade him to take part in any of the battles himself, or to make a decision without consulting him. This meant delays on the battlefield, which the *moriscos* used to full advantage. Many of the places that had surrendered to Mondéjar took to arms again. The countryside round Granada was in a state of revolt. On 19 October 1569 Philip issued the terrible edict in which he authorised his soldiers to plunder wherever they went. He increased their pay.

On 19 January 1570 Don John besieged a garrison of 3,000 poorly armed men at Galera with a well-equipped army at least four times as big. It took him nearly a month of very tough fighting to win, and he himself was wounded. When the defences were broken every creature in the place was murdered, after sexual appetites had been appeased. The soldiers were so exhausted by their knightly behaviour that they were later put to flight by a tiny group of *moriscos*. The war went on intermittently for a year more. A Spanish agent murdered the Moorish leader who had succeeded Aben

Humeja, and the persecution gradually petered out. The crusade was over. The war had a double meaning—death to Islam, and a threat to the Christian heretic more vivid than any placards denouncing protestantism. Some short-term financial advantages also accrued to Philip. He got an annual revenue of 125,000 crowns out of confiscated *morisco* lands. The *moriscos* were now treated like aliens, their movements under close police surveillance. Those in and around Granada were evacuated to other parts of Spain, then dispersed. They were forced to sell their removable goods—on terms well below current Christian prices. Philip had gone to war with the *moriscos* because he knew he could win.

Even when there was no question of heresy, Philip saw any undue vanity or arrogance in his people as a challenge to himself. He was always itching, for example, to trim the claws of Aragonese landlords. A certain John of Aragón, count of Ribagorza, had married a Castilian lady, Luisa Pacheco. After some months of marriage he decided that she had been unfaithful to him and murdered her with his own hands. Philip had him publicly strangled (1572). He did not stop there. He set about to prove, through the Inquisition, that Ribagorza had Jewish blood and that his lands should by right go to the crown. The Justicia decided otherwise and decreed that the lands should go to the count's brother. Philip dropped the case, though to scoop up such a large piece of Aragonese property (17 towns, 200 villages, with 4,000 vassals) would have helped to remove one of the most bitter thorns in his side.

There was also the mysterious case of his own son, Don Carlos, who died after a period of imprisonment. It stained Philip's reputation—and perhaps his conscience—more than any other event of his reign.

In childhood Don Carlos had had bilious attacks and shown signs of an unstable temper. His grandfather, Charles V, had expressed anxiety about him. Both Philip and his queen had been under nineteen at the time of his conception, and some people had thought the queen unprepared for childbirth. Only at the age of five did the child begin to speak. In his youth he seemed aimless and reckless, yet in certain things not unintelligent. Nothing about him reminded people of his Hapsburg blood. He was narrow-chested, with a slight hump on his back at the height of his stomach. His legs were weak, his voice thin. He tended to stammer, and was very pale. His greatest passion was eating. At the end of a gigantic meal he seemed ready to start all over again. At the time of a serious fall he had in the spring of 1562 he almost died of a fever. Blood-letting and trepanning were tried without success. In the end a dead Franciscan, Diego de Alcalá, was exhumed and his remains placed close to Don Carlos in bed. It was hoped that his sanctity would draw off the evil in the prince's system. In ten days the fever did subside (a joint triumph for medicine and theology). But the sickness left him very weak. His fits of fury became more frequent, and people began to suspect that he had inherited something of his grandmother Juana's madness. Charles V too had had terrible fits of depression, alternating with mystical exaltation. In Don Carlos it was the same. No one questioned, least of all his father, his utter devotion to the Church. There was no thought of his being a heretic, however heretical in his father's eyes some of his friends were. In everyday life he was quite agreeable, except that he would now and then order someone in his court to be flogged in front of him. He once had a pair of boots made, large enough to hold two pistols. Philip ordered his shoemaker to cut them down to a normal size. Don Carlos then hacked the boots up and stewed the strips, and forced the shoemaker to eat them.

Madrid was always buzzing with stories about Don Carlos. As a student he had roamed the streets with other youths shouting obscenities at women. Once, he had even attacked the duke of Alva. His confidant, Hermán Suárez de Toledo, was horrified at his cruelty to animals. There were also certain 'abominable' things which the prince did, which were hushed up by those around him. In anyone but a prince they would have been investigated, as Suárez said, by the Inquisition. Since he was laughed at for never having women, it is possible that he went in for homosexual-sadistic practices; the Inquisition certainly had a definite attitude against sexual perversion of any kind. It would have put him outside the pale of

Christianity. All in all, there was enough in the prince to make Philip II morbidly afraid of giving him the Spanish empire. This fear, far more than any threats to his own person, was behind his imprisoning the youth.

Almost always when there was turmoil in his court it was due to Don Carlos. Once, in a quarrel with Don John of Austria, the prince had shouted that Don John 'came of a whore and was a bastard', to which Don John replied that at least his father (Charles V) had been a greater man than Don Carlos's. Don Carlos rushed to the king to tell him this, but Philip told him quietly that Don John was right—his father *had* been much greater than he himself was or ever would be.

At one time Don Carlos had been intended as the husband of Elizabeth de Valois (they were both fourteen at the time). But Philip had married the girl instead. Since then the boy had resented his father bitterly. Matters came to a head when Philip was planning a personal visit to the Netherlands (1565) and then characteristically cancelled his journey. Don Carlos dreamed of going with his father, and for a time it had seemed possible. At court he was watched and wondered at wherever he went. It was not a happy life. And the obsessive supervision may have spurred him to wild behaviour. He was furious when Philip sent the duke of Alva instead of going himself: it was then that he attacked Alva with a dagger, screaming at him that he was not to go. He then composed a satirical book about his father's 'great journeys'—from one palace to another on the outskirts of Madrid, all the year round.

As to the young prince's friendship with Montigny, the spokesman of the Netherlands nobles at the court of Madrid, it has never really been proved: nor has any plot against his father's person. But he was felt to be capable of anything, and his desire to go to the Netherlands was interpreted as an attempt to engage German and Dutch sympathies against Philip. He did negotiate a big loan for himself in Seville, against a possible journey. He also wrote to several grandees for their support in a certain 'plan' which he did not describe. He asked his uncle, Don John, to take him with him to Italy. Most of his letters were shown to Philip. Don Carlos's confession to the prior of a monastery at Atocha that he was unable to expel hatred for a 'certain enemy' from his heart—meaning his father—clinched the matter. The prior contacted the king at once.

He was imprisoned on 19 January 1568, in his twenty-third year, and he did not come out of prison alive. A post-mortem on his body nearly two and a half centuries later, in 1812, indicated that his head had been cut off. At the time it was announced that he had died naturally. This is not altogether unlikely. After fasting for three days the prince drank quantities of iced water and stamped about his cell with bare feet. He then ate an enormous and highly spiced partridge pie at one sitting. Vomiting and a fever ensued.

On the other hand it was usual at that time to murder men in prison by strangulation. It was done with catgut. After two and a half centuries strangulation would perhaps look like decapitation on a corpse. Beheading would have required some preparation, which makes it unlikely. The strangler would have been ushered into the cell and have done his work quickly, from behind the prisoner's back. If the prince was genuinely ill no one wanting to save his life would have kept him in a prison cell, even in the heat of June. It seems possible that he was done away with for reasons of state. The times were too dangerous to permit lenience towards angry court rebels.

Philip watched the boy's funeral from his palace window. There was no grief on his face.

About this time the building of the famous Escorial Palace was reaching its climax. Typically, it was designed by Philip not to house a court or even to cut a figure but to enshrine the remains of his father. He had chosen a site north of Madrid (the capital of Spain after 1561) in the bare arid mountains of the Guadarrama. The palace's shape was that of St. Lawrence's gridiron. The monastery was at its centre. All the rooms except his own were lavishly decorated and furnished. Building had started on 23 April 1563, and ten years later the royal family took up residence in this vast, marvellously serene monument of granite. It was not just another royal palace. Its design was, so to speak, a mystical one.

The massive blocks of stone forming the walls, the marble from southern Spain, the jasper, the gold and silver worked by Florentine and Milanese artists, the Flemish tapestries, the many kinds of wood from South America, the metalwork and the astonishing embroidery were simply the husk of a monastic conception. There is something ecstatic in the hugeness and the repetition of windows and arches.

Above all, it seems the very image of settled orthodoxy. In most lights it is sombre and grey, not festive. Its proportions are fixed and symmetrical, not allowing—not visualising—any argument. There is no hint of the so-called plateresque style, an extravagant amalgam of Moorish, Gothic and Renaissance influences so characteristic of the building under Ferdinand and Isabella. Yet those influences are present—in the cupolas, the steeples, the slender pillars. They are under some invisible, perhaps implacable control. Fervent expression is almost outlawed. In Philip's design there is hardly a suggestion of struggle, much less of fervour. The enormous building simply lies there in the uninhabited and silent spaces, seeming so completely self-realised as to be natural, like the mountains. Even the choice of Madrid (the court moved from Toledo) had something too starkly inevitable about it; Madrid was as near the exact geographical centre of Spain as you could find.

In 1570 the first *auto-da-fé* was celebrated in Mexico. Thirty-one sailors, mostly English, were the victims; three were garrotted and their bodies burned, eighteen were condemned to the galleys, and ten were placed in monasteries for restriction. It seemed on the surface that the faith was being firmly re-established everywhere.

Elizabeth was getting dangerous. She was in close contact with the Huguenots in France. She might soon make a fatal alliance with William of Orange. He had already made a treaty with the Huguenot leader, the Prince de Condé (one of the few great lords of France who was protestant). Also the new French king, Charles IX, was distinctly anti-Spanish. His mistress, Marie Touchet, was a protestant. Charles had all but promised William of Orange's brother that he would help him clear the Spanish out of the Netherlands.

In a world simmering with rebellion a devious and brilliantly astute woman like Elizabeth could be the spark that would set it all alight.

Philip decided that she must be murdered. He made the decision on 7 July 1571. Alva was to have an army ready to occupy England when the deed was done. There was little doubt in his mind that it *would* be done. Mary was the centre of the plot—and, as he well knew, she was a better plotter than politician. The man chosen for the work was Roberto Ridolfi, a Florentine banker in London, who was also a secret agent of the pope. He worked in close contact with the Spanish ambassador. Some time previously, on his own initiative, he had drawn up a list of the Englishmen he felt he could rely on in the event of a rising, some of them hardly known to him, and he had submitted this to the pope. The list seemed authoritative enough, particularly to someone who had never set foot in England. The pope was convinced. And he set to work at convincing Philip, with the help of the Spanish ambassador in London. The duke of Norfolk was drawn into the plot, having emerged from the Tower less than a year before for his part in Mary's marriage intrigues. He had promised Elizabeth solemnly that he would never enter into any transaction with Mary again.

The first plan devised between the Spanish ambassador (Guerau de Spes), Ridolfi, the bishop of Ross (Mary's envoy) and the duke of Norfolk was that Alva should be asked to land a force of 6,000 or 10,000 men at Harwich or Portsmouth with London as his objective. That was long before Philip gave his approval, in the first weeks of 1571. Ridolfi went to Alva in the Netherlands with this plan, but failed to move him. Alva did not consider him a suitable character to lead a rising (Ridolfi thought Harwich was in Norfolk), and wrote to Philip that the English catholics ought to get Spanish support only if and when their rising in Norfolk succeeded.

Ridolfi was something of an indiscreet talker. Before leaving the Netherlands he had sent a quite unnecessary letter to his associate in London saying that everything was going well. The man by whom he sent the message, a servant of the bishop of Ross, was arrested the moment his foot touched land at Dover. Anyone with sense could have foreseen that he would be. The English had their spies in the

Netherlands, after all. The servant was put in prison and then made
to correspond with his master, the bishop of Ross, as if nothing
had happened. Back came letters in cipher, addressed to '30' and
'40', apparently two noblemen, whose identities Cecil, Elizabeth's
minister, could not for certain establish.

Then something quite accidental happened which cleared up the
whole matter. The French ambassador in London gave the duke of
Norfolk £600 to convey to the catholic rebels in Scotland. The duke
passed this money in a bag to a Shrewsbury merchant, with a false
story about the contents. The merchant became suspicious and took
the bag to the local justices. Norfolk's house was searched, the key
to the cipher found, and the whole plot was in this way revealed. The
Spanish ambassador was summoned to the queen's council and given
orders to leave England at once (January 1572). The duke of Norfolk
was charged with high treason at Westminster Hall. After much
hesitation Elizabeth signed the warrant for his execution, but withdrew it. Two months later she signed a second warrant but withdrew
that too. This was partly due to reluctance to cut off a peer's head
(Norfolk was England's only duke). It was also partly fear—that
he was too popular to be disposed of. The House of Commons was
urging her to do away with him. A parliamentary committee
advised her to take away Mary's right of succession to the throne,
or else to charge her with high treason too. Elizabeth politely refused to go along with this, but the duke of Norfolk's execution
became politically necessary as a sop to the Commons. He was
beheaded on 2 June 1572.

The French ambassador begged Elizabeth to spare Mary, but
apparently his king, Charles IX, would have been quite happy to
see Mary beheaded, as he feared that once on England's throne she
might become too good a friend of Philip of Spain.

Suddenly the Netherlands situation exploded in a way that neither
Alva nor Philip expected. The Dutch leader William de la Marck
had for a long time been in Dover with his ships. Alva had protested
to Elizabeth about Dutch attacks on his ships in her waters, and
she had responded (officially) by expelling de la Marck from
England. Legally, so to speak, she was well covered. But hardly was

de la Marck out of Dover harbour when he sighted some more Spanish vessels, attacked them and threw their crews overboard. Then he sailed straight up to Brill and captured it (1 April 1572). This was the key event of the Netherlands crisis. It set off risings in other Dutch ports, the first being in Flushing. The rebels showed themselves equal to the Spanish for sheer butchering fury—so much so that for a time William of Orange wanted entirely to dissociate himself from them. Louis of Navarre with a protestant army (mostly Frenchmen, sent with the secret approval of Charles IX) captured Mons and Valenciennes. Hatred of Spanish soldiery (though it was hardly more than a tenth of the total Netherlands occupation force) did what no leader could have done. It unified the country. Neither the protestants nor the catholics liked to see Spanish soldiers living off the land. Spanish troops had not received any pay for two years, the Germans for over six months. Suddenly there was full-scale revolution. Town after town came out in revolt.

But as suddenly it was knocked on the head by a change in Catherine de' Medici's policy. This change was in the form of the so-called massacre of St. Bartholomew (24 August 1572) when the prominent Huguenot leaders were murdered *en masse* in Paris during a single night. It was all the more unexpected because Catherine—anxious to weaken Philip after his Lepanto victory against the Turks (which was something of a setback to the French policy of befriending the Turks)—had been thinking of giving open support to William of Orange and annexing part of the Netherlands for herself. 1572 was also a year of understanding between herself and Elizabeth of England, though only on the surface, since Elizabeth was nervous of French fingers in the Netherlands and preferred the Spanish there (she secretly told Alva that she would help him against Orange if he let her get into Flanders). That is to say, everyone wanted to weaken Philip, but not so as to strengthen each other. And in the end this determined Catherine's policy towards the protestants.

The man Catherine wished least to strengthen was her own son, Charles IX, at least not until he and she were in agreement. The

Peace of St. Germain which had ended the last civil war in France had made the protestants equal citizens with the catholics. Now Coligny, the protestant leader, was dangerously close to Charles. In fact, it looked as if the French monarchy would go protestant. Only fear of the Guise family had made her tolerate the protestants as she had done. But it was clearly no use putting Coligny into Guise's place as an influence on the crown. Nor did she have any confidence that William of Orange would beat the Spaniards. His armies were less efficient, and Alva was a much better strategist than he would ever be. Alva defeated the rebels at Valenciennes. Then Catherine got wind of Elizabeth's secret promise to support Alva. She was in correspondence with Elizabeth at this time, and Elizabeth may well have told her the secret arrangement herself (hoping to divide Catherine from Charles). Catherine began to feel alone and exposed. She decided to do away with the protestant leader closest to her son, and confided her plan to Henry of Guise (who was convinced that Coligny had been behind the death of his father Francis). An assassin was hired and Coligny was shot at from a window as he was leaving the Louvre on 22 August. This was four days after the marriage between the protestant king of Navarre and Catherine's daughter, Marguerite de Valois. That marriage was designed to heal the protestant-catholic war, and the protestant leaders had come to Paris to witness it. They were also there to prepare a new army for Flanders. The first of 4,000 men, sent by Coligny with Charles IX's connivance to relieve Mons, had been cut to pieces by the Spanish (17 July).

Coligny received the shot in his arm and was carried bleeding to his lodgings. He did not die. There was tremendous uproar at court and all over Paris. But this only proved to Catherine what powerful enemies her son and the protestants might prove, since they were popular. Charles insisted on a full investigation and there was a great danger that her part in the plot would come out. She became even more frightened, and—as much to cover her own part in the affair as anything—she decided that only the removal of all the Huguenot leaders would deliver her at one stroke from her enemies in Paris, from Philip's anger and Elizabeth's duplicity. In this, too,

Henry of Guise was a ready ally. She even convinced the weak if violent Charles that it had to be done—and that he must sign an order for it to be done; otherwise, she argued, Spanish wrath would descend on the capital and provoke a more terrible civil war than ever before. The Swiss Guard began its work at dawn. Most of the leaders were murdered in their beds. Others were dragged into the street. Some were chased across the roof-tops. It went on for several days, and spread to other towns. Not until October did the killing in the provinces stop.

What she did, in the massacre of St. Bartholomew, was to reopen the civil war that she had cleverly mended two years before. Philip is said to have been 'relieved' when he got the news. He even laughed, which was most rare for him. It meant the collapse of the protestant effort in the Netherlands. The French ambassador in Madrid felt so confident of the king's approval that he openly told him that he owed his 'victory' in the Netherlands (Mons fell on 21 September) to Charles (meaning the queen-mother). There were thanksgiving processions in Rome.

The massacre was the real opening of what came to be called the Counter Reformation. First Alva made a settlement with England whereby Elizabeth's trade with the Netherlands was fully reopened and her pirates discouraged (15 March 1573). Then he sacked Mechlin. The protestant army at Zutphen was massacred. The inquisitor-general, Espinosa, was given *carte blanche* to do to the Dutch what he had previously done to the *moriscos*. He was to bring terror to the civil front. Alva's son, Fadrique de Toledo, attacked Haarlem, with orders from his father to show no mercy. But Don Fadrique's troops decided they had been unpaid long enough and mutinied. This encouraged the Netherlanders to come out in arms again, and for a time it looked as if the Spanish effort might collapse. The fleet got a bad beating in the Zyder Zee. Fadrique de Toledo failed to take Alkmaar. Had Huguenot support still been available from France the Netherlanders might well have crushed his army of 60,000-odd troops (including nearly 5,000 cavalry). It was an enormous army to maintain abroad at that time. Certainly the Netherlands were no longer bringing revenue to the Spanish crown

—not enough to maintain armies of that size. In fact, the Netherlands war was rendering the Spanish crown bankrupt.

In April 1573 Philip received a complaint about the behaviour of
his troops from a secretary employed in the Netherlands service
called Esteban Pratz. He wrote that the soldiers constantly took the
law into their own hands. Numberless people had been dragged
from their homes and 'executed' on the spot. The surviving peasants
were treated in the most appalling way—robbed and beaten. Their
women were raped. Nothing like it, he wrote, had been seen 'in
ancient or modern times'. And the culprits were officers and camp
commandants as well as ordinary troops. The bishops joined the bold
secretary in this complaint. It convinced Philip that Alva's policy
of relentless punishment had failed, and he decided to accept the
duke's request—repeated again and again for the past year—to be
relieved of his post. Alva was now a violent, well-nigh hysterical
man. He wrote to Philip that he had never in all his life passed such
days and nights of anxiety, seeing his troops unable to keep themselves in boot-leather and clothing. As civilian hatred of his men
grew, as the rebellion (now almost as strong among the catholics as
among protestants) refused to be put down by the most merciless
behaviour, so Alva's feelings grew more violent. Philip ceased
answering his letters, finding his cruelties senseless (because useless). For Alva the punishment so far meted out was not nearly
enough. He therefore took matters into his own hands. Though the
town of Neerden had surrendered and was given terms he ordered
his son to murder the entire male population. The order was carried
out. Alva told Philip that his desire for less aggressive methods in
the Netherlands was 'a temptation of the devil', which probably
caused Philip some lengthy self-examination, given his awareness
of the devil in everything.

But the Alva repression clearly had not worked. Nor had
Espinosa's. The latter was suddenly in disgrace too. Philip as good
as called him a liar in full council, for having kept news about the
brutality in the Netherlands from him. Espinosa died the day after.
Philip was so far disposed towards conciliation during this year of
1573 that, according to some reports, he offered the protestants

toleration in the Netherlands on the German model if the German princes would elect him emperor.

Luis de Requesens, formerly ambassador in Rome and governor of Milan, was sent to replace Alva in November 1573. By this time Alva was the most hated name in the Netherlands, and he returned to Spain before the year was out. Requesens had his bronze statue in the citadel of Antwerp melted down. He abolished the so-called Council of the Troubles. He returned to the tradition of consulting the Estates-General. He withdrew the hated levy.

Not that Alva's departure altered Dutch feeling. Philip's determination to administer their country from Madrid and make them pay for it remained the same. It took Requesens months to get a General Pardon for the Netherlands out of him (June 1574), mostly because Alva, back in Madrid now, was again trying to sell his policy of wholesale war at court. Nor was his doctrine an illogical one. The pardon did fall completely flat as he predicted. Requesens, no less than he, had to continue fighting. A number of rebel towns were still defying the Spanish. And then fighting was the only way to apply Philip's policy. The Netherlanders saw to that.

William of Orange occupied Middleburg on 18 February 1574, but an army of 8,000 Spaniards defeated Louis of Nassau with his German mercenaries at Mook, killing Louis himself. The whole situation was complicated by the mutinous temper of the Spanish troops, who continued to take their unpaid wages in plunder wherever they went. Fighting went on until the autumn of 1575. It began to look as if Alva's plan for castrating the Netherlands was the only answer. Requesens died in March 1576. The situation was even more dangerous than it had been under Alva. The Estates of Holland and Zeeland decided to publish their edicts in their own name and no longer in that of Philip II.

Now that there was no governor mutiny broke out among Spanish troops quartered in Brussels. Most of the Council of State, despite the fact that they were Philip's chosen men, came out against his policy. For a time they were the only government. The gap was eight weeks long. In that time William of Orange managed virtually to replace the council with his own government, by the simple

expedient of entering the city and putting most of the councillors
under arrest. The Estates met and began to plan a national army
under him. He was in close contact with Elizabeth, though all he
got out of her for the time being was a down payment of £20,000
and the promise of a loan later on.

It was clear now that Philip's methods had brought a nationalist
Netherlands into being. Until then there had only been pockets of
heresy and rebellion. Spanish troops now took matters into their
own hands. They had already created terror in Antwerp, but
Requesens had managed to drag them off the prey for a time with a
promise of wages soon. For weeks the citizens of Antwerp had been
terrified in their homes at night by the sound of marauding troops
outside (they had marched on the city from Mooker-Leyden). These
men were the best arquebusiers of the army, and Requesens found
it necessary to take up his headquarters among them and talk to their
'soldiers' council' as if it were his own. There were daily brawls and
murders. Troops cut one citizen to pieces, tearing him from the
protection of a Spanish officer. They attacked a church, removing
its altar to the square outside, so that Mass could be celebrated in
the open.

The promised wages did not arrive. Raping and pillaging
went on. At least 7,000 people were murdered on 4 November
1576.

More than any previous event this new 'occupation' of Antwerp
made hatred of the Spaniard a necessity for every proud Netherlander, whether protestant or catholic. Four days after this 'Spanish
fury' the protestants and catholics joined in an alliance called the
'pacification of Ghent', by which the Spanish were to be driven
out.

Philip's money-problem was getting worse. In 1571 and 1573 he
had told the Castilian Cortes that he had already spent his income
for the next five years. On 7 November 1574 he asked for an increase
in the annual subsidy called the *encabezamiento* and in September
of the following year he suspended interest on all state debts. This
was really a suicidal step. This alone would have involved him in
policies of aggression, even had he not felt them to be justified by

the religious state of the times. His creditors all over Europe were astonished—and of course his credit position was damaged permanently. The German bankers began to be wary. The Genoese stopped their credit. And he was forced to supply interest by the only expedient left to him—that of piling up more debt.

Chapter 11

Murder in High Places

Philip wanted to mend his image in the seventeen provinces of the Netherlands. Don John of Austria seemed just the right man to do the mending. He was Philip's own half-brother. He was also more than half a Netherlander, being the illegitimate son of Charles V and Barbara Bomberg. He had been brought up in ignorance of his origins in the household of a Castilian nobleman called Luis Quijada, and had been given the Spanish name Jerónimo. Philip discovered who he was from his father's will and began showering affection on the boy, providing him with a household of his own. Don John was now thirty and handsome—and blond too, the opposite of Spanish in appearance. At this moment he was everyone's hero, for the recent victory against the Turks at Lepanto had been his, on the military side. He was short in stature but elegant and fine-looking, with a powerful moustache. He was also upright, brave, affable, courteous, handsome, reliable—in fact all the things likely to make Philip choose him and then watch him like a hawk.

Almost at once there was a snag. Barbara Bomberg of Ratisbon, Don John's mother, was famous all over the Netherlands for her sexual extravagances. It hardly helped him when he arrived. Where Spain had considered him the son of a king, the Netherlands saw him as a plain bastard.

And then he had an impatient nature. While not another Alva, he was still more of a soldier than a statesman. As for Philip, he did not believe in killing people unnecessarily. Above all he liked his troops to behave. And then a period of respite in the Netherlands was economically necessary. He still had no money to pay his troops. He looked to Don John for the impossible—peace in the Netherlands under Spanish control.

Don John disliked his appointment intensely. He tried to get out of it. But Pope Gregory XIII supported his nomination warmly. He had a strange plan of offering Ireland to Don John, once a silly plot of his own hatching had pushed Elizabeth off the throne of England. The Ridolfi affair was only the first of several papal intrigues. But the promise of the Irish throne persuaded Don John that it was right to take the Netherlands job. It was little wonder that Philip began to watch him with less than brotherly trust.

Don John was to go direct to the Netherlands from Milan. He must, Philip wrote, 'take wings and fly there'. Don John would have preferred to invade England, and put Mary Stuart on the throne as his wife. Elizabeth heard every detail of this plan and later asked him for an explanation of the presence of some highly suspicious Englishmen in his court, and he wrote her a letter of explanation which she pretended to accept.

Pretended—in fact she decided to have him murdered. A man called Ratcliffe was released from the Tower by Walsingham on condition that he would do the job. He was sent with an accomplice across the water, and managed to get access to one of Don John's audiences. In the meantime the Spanish ambassador in London had got wind of the plot through his secret agents. He sent Don John a portrait of Ratcliffe. Don John recognised him as soon as he walked into the room and had him arrested on the spot. Ratcliffe was executed. It is said that he had received his instructions from Elizabeth's own mouth.

Don John had made his acceptance of the Netherlands post conditional on Philip's approval of his plan to invade England. He had hurried not to Brussels but to Castile to get this approval. And Philip had agreed cautiously. And then he had given Don John his briefing. Spanish troops were eventually to leave the Netherlands, and there was to be a measure of self-government. Don John was to enter the Netherlands on horseback from France, disguised as the servant of the man sent to attend him, Ottavio Gonzaga.

He arrived precisely on the day of the 'Spanish fury' at Antwerp. Nothing he did afterwards could disconnect his name from that. He tried to negotiate with the Netherlanders but was told that discussions could only begin when Spanish troops had left the country.

The catholic south-west and the protestant north-east were united
in this. He had no alternative but to give way, and by an edict of
12 February 1577 he promised the departure of Spanish troops
within twenty days. He hoped to use these troops against England
by sailing them down the English Channel, but the Dutch and the
Zeelanders refused to have them passing through their territory to
the ports. The troops were thus obliged to leave by the overland
route to Italy.

Within two or three months Don John was asking for them back.
Negotiations had broken down. The Estates-General had recognised
him as the governor but only by a majority of one.

By December of the same year Spanish troops were once more
back in the Netherlands. The policy of war necessarily returned
with them. Don John went into the attack at once but only succeeded
in reviving the determination of the rebel army against him. He
wanted to press on to Brussels but had neither enough troops nor
the money to pay them. Alva's recall to Madrid had achieved nothing
except to strengthen the rebels and open up a series of new mutinies
in the Spanish army itself.

Despite the massacre of St. Bartholomew, the protestant movement in France was still strong, and it still had support in high
places. There was as much danger now as ever before of an alliance
between the king and the rebel leaders in the Netherlands. The
king's younger brother, the duke of Alençon and Anjou, had also
turned out a rebel, to his mother's disgust, especially as he had long
ago been promised to Elizabeth as a husband. At the head of a group
called the 'malcontents' he more or less forced Catherine to agree on
an advantageous settlement for the Huguenots, though he was a long
way from being a convinced one himself. William of Orange contacted him, and the young duke was promised the Netherlands
throne when and if it came into being, in exchange for his help. In
August 1578 they made a treaty by which the duke of Anjou was to
keep an army of 10,000 men and 2,000 horse in the Netherlands at
his own expense. His title for the time being was to be 'Defender of
the Liberties of the Netherlands'.

Don John died in October 1578. Rumours began circulating as

to the manner of his death. Some said he had been murdered at the instigation of Don Carlos. There was a story that he had died of syphilis, another that he had died of a broken heart, seeing all his plans to invade England in ruin. It was true that Philip had rejected the passionate arguments put to him by Escovedo, Don John's brilliant secretary, sent to Madrid to argue his case. In fact Philip was stung and insulted by Escovedo's sharp and unhesitating criticisms of his policy.

The truth was that Don John died of a fever. He was ill for at least a fortnight before. There had been a serious outbreak of typhoid among his soldiers, and this could well have been the cause.

Not that a murder in high places was unlikely. A murder did take place. The victim was Escovedo, and it was at the instigation of Philip's most loved and trusted minister, Antonio Pérez.

The Madrid court was rotten through and through at this time, ever since the thirty-nine-year-old Pérez had succeeded the prince of Eboli in 1573 as the closest man to Philip. With Philip's tacit consent he had turned the state into a kind of sinecure-market. The sale of offices had gone up catastrophically, for the exchequer needed the money. The grandees were in league with foreign bankers to rob the state of its revenues. A lot of the revenues that did arrive went into private pockets. There was an increasing national debt. It is little wonder that conspiracy and murder—progeny of corruption—crept into the court and closely touched even Philip's life.

The widowed princess of Eboli had fallen in love with the dazzling and perfumed young Pérez (opposite in type to her late husband's chief enemy at court, the duke of Alva) the moment she clapped eyes on him. Escovedo, who knew them both, became (vociferously as always) concerned about their affair, and threatened to find it his duty to expose it to the king, who liked sexual extravagance to be marital. Escovedo was a clumsy psychologist. It was not difficult for Pérez and the princess (an intelligent as well as handsome creature) to persuade Philip that Don John and above all his secretary had dangerously grandiose schemes afoot for challenging his authority. On 31 March 1578 Escovedo was stabbed to death in a dark side street in Madrid. This was to have severe repercussions later for both Pérez and Philip, ones they could hardly foresee at the time.

But meanwhile life went on as before. England remained un-invaded. The pope's madcap scheme had been tried out. Early in the year (1578) he had sent off his first 'expedition' in a leaky ship under the command of an Englishman called Thomas Stukeley, said to be one of Henry VIII's many bastards. Stukeley had been described as a 'ruffian, a spendthrift and a notable vapourer'. He had obtained an audience with Elizabeth before setting out 'to establish a colony' in America. He got as far as Dublin, where he began discussing with a Shane O'Neil (who was in touch with the Spanish embassy in London) a plan to make Philip king of England. As for the pope's expedition to England, it ground to a halt in Africa, and Stukeley got caught up in the battle of Alcazar with the Turks. He had both his legs shot off.

The pope tried again the following year, in July 1579. This time the command was in the hands of an Irishman of noble birth called James Fitzmaurice Fitzgerald. An English catholic priest, Nicholas Saunders, acted as the pope's agent, charged with bringing England back into the Church. The purpose of the expedition was to land in Ireland, using it as the springboard for an attack across the water. This time the ships at least got to Ireland, and it even began to look as if it would become another occupied area, much like the Nether-lands. Philip allowed himself to be persuaded to take part in it, urged by Irish catholics as well as the pope. A second stronger force of Italian and Spanish troops was equipped in Spain and set off in September 1580. They were killed almost to a man within two months of landing in Ireland. Six hundred creatures were killed in cold blood, including women and children, and the whole thing fizzled out. The English had been waiting for them. An occupied Ireland was too close a danger to be even thinkable for Elizabeth. The pope never tried again.

Philip definitely did not enjoy this kind of thing. He liked a plot to be in the hands of competent agents of his own choosing. Only the hope of establishing the Spanish presence in Ireland with the blessing of the pope (better than going it alone) had made him fall in with the plan. Also, if the pope had been successful it would have meant a dangerous increase of papal prestige. This way, even with a failed expedition, the pope simply became an extension of the catholic command in Madrid.

During 1580 the first official Jesuit mission arrived in England. It was in the hands of two powerful men, Thomas Campion and Robert Parsons. Twelve years before, an English college had been opened by a Jesuit at Douai in the Netherlands. A second had been started in Rome in 1579. Londoners saw these first arrivals simply as agents of the pope (or the devil). They were not far wrong. Shortly after their arrival the English Jesuits were given to understand by the pope that anybody who murdered Elizabeth would not be considered a sinner but *might* be considered a saint.

The courage of these Jesuit priests, moving about secretly under the protection of catholic families, had an extraordinary effect in promoting a sense of catholic unity in England for the first time since Henry had sacked the monasteries. A particle of real dedication stimulated terrific forces. These men had learned to smile at the idea of being burned alive. Naturally the comfort-loving merchants of the City (the treasurers, so to speak, of the protestant movement) had everything to fear from them. The Commons called them 'a rabble of vagrant friars newly sprung up and running through the world to trouble the Church of God'. And it became clear that one day the Jesuits would have to be banished, or else the throne would go to Mary Stuart. Leicester wrote to Walsingham in 1582, 'If she [the queen] suffer their increase but one year more, as she hath done these two or three years past, it will be too late to give or take counsel to help it.'

There is no doubt that Philip felt relief at Escovedo's murder. While he disliked lawless acts he had come to distrust Don John even more for trying to run a foreign policy of his own. He knew that Don John had been in secret talk with the Guise family. As for Escovedo, he had called Philip's policy in the Netherlands 'disconnected' to his face, and the princess of Eboli had been in the room too. Philip never forgot a slight of that kind.

Pérez afterwards maintained that Escovedo had been murdered on Philip's orders alone. What we do know is that Pérez gave a full account of the murder to Philip afterwards, and that Philip felt a safer man for it, as he no doubt did when Don John died too.

Ruy Gómez, the prince of Eboli, had introduced both Escovedo and Pérez to the court when they were young men. They were all friends. And it was natural that Escovedo should open his heart to Pérez in a series of letters from the Netherlands about his and Don John's dreams of future glory. It was equally natural that Pérez should divulge the contents of these letters to Philip, especially after Escovedo took too strong an interest in his love affair with the princess. Pérez was a courteous as well as a clever young man, and he had made himself indispensable to the royal council. He had always belonged to Prince Eboli's anti-Alva faction. Eboli's and Alva's were the two principal factions at court; Charles V had taught Philip to keep two going at all times, and to play one off against the other. It was a good way, too, of hearing both sides of any argument.

Together with the princess, Antonio Pérez continued to believe in Charles V's policy of conciliation and compromise where possible. And for many years Philip was inclined to agree with him. But lately he had been showing signs of a new attitude. And Pérez may have begun to fear that the Escovedo school would win him over. That policy was to plant new kings abroad.

Pérez naturally had enemies. After the Escovedo murder these enemies began to persuade Philip, mainly through their leader Monteo Vazquez de Leca (who had started his political life as a common informer and was now one of the king's secretaries), that Pérez had accused Escovedo falsely. He had, they said, even made trouble deliberately between Philip and Don John. That Philip listened to these men simply meant that Pérez had come to the end of his usefulness as a minister.

In April, just one month after Escovedo's murder, Philip wrote to his sixty-year-old favourite Antoine Perrenot de Granvelle, now living in retirement in Rome (and no doubt thankful to be out of the Netherlands), telling him to return to Madrid at once. Philip had a new military programme in mind—Portugal. Neither Pérez nor any other prominent minister could help him in this. It required the understanding of a Burgundian of proved integrity, from the old guard, a monument of the imperial past. Granvelle was the man. Nowadays such men did not grow on trees.

On the night of 28 July, Philip had Pérez arrested, and Princess Eboli was sent to a castle under house arrest. A few days later Philip received Granvelle at the Escorial. Pérez was tortured, and gave it out that Philip had said to him, 'You will see that we shall have to kill these men.' It was no wonder that Don John's death excited so many rumours when it came in the autumn of that year.

Alva was back in royal favour—though only because there was no one else for the job Philip had in mind. For years Pérez remained in prison without trial. Not until 1584 were his private papers seized and his trial for corruption started.

The job Philip had in mind was the invasion of Portugal. That country was no longer the modest strip of territory it had been at the time of its first independence in the twelfth century. It was nowadays the centre of a vast empire stretching from the Azores to Japan. Lisbon was one of the most luxurious cities in Europe, decidedly imperial, and much more so than Madrid. The Portuguese held the Azores, the group of islands round Madeira and the Cape Verde islands. In the previous century they had rounded the Cape of Good Hope. They had discovered Brazil. Above all they had explored the east coast of Africa, under Vasco da Gama, and penetrated to India. At the beginning of the century Francisco de Almeida had established himself firmly in India, after defeating the Egyptian fleet at Diu. After him Don Afonso de Albuquerque had discovered Madagascar, and then laid hold of Goa in India as the headquarters of Portuguese power in the east. The Red Sea and the Persian Gulf were discovered, then Java, New Guinea, Borneo. China was reached (Canton, 1518), and twenty years later Japan.

The Portuguese were unashamedly seeking trade—at any price. They were swift in the attack. They were corrupt in their operations, and required conversion to Christianity as an insurance policy to secure the trade. They were no more cynical than the Spaniards. They simply bore no responsibility towards the men they colonised.

Nowhere did they establish a 'New Portugal'. Their affairs were directed by no great figure in Lisbon. The Empire brought tremendous wealth but no order. The Portuguese flocked to Lisbon to share in the good life and left their land either abandoned or in the hands of African slaves. What could have been a strong Portuguese army at home was used to man the trading outposts. And it was natural that when King Sebastian of Portugal was killed in his second hopeless crusade against the Turks in Morocco, Philip should have begun pressing his claims to the Portuguese throne. He was after all the son of Isabella of Portugal. She had been the eldest daughter of Emmanuel the Fortunate.

He began by injecting agents and bribe-money into the neighbour kingdom. The people of Portugal were against him, but that became less and less important as time went on.

Besides needing a vast eastern empire to add to his vast western empire, Philip felt nervous at having such a wealthy country so much on his doorstep. It never asked his advice. This was especially so under Sebastian, who kept his own—often mad—counsels. His crusade had been doomed from the outset. Sebastian was an appalling strategist. In his last fatal battle he left the rear of his army and both flanks exposed. Deprived of its king, Portugal now seemed (to Philip) to be in crying need of him. Sebastian had been a brave and devout man but entirely incompetent as a ruler. His court had been honeycombed with Jesuits. His Jesuit father-confessor had probably initiated the idea of the mad crusade—mad not because Sebastian's army was weak (20,000 men from Portugal, Germany and Italy) but because of his bad generalship. The defeat at Alcazar el Kebir (June 1578) was due to him alone. Philip had warned him of the dangers at their meeting in a monastery at Guadalupe in Estremadura. He had refused to give Sebastian help, apart from a few weapons. He may even have hoped quietly for Sebastian's death, rather as he may have hoped for Don Carlos's death some time before. Sebastian and Don Carlos were similar results of inbreeding —erratic, weak and frequently wracked with fever (as well as with genuine mystical exaltation too).

Philip had begun his campaign of softening Portuguese public opinion before Sebastian's death—and precisely at the moment when he heard that Sebastian was sexually impotent. He sent one of his counsellors, Cristobal de Moura, a Portuguese, to Lisbon with plenty of money to argue his case. The prince of Eboli too was Portuguese in origin and through his relatives kept a close eye on what was going on behind the scenes at Sebastian's court.

There were several other candidates for the throne, including Catherine de' Medici, who claimed King Afonso III as one of her forebears some centuries back. But none had Philip's power or money. His most obstinate enemies were the Portuguese people themselves, under a popular candidate for the throne called Don Antonio—an illegitimate nephew of the Cardinal Henry, regent of Portugal since Sebastian's death. Cardinal Henry disapproved of Don Antonio because he was said to have many bastards by 'New Christian' women. He feared that, once king, Don Antonio would advance New Christian interests above those of the nobility. The duke of Braganza, another candidate, was rich and powerful (he was favoured by the Jesuits) but not popular, nor did he have Don Antonio's rhetorical powers.

Cardinal Henry was Sebastian's great uncle, and the last of the Avis house. He was now sixty-seven, and was toying with the idea of getting a special dispensation from the pope to marry and produce an heir. When Philip heard this he thought of offering the cardinal an already pregnant woman as his wife so as to secure a Spanish succession. Finally Henry was won over by the Jesuits at court, who had veered to Philip—and to the idea of a Spanish take-over, which seemed the safest thing for the Holy War.

Three members of the royal council in Lisbon were bribed to support Philip's claim, but they could not sway the people. The Portuguese ambassador in Madrid told the Venetian envoy there that he would rather be 'ruled by Turks than by Spaniards'. But the royal council effectively hampered all attempts to muster an army or any kind of united opposition to Philip, under cover of doing precisely this. The rest of Europe was watching with great if rather academic interest. Catherine de' Medici had put herself forward as a candidate only in the hope of being bought off by Philip.

Her price was his daughter for the duke of Anjou. She indicated to his ambassador in Paris that the marriage would keep her arms and her agents out of both the Netherlands and Portugal. As it happened she went on making trouble for Philip wherever she could, and the marriage did not take place.

Philip was the only candidate willing to send an army into Portugal. In fact, Granvelle set about preparing a force under Alva the moment he returned to power. He reorganised the country's pitiful finances. He mustered Spaniards from Sicily and Naples and Milan, together with Italians and Germans. The grandees suddenly began to co-operate, and the cities of Castile raised troops. Something of the excitement of the old crusades was aroused—this time against fellow-Christians in the same peninsula!

Granvelle urged Philip to cross the Portuguese border after Cardinal Henry's death. This happened less than eighteen months after he had been declared regent, on 31 January 1580. But Philip (as always too slow in his decisions to achieve surprise) preferred to find out first whether or not the Portuguese would receive him of their own accord. The last thing he wanted was a second Netherlands, with England and France egging the rebels on. But all that his delay achieved was a stiffening of resistance—inside and outside Portugal. Even the monks and clergy took to arms. Catherine urged Elizabeth to help her. A French ship loaded with arms left for Portugal. A French secret agent called Jean Pierre de Abbadie worked hard with the French consul in Lisbon to centralise resistance. The illegitimate Don Antonio was also active, with a large following. He told everyone that the Spanish army was too small to be effectual, and that if necessary he would call in the Turks to help him. All of Philip's efforts to buy him off failed—in fact, they made Spain even more unpopular.

On 16 April 1580 Philip sent the Portuguese an ultimatum: either they accepted him as their king or he would take the throne by force. They had twenty days in which to decide. The action was to be a pincer-movement. While Spanish ships came up from the south and took what ports they could, the army was to invade at Badajoz in southern Portugal. The two were then to join up.

Don Carlos, Philip II's son and heir

The Infanta Isabella Clara Eugenia

The Portuguese fortress at Elvas, just on the other side of the border from Badajoz, surrendered on the news that the Spaniards were close by (though still in Spain). In June Philip's army crossed the border. At once Don Antonio was declared king of Portugal by his group. He was supported by the bishop of La Guarda (in a sermon given on the day Elvas surrendered). He went to Lisbon, and tremendous enthusiasm for him began to generate. But the Portuguese army was poor and weak. The country was divided in its loyalties, mostly between Don Antonio and Braganza. Many of the nobility had been bribed by Philip. Also Spain was in a position to cut off Portugal's wheat supplies from Andalusia and Castile at any time. The people could be starved into submission.

The Spanish advance on land and sea went according to plan. The resistance was small. At Setubal on the Portuguese coast, quite close to Lisbon, Spanish troops went in for murder, rape and plunder. Then Alva decided to attack Lisbon from the sea, when the Portuguese were expecting him to come from inland. It was a dangerous action, as the shore was steep and difficult for a landing. But there was no one waiting there. All the way to Lisbon the fortresses fell, and Antonio's general was captured and put to death.

The pope came out firmly on Philip's side. The Spanish ambassador put it to him that Don Antonio would only cause unnecessary bloodshed by staying in Portugal. The pope advised Don Antonio to leave. Success being nine parts of any political argument, the English and French also cooled towards Antonio.

Even after the Spaniards had overrun the country Don Antonio went about in disguise. He was betrayed by no one. But his case was hopeless. He had to leave. For years afterwards he went between France and England as an outcast, still believing that he could drive the Spaniards out of his country. He put down the crown jewels of Portugal as a guarantee for loans. He was the kind of gallant individual that the new era had little time for. Yet he probably did more to harm Philip's image in the courts of northern Europe than any other man, apart perhaps from Antonio Pérez later on.

Alva was shelved, now that he had served his purpose. At the end of 1582 he died. Philip's mourning (he was still in Lisbon) was

9

perfunctory, considering that Alva had served him with unstinted loyalty. Philip never perhaps forgot that Alva had once burst into his room without permission and begun shouting at him. Of all the possible threats to the Spanish throne, a powerful and obstinate grandee was the greatest. The occasion of the shouting had been King Sebastian's plan for a crusade. Philip had borne with the rudeness and taken Alva's advice. But he did not forget the lack of proper awe for the royal presence.

Philip went to Portugal himself despite the death of his fourth wife, Anne of Austria, in childbirth, and he almost died himself on the way. He went through the farce of being officially accepted by the people whose faces he had just rubbed in the dust. On 16 April 1581 he was crowned before the Portuguese Cortes at Tomar, dressed in brocade, in the Portuguese fashion, and finding it very uncomfortable. He ordered his court to do the same. He declared that no new laws were to be made for the country. Portuguese law was to be respected. He also agreed that Portugal was not to be Castilianised, and that official posts—including the governorship—were to remain in Portuguese hands. The army, the Church, the eastern empire, the trading fleet were to remain as before, entirely peopled by the Portuguese. He removed the customs barrier between Castile and Portugal (though he did restore it some years later), and undertook to help Portugal in the matter of defending its outposts. In fact thousands of ducats poured into Portugal from Spain annually.

He never entirely stood by his agreement that Portuguese fortresses were to be manned only by natives of Portugal. And, while the highest offices in Portugal remained in native hands, he saw to it that they were men who might as well have been Castilians. Yet his last wish was to squeeze the country dry, or even to change it. The whole scope of the exercise had been to draw Portugal inside the Spanish orbit, not to exploit it for Castilian interests. Above all, he had wanted to prevent Portugal from going to a foreign power.

The invasion of Portugal was his second aggressive act, after the Netherlands. And it was just as unwise. His father would probably have been against it. A tremendous empire was the result, with an unprecedented pressure of business on a tiny headquarters. The exchequer was simply not organised to take this load. More than this, all the fears that Charles had aroused in Europe—of a 'universal monarchy'—were now brought to well-nigh panic point. It produced a determination in all the seafaring countries to weaken him at his outposts whenever a chance came up. And this was what began to dissolve his empire at a time when it was expanding to its fullest limit. Charles had advised him to follow a 'defensive' policy. But this would not have kept Spanish zeal alive. Philip felt the need to regulate the world of Christ, not in a mediaeval fashion, through dynasty, but by control of men's minds. For him it meant a mounting programme of indoctrination (by force, bribery, plot or persuasion). This had by no means yet reached its climax.

There was trouble in the Portuguese Azores, due to the French. The nine islands were divided in their loyalty. The chief one, São Miguel, supported Philip. In the second largest, Terceira, the Franciscans supported Don Antonio while the Jesuits supported Philip (enough in itself to make the clergy distrust him). The Don Antonio side quickly got the upper hand. Don Antonio's scheme of getting together a fleet and establishing some kind of headquarters on the islands, with which both to worry Philip's shipping and to prepare an invasion of Portugal, appealed to both Elizabeth of England and Catherine de' Medici. But Elizabeth was willing to provoke Philip only on utterly essential details which could bring her immediate gain. So the jewels Don Antonio gave her were wasted, in spite of the hot support he received from the admirals Hawkins and Drake. The French were more helpful. Their new king, Henry III, knew about the plan, though not officially, and an expedition was assembled that finally sailed on 16 June 1582, under Filippo Strozzi.

Philip knew every detail of the operation before it started, since he had an agent planted very close to Don Antonio himself (in fact he was one of Don Antonio's most trusted men). A Spanish fleet arrived at the Azores after the French, and won a five-hour battle in which the leader Strozzi and Philip's agent at his side were killed.

The Spanish commander, the marquis of Santa Cruz, then gave
orders that all French prisoners should be killed—officers beheaded
and the men hanged. It was a warning to foreign adventurers and
monarchs alike to keep out of Spanish waters. But the hint was not
taken. Almost precisely the same battle, with the same result, took
place a year later.

From Portugal Don Antonio had gone straight to England (June
1581), where there was still much sympathy for him. Philip at once
demanded an explanation of this from the queen, through his new
ambassador in London, the skilful Don Bernardino de Mendoza
(already regarded there as akin to the devil for his part in trying to
stir up rebellion in Ireland). On the other hand Philip still very
much wanted peace with Elizabeth. With his invasion of Portugal,
he could not afford to have her helping the duke of Anjou in the
Netherlands. On her side, to avoid trouble, she advised Don Antonio
to slip across to France, which he did.

Drake had got back from his trip round the world in the previous
autumn with a lot of booty from Spanish America. The queen refused to give it up. And it did Mendoza's liver no good when he
was offered a large portion of it himself if he could smooth things
over with Philip.

Towards the end of 1581 the duke of Anjou went to England to
seek help for the Netherlands. His brother Henry III had signed a
secret pledge to support him officially if he could manage to win the
Netherlands from Philip—and to recognise him as the 'prince and
lord' of that country. Holland and Zeeland, on the other hand, still
refused to recognise anyone but William. But the chance of France
intervening in the Netherlands was not strong. The Valois house
was too busy defending itself against the Huguenots on one side and
the Guise family on the other. This weakening of France was what
made it possible for Philip to clear up the Netherlands, at least
temporarily, and later to launch his attack on England. His agents in
Paris were doing their best to make the divisions worse, with bribes
and intrigues.

He had sent Alexander Farnese, son of Margaret of Austria and
Ottavio Farnese (a general in the imperial army), to succeed the late

Don John of Austria. Farnese was a diplomat as well as a soldier. The situation in the Netherlands was favourable to him, in that the old religious quarrels were starting up again, after a brief period of anti-Spanish unity. That compromise union of the seventeen provinces, made in Ghent back in 1576, had really been the work of the Spanish mutineers and pillagers. After hours of disagreement at the conference table the two sides had suddenly come to terms on hearing about Spanish violence in Antwerp. The resulting 'pacification' had recognised protestant worship in Holland and Zeeland, and catholic worship in the other fifteen provinces. That had been before the arrival of Don John and before the explosive situation had forced him to accept the pact, if not officially to recognise it. The compromise was clearly not going to last long. The catholics would soon want their forms of worship recognised in Holland and Zeeland, and the protestants theirs in the other provinces. It only needed the Spanish terror to abate. Alexander, duke of Parma, subtle and patient, saw to it that it did abate.

In the authentic Italian spirit he dealt with his enemies without hating and therefore without discounting them. He saw that the Netherlanders were a divided people and that no use had hitherto been made of this division. He set about making it deeper. Some of the German mercenaries on the protestant side (financed by Elizabeth) had behaved quite as furiously as the Spanish, and the catholics had begun to think that they might as well be under Philip after all. A group of catholic 'malcontents', from the Walloon provinces—Artois, Hainault and French Flanders—had got together not two years after the Pact of Ghent and demanded that confiscated Church property be restored to the priests, and that half the catholic churches be brought back into use. The prince of Orange accepted this but the Dutch people did not. When they saw catholic priests once more in their towns they began to strip catholic churches of their altars and threaten anyone who entered with death or torture. So internal hatred was greater than hatred of the foreigner. The result, on 3 January 1579, was the so-called Union of Utrecht, a treaty that definitely prohibited the practice of catholicism in Zeeland and Holland, yet asked for freedom of worship in the other provinces. The catholic answer was the Union of Arras three days later. In May the catholic provinces reaffirmed their loyalty to Philip. The Netherlands were thus virtually divided into two nations, protestant in the north-east and catholic in the south-west. At the same time the Pact of Ghent still operated officially. Parma got Philip to recognise it, now that it was just a piece of paper. And he started a civil war. It was Philip's only hope of getting his way.

The Holy Roman emperor, Rudolf II, had already, in March 1580, formally declared William of Orange a traitor, and had put a price of 25,000 gold crowns on his head. Anyone who murdered William would be made a nobleman and—on the papal side—be given an indefinite reprieve from hell. All this was at Philip's instigation.

Alexander of Parma recaptured Maastricht with 30,000 German mercenaries. But by treaty he was obliged to send all foreign soldiers out of the country. It meant that he was too weak to prevent the duke of Anjou from relieving Cambrai. Yet he was so successful in his general policy that Philip began to see him as a potential Alva, and quickly tried to substitute Margaret for the second time as regent. But Alexander was too deep in the country, psychologically speaking, for this to be possible—at the moment.

The duke of Anjou came off better in England than William of Orange, with £40,000 down and the promise of £50,000 more in 1582. When he returned to the Netherlands he was perhaps the only hope they had of unity. He was in with both sides. The catholics saw him as one of them, if a bit of a protestant. The Calvinists, who thought of him as one of them, complained that his suite practised catholic rites. It made him especially dangerous from Philip's point of view. But what Philip could not do by military action—Alexander's native army was not yet strong enough—he tried to do by murder. A great deal of money changed hands to manipulate the duke of Anjou into a place where he would not be able to defend himself. Hired murderers were now quickly becoming Philip's unofficial army. A certain acceleration of the terror machinery was noticeable after the resounding success of the Portuguese invasion. A Basque called Jean Jaureguy shot at William of Orange and wounded him. William's attendants killed the man on the spot. Two other agents, an Italian and a Spaniard, were arrested for trying to poison both Anjou and William. They confessed under torture that Alexander of Parma had hired them.

A new plot to murder Elizabeth of England obtained Philip's reluctant support. The duke of Guise thought it up. Mendoza, Philip's ambassador, organised it. As before, Mary Queen of Scots was its focal point. A Spanish agent disguised as a dentist was arrested on his way to Scotland, and in the back of his looking-glass the first evidence of a plot called 'The Enterprise' came to light. Sir Francis Walsingham, the queen's secretary, set a spy on the French ambassador and began intercepting correspondence between him and Mary, hoping to get more news of 'The Enterprise'. But no new clues came his way. Then he used his intuition. He came to learn that one of Mary's agents, a catholic gentleman called Francis Throckmorton, was in the habit of visiting the French embassy after dark. For six months he put spies on him. In November 1583 Throckmorton was arrested. Under torture he confessed that he had acted in close consultation with the Spanish ambassador, and that a number of places along the English coast had been selected for the landing of foreign troops. Several catholic noblemen fled the country when his arrest became known. Others were thrown into gaol. Mendoza, the Spanish ambassador, was given fifteen days to get out of England. He went—after promising Elizabeth to face her again as a 'minister of war' since he had failed to satisfy her as a 'minister of peace'. And he became the principal mover behind Philip's Armada preparations against her.

Meanwhile the duke of Anjou was getting unpopular in the Netherlands. He made it too obvious that his only interest in the country lay in becoming its king. His awareness that he was no longer among friends—despite William of Orange's arguments in his favour—turned him into a third factor in the civil war. He started fighting Netherlanders. He tried to attack Antwerp and there was some bitter fighting in the streets, but William managed to hold the town against him. By June 1583 he was obliged to retire to Paris again. He died just a year later. And a month after his death, at the end of June 1584, one of the Spanish murder-plots against William of Orange succeeded. He too died—from bullet wounds fired in his own home at Delft. The murderer was Burgundian and a fanatical catholic.

Two months later a boat bound for Scotland was intercepted by the Dutch (acting perhaps on a tip from Walsingham). It had William Creighton the Jesuit on board. On his person was found more evidence of 'The Enterprise', and it began to look as if England had only narrowly escaped a full-scale Spanish invasion. Creighton confessed everything in London. The queen's council drew up a 'bond of association' by which anyone trying to usurp the throne after having organised Elizabeth's murder should himself (or, more likely, herself) be murdered. This 'bond' joined all the members of the council—and all those other noblemen who cared to sign it—in a common pledge. The response was overwhelming. Even Mary herself offered to sign! But it looked too much like an official advocacy of murder for Elizabeth's taste. She made suitably grateful noises and hoped for the hysteria to pass quickly. It showed how far the murder-plot, engineered by a powerful government, under-mined law everywhere. Politics by murder spread at the expense of the *status quo* it was designed to protect. The cleverly organised conspiracies of the sixteenth and seventeenth centuries resulted not in the consolidation of Madrid or Rome but in the ascendancy of the small powers, who made good use of the collapse of law wherever they could, particularly on the seas.

Elizabeth managed to get the 'bond of association' toned down before it passed into law. The bill introduced a tribunal to try Mary. It ordered all Jesuits and priests ordained outside England to be out of the country within forty days.

Another murder-plot was then discovered. This time it involved one of the queen's own spies in France, a man called Dr. William Parry. He was in fact a double spy. This plot again involved Mary (through one of her agents in Paris) and also the pope. Mary was sent to Tutbury Castle in Staffordshire at the beginning of 1585, and was cut off completely from her correspondents. The heels of her shoes, the linings of her trunks, her books, her clothes, her paper (which showed writing only when dipped in water) now underwent the strictest surveillance.

Elizabeth was feeling stronger and therefore bolder. She made a treaty with the Netherlanders and began sending troops across the water. Now that they had no leader capable of uniting them it looked as if she might get something out of the situation for herself. Alexander of Parma had meanwhile taken full advantage of the duke of Anjou's unpopularity, before his death. The pledge to use only native troops in the Netherlands was shelved. Spanish troops, supplemented by Italians, were brought back. Parma decided to starve the country into submission by stopping up all the rivers. Communication with the sea was now impossible. Ypres was the first city to surrender to famine. Then Bruges, Ghent and, on 10 March 1585, Brussels itself gave in. Parma allowed no terror this time. He issued a general pardon, and pledged himself to respect the ancient liberties. Antwerp still held out, supported by French and Scottish protestants. The Scheldt remained open, Parma having too few ships to close it. But his engineers managed to build a block across the whole width of the river. The city's efforts to break a hole in it (under an Italian engineer) failed. And in August Antwerp too gave in. When Parma entered the city he made sure to do so with Netherland noblemen, and to leave his Spanish entourage behind. His success was so perfect that there was something uncanny about it. It looked like the climax of the programme of catholic restoration. It seemed to Philip that only a few quick strokes more were needed to squash the last traces of heresy everywhere in Europe.

The death of the duke of Anjou meant that the heir to the French throne was the protestant Henry of Navarre, a Bourbon, which so alarmed the Guise family that it decided to go in with Philip in the Treaty of Joinville (31 December 1584). It was a treaty to root out heresy in France and the Netherlands, and to exclude the Bourbon family from the throne. Philip agreed to provide a subsidy of 50,000 crowns a month to this end. He was now sufficiently strong (and so was Elizabeth of England) to befriend the Guises without apprehension. That was another successful development in the catholic programme. But power and politics can be stupendously deceptive. They can display the greatest security at the moment of greatest danger.

Chapter 12

'Best not to Talk of It'

Two things decided Philip to adopt the Marquis de Santa Cruz's scheme for a full-scale invasion of England. First there were Francis Drake's piratical attacks round the Jamaican islands and along the coast of Florida. Then there was Elizabeth's expedition of 6,000 men to the Netherlands under the earl of Leicester.

The fact too that James, son of Mary Queen of Scots, was offered the governor-generalship of the Netherlands by the protestant leaders there (to Elizabeth's horror) also played its part. James might one day be king of England. Already in 1585 he had declared himself a protestant and made it clear that he did not wish to see his mother released from prison. He had no desire to share his throne with her.

France was safely under Spanish control for the moment. So there was no danger of any help coming to England from Paris. Philip's ambassador there, Bernardino de Mendoza, had frightened Henry III into making an agreement with the Guise family which gave them virtual control of his throne. Since the Guises depended on Philip for money and troops, this put French politics neatly into Spanish hands. Mendoza worked night and day to divide Henry from the Guises, and both from the Bourbon Henry of Navarre. The result was the 'War of the three Henrys' (1585), with Henry of Navarre in the field against Henry the king and Henry Guise.

In England the Spaniards were less successful. Mendoza intrigued there through his agents. But he could not divide the country. This made invasion the only solution, also for the conquest of the Netherlands. If he was to pour men into the Netherlands and patrol her seas with a powerful fleet, the men must be based in England, and the fleet must lie up in English ports.

In January 1586 Philip, urged on by Granvelle and Mendoza, asked Santa Cruz to prepare for him an estimate of what he would need to invade England effectively. The marquis asked for what was gigantic equipment in those days—about 150 ships, not counting merchantmen, to carry over 50,000 infantry. It was the biggest operation of Philip's career. The soldiers were to be Spanish, Italian and German. The scheme was to be financed by Castile and the Spanish possessions in Italy. Philip signed the document, and preparations started in the ports of Sicily, in Lisbon and Naples, with as much secrecy as was practicable.

A few months later Mary Queen of Scots wrote to Bernardino de Mendoza that she was handing over her rights to the English throne to Philip and not to her son. Philip instructed him to reply that he was grateful (mostly for her devotion to her religion). She was to be given 4,000 crowns, on top of the 4,000 crowns he had given her not long before. It made the whole invasion scheme look too inviting to fail.

The pope released Church revenues in Spain to the tune of nearly 2,000,000 crowns a year, and a large grant from papal funds. He was horrified by the idea that Philip might reign in England but the prospect of England becoming permanently protestant under James horrified him even more.

But the invasion scheme was based on a number of grave miscalculations. A catholic nobility in England was expected to remove Elizabeth at a stroke. Philip saw England as he had seen it thirty years before—a much weaker, a much more divided country than it was now. He had little conception of the fact that every new plot and attempt to invade England made Elizabeth's popularity the more solid, uniting the country as it had not been united since her father's time. The Jesuit plots were blamed on Philip. Even a lone would-be assassin who told his Warwickshire friends that he was going to London to 'shoot the queen', after which her head would be set on a pole 'for she was a serpent and a viper', helped the mounting anti-Spanish feeling. The man was arrested and flung into the Tower.

But Philip looked on every capital of Europe, every aristocracy, every monarch as having their price. He poured out immense sums in pensions, money for espionage and outright gifts. Wherever he found imagination and power in deadly conjunction, abroad or in his own country, in his council, in his family (Alexander of Parma was one latest example, the venerated Granvelle another), he took steps to trim it or remove it, if necessary by murder. The way he preferred was to buy it off. But the persecution of imagination only stimulated imagination. Much of the 'heresy' in England and the Netherlands was stimulated by the Spanish threat, under its veil of formality and legal order. At the beginning of her reign Elizabeth had counted for no more than a strip of island which the Guise family might easily annex. But she had used the protective wing that Philip had offered her until she was strong enough to give his empire the hardest blow it ever received. She did it without moving her fleet outside her own waters.

Another plot was uncovered in England in the first months of 1586, a further step in the development of 'The Enterprise'. Like the earlier plot it had Philip's reluctant and sceptical support. 'As the affair is so much in God's service,' he said, 'it certainly deserves to be supported, and we must hope that our Lord will prosper it, unless our sins are an impediment thereto. Perhaps the time at length has come when He will strike for His cause.' Mendoza had asked him to hold up his invasion plans until the plot had been carried out. On 4 August Walsingham arrested Anthony Babington, a wealthy young man from Derbyshire, and a catholic priest called Ballard, who had conceived this particular plot. Since January Walsingham had been following Mary's secret mail, using a priest called Gilbert Gifford as a double agent. Gifford had Mary's confidence (coming as he did from her own agent in France) as well as Walsingham's. The mail travelled to Mary's new home at Chartley in waterproof bags. These were hidden inside full beer-kegs. Her answering mail returned in the empty kegs. The brewer was paid by both sides. Further details of 'The Enterprise' emerged. Babington himself was responsible for the collapse of the plot, through writing an unnecessary letter to Mary. Under his leadership six men were to have murdered Elizabeth. Others were to have gone to Chartley to release Mary. A foreign army was then to have invaded the country.

The execution of these men was celebrated throughout England with bonfires and dancing in the streets. Babington and six others were given traitors' deaths—mutilated and then hanged. The remaining seven were hanged before mutilation. The plot served to put London and indeed every town and port in England on the alert. Rumours went to and fro. Hawkins went out to patrol the coast. Catholic priests were put under lock and key wherever they were found. There was a call to arms in every county. Mary was put on trial at her new home in Fotheringay Castle, and refused counsel. She was sentenced to death.

Elizabeth went through the same agonies of indecision over this death-sentence as she had over the duke of Norfolk's. She was aware that if she endorsed parliament's unanimous will to do away with Mary it would make a full-scale Spanish invasion, supported by the pope, inevitable. At the same time she had to think of her own position on the throne, with two houses of parliament clamouring for execution. Mary's existence also centralised catholic feeling and gave purpose to an invasion. If she allowed Mary to go on living the plots against herself would multiply, and one day they might succeed as had those against William of Orange. On the other hand a bold stroke against Mary, and emergency measures against the catholics, might get rid of one danger and unite the country against the other. That was the feeling in parliament too.

Then in January 1587 another plot against her was revealed, this time involving the French ambassador. It served to stimulate more alarmist measures than ever before. It was said that Spanish troops had already landed in Wales, that Mary Queen of Scots had escaped, that London was on fire. Elizabeth decided in favour of the death-sentence (1 February). It was not at once clear whether Mary would be quietly murdered or subjected to the shame of public execution. The king of France and most other people on the Continent thought murder the best way. But no one would take responsibility for doing it, since Elizabeth was quite capable of condemning the murderer afterwards as a scapegoat. Public execution was decided on. Precisely a week after Elizabeth had signed the death-warrant Mary was executed. At the execution the dean of Peterborough read protestant prayers while Mary read her own in a louder voice. Her death produced as much of a shock on the Continent as did the massacre of St. Bartholomew, and perhaps more hatred for Elizabeth than Catherine had got. And as her councillors may have expected, she now denied that she had ever sent the death-warrant to the Tower after signing it. She chose her scapegoat—William Davison, one of her secretaries (he had been chosen to do the murder if necessary). He was tried and put into prison. She did not do away with him. She waited until the Spanish invasion was over and then released him with a reward.

Paradoxically the execution of Mary made the Spanish invasion harder, not easier. The loss of their leader and figurehead dismayed the English catholics. And the prospect of a Spanish king of England frightened catholics even more than protestantism did. There were many English catholics who would have been happy to retain Elizabeth as their queen on certain conditions—for instance that she got rid of men like Cecil and Walsingham.

But Elizabeth was made the butt of the Spanish attack just the same. Cardinal Allen (who had founded the Douai seminary) made the mistake of publishing a tract against her the day before the Spanish fleet set sail, in which she was described as 'an incestuous bastard' who had exalted Leicester to his present position out of 'filthy lust'. Her ministers made great use of this tract as propaganda against the Spanish, and lurid stories spread. The Spanish were going to hang Englishmen by their thousands. The Armada was bringing a shipload of halters for this purpose. English children were to be branded with hot irons.

Elizabeth knew that her execution of Mary really obliged Philip to invade her. From his point of view England was in the same be-devilled situation as the Netherlands. Heresy looked like becoming a permanent state of affairs. Only quick, ruthless action could root it out. Above all he now had an excuse for absorbing England into his empire much as he had done Portugal. By catholic law he was now the rightful king of England. Or at least clever arguments could

be adduced for this. The pope showed his dislike of this idea, and
Philip suggested one of his own daughters, Clara Isabella Eugenia,
for the English throne instead. His alliance with the pope (for-
malised in the summer of 1587) required him at least to discuss the
matter beforehand. Had his invasion of England succeeded he
would conceivably have dispensed with the pope's approval and had
himself invested. It would have given him perfect control of the
situation in France and the Netherlands (mostly by removing the
possibility of a useful ally from both of them), and of course it
would have cleared up the distressing problem of English piracy in
Spanish waters across the Atlantic. It would have given him a fleet
in northern seas, too.

While her soldiers were fighting in the Netherlands against Parma,
Elizabeth secretly tried to come to terms with him. She certainly
had an inkling that he would be strategically involved in Philip's
invasion plan. Certainly too she knew about Philip's 'secret' preparation—though a number of Englishmen thought that his carefully polite letters were fooling her. In fact she spent over £160,000
to prepare to meet the Spanish fleet. And she followed Drake's
advice that the best way of defending England was to attack first—
and with light vessels of the kind that had been designed for fast
movement in the time of Henry VIII.

In April 1587 Drake took a small squadron over to Cadiz and,
with what was for that time astonishing eccentricity, burst his way
into port and began destroying ships and supplies meant for the
invasion of England. He seized Cape St. Vincent, and stopped the
enemy fleet assembling at Lisbon for a time. He then made a swift
voyage to the Azores and carried back to England Spanish treasure
worth about £114,000. Philip was furious, and urged the invasion
preparations on.

But he himself was the chief obstacle to their success. All round
him councillors were talking against Alexander of Parma. Yet Parma
was necessarily the key to the whole invasion enterprise. An occupation army would have to be transported from the Netherlands to
England. It would have to meet the invading fleet in the Channel.
But because Philip was highly suspicious of Parma's ambitions (so

many people wanted to be kings, it seemed), he let that part of the plan drop. This it was that doomed his scheme from the start. He chose a purely naval attack, with the army fighting it out in ships. In this way, too, he could improvise every aspect of the fleet's preparations himself. But even here he had his jealousies. His naval commander Santa Cruz was disturbingly popular. But then he had the good grace to die when the fleet was ready, in February 1588. Because Philip only felt safe with mediocrity he put a man in his place who could be relied on to toe the line even when the orders he got were wrong. The duke of Medina Sidonia, the richest lord of Andalusia and former viceroy of Naples, knew almost nothing about naval matters. Even he was shocked by his appointment and tried to persuade Philip that he was unfit to command anything afloat, quite apart from an invasion fleet. Philip, however, stood firmly by his decision, after making sure that the experienced Diego Flores Valdes would sail in the flagship *San Martin* with Medina Sidonia to control tactics on the spot. Even here his choice was a diffident one. Other men in the same expedition could have done the job better. As it turned out, this was the crucial appointment of the whole operation; it transformed into a rout what might have been a temporary setback. And then Medina Sidonia's slowness, his almost obsessive attention to worthless details threw away any chance of a surprise attack (which Parma had been advocating passionately). He postponed the attack again and again. His slow hand was felt in every shipyard and warehouse. Poor weapons, underweight food-supplies were despatched by wholesalers in connivance with the receivers. Medina Sidonia had to reorder masses of material. But Philip's recent successes had perhaps begun to persuade him that God was not likely to smile on other princes. He believed that the moral purpose of the Spaniard shone everywhere, even where it was hated, perhaps most where it was hated. And he had come to believe in brute power. England was simply not strong enough.

By the time Medina Sidonia was ready to set sail most of the food had gone bad. Two months had passed since Santa Cruz's death. The postponement of the invasion from the previous year had also given the Dutch time to mount a blockade against Alexander of

Parma. This prevented him from getting to the sea with the flat-bottomed boats he had been building in Flanders.

Philip's strategic calculations were based on an assumption that the major part of the English fleet would be found in Channel harbours waiting for Parma from the north instead of a huge Spanish fleet from the south. The southern ports, he assumed, would be empty. But the English had had a change of plan. Lord Howard of Effingham's fleet in Calais Roads was thought too big to be patrolling for Parma's boats. It was replaced by a smaller squadron under Lord Seymour, while he moved south. Most of the English fleet was now concentrated around Plymouth, precisely where Philip expected it not to be.

The Spaniards put out to sea on 30 May, with the wind against them. They found themselves drifting backwards instead of forwards, and it took a fortnight to return to the starting point. Meanwhile dysentery had broken out among the troops, and the food began to go bad. A gale sprang up, and the fleet—or such of it as could keep together—had to put in at Corunna. It took another two weeks to reassemble in port, and there were many desertions. Medina Sidonia wrote advising Philip to abandon the expedition. Philip refused. He well knew that he had most of the other commanders behind him.

The ships were refitted, and fresh supplies were taken on. Towards the end of July they set sail again, and this time the wind was favourable. It carried them over the Bay of Biscay in three days. But when they reached the mouth of the Channel there was a storm, and some of them had to shelter in French ports. This was providential for the English. It gave Drake time to get his ships out of Plymouth to face the Spaniards before they concentrated. Fog and rain then covered the English ships (fifty-four in number) from view. Howard with his smaller fleet managed to slip past the left flank of the Armada between the Spanish ships and the shore to join Drake without it becoming clear to Medina Sidonia what had happened. He expected—he had been drilled by Philip's instructions to expect—that the bulk of the English navy would be in front of him, towards the narrows of the Channel, though he knew well

enough that Drake lay in Plymouth. He therefore took no notice of
Drake's presence behind him and to the south-west, out to sea, even
after Howard had slipped past him.

With Howard's force, the English were not much less powerful
than the Spaniards, whose battle-worthy vessels numbered little
more than seventy. The English had superior gun-power. And they
had the advantage—and used it to full effect—of lightness and
mobility. The Spanish boats, on the other hand, stuck up out of the
water like terraced palaces, each terrace containing soldiers who
hoped to board the enemy vessels and fight it out by hand. The
English vessels never obliged. They refused to come close enough.

But essentially the day was lost by Medina Sidonia's inability to
escape from Philip's imagined battle and face the one he had to
fight. He put his main squadrons up in front with the flagship, to
face an enemy that was not there. Thus when the battle started, from
behind, there was no time for his vessels to turn round and pass
through the supply ships to the south, in order to engage. His second
mistake was to assume that in all naval battles the enemy let you
board their ships. The English showed that this was not the case.
They were fighting what was to the Spaniards a pirate's battle.

Drake and Howard spread out in a line and bombarded the
Spanish rear while Medina Sidonia moved his shore-flank closer to
Plymouth so as to prevent any more vessels joining the English.
But he soon had to release this hold, as his rear squadrons began to
feel the English cannonades and edge him further towards the
narrows. That was on 31 July. Two days later the wind changed
and the Spaniards succeeded in bearing down on the English, in a
south-westerly direction, and cutting their line in two. Medina
Sidonia then decided to chase the end of the English line which
was out to sea, instead of forcing the other further into shore and
dealing with it at close quarters. His flagship got a severe beating,
and failed to pursue the much faster English vessels. What advantage
he had gained in the morning was turned to disadvantage by sunset.

Meanwhile English ships in other ports had seen Drake and
Howard and joined them. It was now an equal, if not a superior,
force that faced Medina Sidonia's rear and continued to bombard

him. He had already lost seven vessels. He had hoped to land troops on the Isle of Wight and wait for Alexander of Parma there. But he was forced to edge towards Calais. Even where he had a tactical advantage, as when he cornered part of an English squadron close to the Isle of Wight, he lost it through the enemy's speed.

Meanwhile Parma refused to come out with his boats until Medina Sidonia's fleet was in a position to break the Dutch blockade. Lord Seymour, who had been posted to watch for Parma, now slipped past the Spaniards with his squadron and joined the rest of the English fleet. Medina Sidonia had little alternative but to drop anchor, and this he did on 6 August. His entire fleet was now squashed together at the narrowest part of the straits. The following night Drake sent eight small ships hastily equipped as fire-vessels bearing down on them. These were floating balls of fire like those recently used by the Dutch at Antwerp to break Parma's blockade. The Spaniards were unable to get away fast enough. Medina Sidonia gave orders for the cables to be cut. He was forced further into the narrows. At Gravelines fifty Spanish vessels turned round and engaged with the English. They suffered a stiff bombardment and again their soldiers were unable to get among the enemy with their swords. The fleet was still being forced up the Channel. They were now beyond the point where they could land troops along the English coast, and beyond the point where they could meet up with Parma. They had come too far to do any more useful fighting. And there was a strong chance of their running aground. Parma had warned Philip long before of precisely this possibility, through his representative, the historian Cabrera de Cordoba. He had pointed out that Spanish galleons drew twenty-five and thirty feet of water and that in the seas round Dunkirk this much depth was lacking for several leagues. It had made the idea of a two-pronged invasion impractical from the start, because the two fleets could easily be divided by the shallower English vessels.

A slight change of wind helped Medina Sidonia to get out to the North Sea. There he assembled his fleet again. He could have turned round and engaged the English had his ammunition not been low. He decided to return to Spain, seeing that her ports were at present virtually undefended. But his way south was of course barred. The only route was round the Orkneys and down the coast of Ireland, a long voyage that involved grave supply problems. Those vessels which had been all but wrecked in the Channel were helpless in the Atlantic seas. Some crashed into the rocks off the Irish coast. Those soldiers who reached the shore were shot by English garrisons, or caught by those of the Irish who obeyed the Lord Deputy William Fitzwilliam's order to kill all Spaniards on sight. A government secretary, Sir George Fenton, said he saw thousands of corpses along a five-mile stretch of beach at Streedagh strand in County Sligo. Spaniards were massacred in hundreds even after they had made formal surrender, so great was the English fear that the remainder of the Spanish fleet would use Ireland (with the bulk of the Irish in support) as a springboard for a second attack. The idea was to leave no Spaniard alive.

Towards the end of September the remnant of the Spanish fleet got back to Spanish waters. Medina Sidonia had only eleven vessels with him. Fifty-five more managed to follow him in the course of the next few weeks. This meant that over sixty vessels—including the supply-ships—had been lost. Out of a total of 30,000 soldiers fewer than 10,000 came back.

Philip sent Medina Sidonia to his estate and put Diego Flores Valdes in prison. Apart from that he did and said little about the whole thing. He simply remarked that setbacks were to be expected and did no harm. He did not even deprive Medina Sidonia of his nominal command. Almost certainly he recognised that he himself had caused the failure of the enterprise. He had foreseen that the English would prefer to fire from a distance, and he had warned Medina Sidonia of this, but he had not explained how to get at close quarters with ships that refused to close. He had told him to get level with Margate and then to hold the Channel for Parma's descent; but he had not explained what was to happen if the English fleet attacked from behind and forced his ships into shallows where they could either accept systematic bombardment or move beyond the point where Parma could meet them.

Philip could easily—as he himself said—have put another fleet

to succeed where Medina Sidonia's had failed. His losses were great
but not fatal. He remained master of the seas. But he knew now that
the English catholics could not carry the rest of the country with
them. The defeat was his way of learning that Elizabeth commanded
more loyalty than he or his advisers knew. It had been an unsuccessful attempt to deal with heresy. He took the message. He looked
after the soldiers who managed to get back, and there was no
recrimination. 'In God's actions reputation is neither lost nor
gained,' he said. 'It is best not to talk of it.'

Parma had asked him a number of times to abandon the expedition. For this reason he had opened up negotiations with Elizabeth
which Philip had tolerated only as a blind for his invasion preparations. Philip had refused to allow Parma to take Flushing, when he
was as near as Sluys. The taking would have been easy. Parma
needed a port from which to launch his attack on England. Philip
was too anxious to trim Parma's wings. So he put a series of impedi-
ments before his own design, and more or less ordained its failure
himself.

He now set about producing new light vessels of only 200 tons,
the *gallizabras*, capable of carrying treasure back from the Indies
but avoiding piratical attacks. A new attitude towards England was
necessary too. She could, he now acknowledged, become a rival in
the Atlantic. Elizabeth had proved herself a 'great queen'. Even the
pope said of her, 'Just look how well she governs! She is only a
woman, only mistress of half an island, and yet she makes herself
feared by Spain, by France, by the Empire, by all.' She could easily
have been called, like Philip himself, 'the prudent'. But a serious
rival to Spain she could never become. Her annual revenue from
crown lands and customs and various taxes was only £200,000 in
the first twelve years of her reign, and never more than £300,000—
a fraction of what came into Philip's exchequer. He still meant to
deal with her but in time, and without straining his other sectors of
power. She was strong enough not to be forgotten but weak enough
to allow him to wait.

Elizabeth on her side was perfectly aware of this. She did not cease
to fear—and expect—the 'invincible Armada'. Nor did the legend

of Spanish invincibility cease because of the defeat. It was in fact
hardly dented by what happened in the Channel. 'Spain' was still a
fearful word in London for at least twenty years more. There seemed
no reason why the Spaniards should not mount their most terrible
invasion force to date, and with vessels fast enough to cope with men
like Drake. Ireland was England's naked side, which the Spaniards
might very well revisit. A terror-system, once successfully moving,
sets a legend in motion that in the end is more important than the
power. It even survives the running-down of the power. In the
following century few people realised that the Spanish empire was
not precisely what it had been in the 1580s.

Elizabeth had stopped Drake from chasing the Spanish fleet
round the top of Scotland. She did not mean to let the war run her
into the kind of debt that France and Spain had accumulated. But
she had to give him his way in one thing. He was desperate to take
an expedition to Portugal. The idea was to stir up revolution there.
Don Antonio swore that this was possible.

Philip got warning of this through his agents in London, but
Drake still surprised him with his choice of place—Corunna (April
1589). The English fleet was 130 vessels strong, with over 15,000
men. A force of 7,000 men landed and did a lot of damage, though
with the loss of over a thousand men. Drake went on to a place
called Peniche a few miles north of Lisbon, and landed 6,000 men.
This was designed as part of a two-pronged attack on Lisbon. Drake
was to support the land attack by entering the River Tagus. But
disease and short supplies (the Spaniards stripped the countryside
of supplies along the English line of advance) forced a withdrawal.
The fleet got back to Plymouth with thirty fewer ships, 9,000 fewer
men. It showed that Elizabeth had been right to disband her forces
immediately after the Spanish flight up the Channel. But at the same
time it convinced Philip—since the English embryo-invasion had
not been at all a fiasco—that something like stalemate between the
two countries had been achieved. When he was strong enough he
would again mount an invasion force (in fact, he mounted two
more). But, as he told the Cortes, the defeat in the Channel had
cost him at least 10,000,000 ducats. This loss led to another tax, the

so-called *millones*, a direct subsidy to the crown, to be collected over
a period of five or six years and amounting to about 8,000,000 ducats.
On the face of it this looked like the fairest tax so far, in that no one
could escape it. The *millones* was so called because it was reckoned
in millions of ducats and not the usual *maravedis*. Cities could raise
the necessary sums in their own way. At the end of the first six years
it was prolonged—and increased to nearly 1,500,000 ducats a year,
to be derived from taxes on essential foodstuffs (meat, wine, oil,
vinegar). But again the grandees came off free, since they drew these
supplies from their own properties.

Philip could no longer go to foreign creditors. Too many of them
had been ruined by his pledges. With a population of just over
9,000,000 (twice the population of England and Wales) Spain was
under-populated for the kind of production it needed to balance the
outgoings. Emigration to the Americas and the constant drain of
manpower to fight in France and the Netherlands accounted for this.
The disappearance of the *moriscos* removed a source of much of the
country's commercial initiative. The religious policy was thus a
wrecking policy; it took little account of the prevailing facts. Above
all, the country needed an active agricultural policy from the government, backed by subsidies, at a time when the rest of the trade
picture looked bad. But this did not come about. Instead, people
left the land in thousands—until only a third of the labourers remained. It was beyond Philip to understand that something must
be done. Food prices went up. The fortune pouring in from the
Americas went mostly to pay off Spain's debts abroad.

Chapter 13

The Catholic Restoration

It must have seemed to Philip that his defeat in the Channel was a necessary reminder of mortality at a time when he—the spearhead of the Church—was having success after success. Between the 1560s and the 1580s the catholic-protestant situation had changed in every part of Europe. There was now a visible catholic restoration, not many years after it had seemed that Rome was finished. A book that Thomas Campanella published on Philip's death, *De Monarchia Hispanica*, maintained that Spain was the new Holy Roman Empire. Even during Philip's life the claim would not have looked absurd. The Jesuits had by this time established themselves everywhere, and they had become—much more by the destiny of events than the intentions of their founders—the order of catholic restoration *par excellence*. The protestants were not nearly as confident as they had been in the first half of the century, now that their doctrines had settled more or less into convention. The catholic side had taken proportionate courage.

When the Jesuit Peter Conisius published his *Catechism* (1555) it seemed that catholics had at last learned from their enemies how to explain the Bible and even the faith in simple, lively language for ordinary people. The book gave a lot of German catholics new heart. The faith began to be separated with more confidence from the physical state of the Church. It came to be seen that the only way to prevent collapse was to reform the Church. And this was done mostly under the guidance of the Jesuits. In Bavaria Prince Albert invited them (they had been established since 1549 at the university of Ingolstadt) to help him clear his country of heretics on the one hand and Church corruption on the other. The university of Ingolstadt was becoming more important than protestant Wittenberg.

A typical example of how things now went was in Graz, which until the Archduke Charles founded its first Jesuit college had been a largely protestant city, just as Austria had been a largely protestant country. The archduke had promised the citizens of Graz freedom of worship in 1578, but three years later he expelled the evangelical pastor from the city. Four years after that the Jesuit college was made into a university. Citizens were forbidden to send their children to any but catholic schools. In the end citizenship was only granted to catholics. Under Ferdinand, in the 1590s, all the protestant churches in Graz were closed.

In Poland there had been as much protestantism as in Austria, due in this case to the loose control of the Church over Poland's highly individual landowners. Their estates were all but independent townships, and they found it unthinkable that religious conscience should be dictated from elsewhere. Their already protestant disposition was influenced still further by the Anabaptists, when they were fleeing eastwards from the persecutions in Germany and the Netherlands. Poland achieved at this time an astonishing freedom and toleration, amid the most bitter religious conflicts everywhere else. Prince Radziwill, the chancellor of Lithuania, was an Anabaptist, and together with a number of other powerful landlords he had founded the Minor Reformed Church of Poland. Under King Stephen Bertory, who came to the Polish throne in 1574, catholics and protestants lived side by side with as much mutual respect as was possible between two declared enemies. The Jesuits used this beneficial atmosphere in order to establish themselves. They influenced Bertory's successor, Sigismund III, to exclude protestants from all public offices, and to urge catholic landowners to evict protestants from their estates. By this time there were nearly 400 Jesuits in the country. Churches that had been taken over by the protestants, even in places where the protestant doctrine was the only practised one, were absorbed back into the catholic Church by legal actions. Gradually the Jesuits won control of education, especially in the universities. By the first years of the next century the Roman faith was fully established again.

In France Henry III looked like becoming a vassal of the Guise family. The heir-presumptive to the throne, Henry of Bourbon, king of Navarre, was once more a 'heretic'. His life had been spared in the massacre of St. Bartholomew on his promise to revert to the Roman faith. But he had gone back to the protestant ideas of his mother, Jeanne d'Albret, once he was free again. He was now successfully isolated from the throne, especially after the pope had issued a Bull of excommunication against him. But, in the 'war of the three Henrys' he had shown that he could put up a good fight, while Henry the king had shown that he loved Navarre more than he did his official ally Guise. This was not at all depressing for Philip. There was in fact every reason why he should want to preserve the 'heretic' Henry, for fear that either the Valois family or the Guise family should become too strong. In the meantime, at the behest of the Guises, angry edicts against heresy were displayed everywhere in Paris.

Henry III suddenly rebelled. When he saw that the Guise family had virtual control over the Estates-General he took the unexpected step of sacking his own chancellor (who was taking his orders from the Guises). Then, on 23 December 1588, he invited the duke of Guise to court and had him murdered by the royal guard.

The next day Cardinal Lorraine, the duke's brother, was murdered too. A fortnight or so later Catherine de' Medici died. For Philip the murders were a much worse defeat than that of the Armada. But things were less grave than either he or Mendoza thought. Henry III had made too many enemies with these murders. The surviving Guise brother, the duke of Mayenne, led a revolt against him, and Henry had to flee the capital. Mayenne was declared 'lieutenant-general of the state and the crown'. He expected Spanish help. But Philip recoiled from the idea of supporting open rebellion (though only because he failed to see its chances of success). Also he still feared the Guises. The result was that once again Henry III reached an understanding with Henry of Navarre, and together they marched on the capital. The French were thus at war with themselves without knowing precisely what they were fighting each other for—an unmistakable sign that a powerful third party was present, manipulating feelings from behind the scenes.

The two Henrys published an appeal to the French to unite against the Spaniards. The siege of Paris went on. Then Henry III himself was murdered. A Dominican friar called Jacques Clement managed to get out of Paris to St. Cloud, where Henry was staying. He stabbed the king to death. Henry, before he died, declared Henry of Navarre his heir.

Mendoza was happy (the murder being God's will). Philip was not. Like Elizabeth he could see his own murder in any knife that touched a legitimate king. Above all, he was horrified that a Dominican (he much preferred the Dominicans to the Jesuits) should have done it. The murder left him only one course of action —to try to get direct control of France himself, by force, and become king of France as he had become king of Portugal. As the son-in-law of Henry II he had some claim to the throne—enough to clothe a naked invasion with good intentions. It looked as if Henry of Navarre might be easy to deal with, too. He had issued a promise (on 4 August 1589) that he would maintain the Roman faith on becoming king. This failed to reassure the catholics and aroused the suspicion of the protestants (many of whom defected from him).

Philip now did in France what he had done in Portugal—he supported the candidacy of an aged cardinal, the cardinal of Bourbon, hastily made 'Charles X' by the duke of Mayenne. This was an interim act until his own candidature should gather support. He despatched agents to France with plenty of gold. The pope refused to support Mendoza's suggestion that Philip be declared 'Protector of France', and here he knew he could rely on the duke of Mayenne's opinion too.

At this time Alexander of Parma was just about to clinch his victory over the protestants in the Netherlands. Early in 1589 he had got possession of Gertruy-Denberg, with the result that Zeeland and Holland were isolated.

Philip now required him to invade France. Parma was unable to move at once because of mutiny in his unpaid armies. Meanwhile Henry of Navarre, to everyone's surprise, since his army was now much smaller than the duke of Mayenne's, managed to push Mayenne back to Paris, and enclose him inside. Gradually the capital was brought to starvation and over 13,000 people died in the two months before Parma managed to join forces with Mayenne and break Navarre's siege. Navarre withdrew to Tours.

Parma's presence in Paris brought Philip no satisfaction. He sent him back to the Netherlands instead of asking him to quell the whole of France. Apart from his wariness towards Parma, he may have felt that the French would rise against the Spanish presence even more successfully than the Netherlanders. And he felt perhaps that France must be divided before it could be swallowed up. This could be done with smaller forces under his own supervision, from the south.

Besides, there was trouble in Aragón. Perhaps the time had come to Castilianise that province at last. The nobles there lived as if no authority beyond theirs existed. They resented foreign adventures unless they brought immediate profit. They clung to their often brutal privileges. One of these was the right to strangle any vassal for any misdemeanour, without even specifying the misdemeanour. Unlike his father Philip was too busy to make repeated visits to Aragón. The vassals constantly claimed royal protection against their lords. In the Ribagorza case Ribagorza himself had accepted the verdict of the Justicia—that the count's lands should go to the count's brother and not to the crown. But the vassals had not. They had rebelled (the count's brutalities fresh in their mind) and had all but taken control of his territory. The situation had never really been cleared up.

In 1585 Philip decided to repair his long absence from Aragón by a visit to Saragossa in the company of his daughter, Catherine. There he gave her away to the Duke Charles Emmanuel of Savoy, who hoped that the marriage would turn Savoy into a great state. His hope came to nothing. Perhaps Philip had no wish to engage with Savoy's powerful (and seafaring) neighbour Venice, or to make any Italian state strong enough to unify the peninsula. But for the moment he treated the duke with enormous favour. There were processions, illuminations, dances. Philip rode out of town to meet his future son-in-law, with mounted archers from the Burgundian guard. Then he returned to the workaday problems of his own state. He never lost a moment in sentimentality.

At Monzon he acknowledged the right of Count Ribagorza's brother, the duke of Villahermosa, to his own land, but carefully omitted to put down the rebels. In fact his presence encouraged the violence. He made use of this and, offering his protection, neatly scooped up two towns, Tervel and Albarracia, for the crown.

When he returned to Madrid the violence on the Villahermosa estate became worse, growing into a civil war which involved the *moriscos* as well. These *morisco* risings were put down by the vassals with the same brutality that the count himself would have used.

Philip's adviser on Aragonese matters, the count of Chinchon, his Grand Constable, was one of the duke of Villahermosa's most bitter enemies. He began a personal campaign against Villahermosa, accompanied by the usual bribes and murder-plots. Finally, Villahermosa thought it best to renounce all title to his lands, and to hand everything over to the crown. Philip, the land now his, promptly changed his attitude to popular rebellion. He quickly suppressed the vassals.

The whole operation was an example of how he increasingly used legality as a blind for the credulous. If he found a legal verdict against his interests he now worked illegally to undo it. But the illegality was always hard to prove, since nothing more overt than threats and money-persuasions took place, without the slightest official encouragement.

It looked like a successful Castilianisation of Aragón, on a par with that of Milan and Naples. Philip even drove the message home by sending the marquis of Almenara (a Castilian and a Mendoza, and a first cousin of the count of Chinchon) as virtually his viceroy there. This pleased neither the noblemen nor the vassals, who now saw how innocent they had been of Philip's real intentions. The new man was ridiculed. He could not be declared viceroy officially because of the law which said that royal officers in Aragón must be Aragonese. Here again Philip accepted the legal verdict against him while preparing secretly to undo it.

But it was now (1590) that Antonio Pérez, the disgraced minister, escaped from his Madrid prison. He went straight to Saragossa. During the five years of his imprisonment Philip's agents had been trying to extract a confession from him about the murder of Escovedo—not in order to establish the truth but to implicate Pérez at all costs. He was too dangerous a man to live. He had enjoyed the royal confidence for too many years. But to have him quietly strangled in prison would have made Philip's role in the Escovedo murder too obvious. Above all, Pérez had some state papers hidden somewhere which Philip was dying to lay his hands on, since they no doubt contained a documented history of the Escovedo affair, and a record of his own secret conversations with Pérez. He had been playing cat and mouse with Pérez for the last five years. He had even released him from gaol for a time to give him a sense of false security. He may even have been behind Pérez's recent escape. Pérez, on the other hand, knew Philip's mind far too well to be trapped. His home had been raided and some state papers removed. But they were not the state papers Philip was after.

The official charge against Pérez was corruption. He had become too wealthy when in office. Not that it was unusual for a minister to become wealthy, but the charge was sufficient to keep him in prison. Meanwhile Philip had concentrated on building up another and far more important case against him, that he had murdered Escovedo. He went so far as to write to Pérez personally that he acknowledged having given him the order to murder Escovedo but now wished to refresh his mind about the details. It was of course a trick. Pérez refused to be drawn. He kept on denying the slightest complicity, the slightest knowledge. He was put to the torture, and then confessed. But his confession dealt only with his own part in the murder. It made no mention of Philip. Yet it left it quite clear that Philip had played more than a conniving role. The confession had if anything put him in a worse light than before. Had he allowed Pérez slowly back into favour, as Pérez himself wished, the Escovedo matter would probably have been forgotten. Philip could have made it part of the bargain that the state papers in Pérez's possession should be handed over. But now he got more publicity for his role in the Escovedo matter than he liked, while the sympathy went to Pérez.

Pérez escaped from prison in his wife's clothes (20 April 1590). In a matter of hours he was in Aragón. And it was not long before he had become virtually the figurehead of an Aragonese movement of independence. As a born Aragonese he claimed asylum—and protection against the king. By law he was entitled to it.

Philip sent immediate orders to have him taken dead or alive. The marquis of Almenara sent a force to the Dominican convent where he had taken refuge, but it was too late. One of Pérez's men had contacted the Justicia, who had sent a deputy with fifty men to escort Pérez from the convent to Saragossa, where—in accordance with ancient Aragonese privileges—he was lodged in the *carcel de los manifestados* or rebels' prison. His entry into the town was more or less a triumphal procession.

Philip's answer was to lodge a formal charge against Pérez with the Justicia, in the hope that Almenara would be able to lay his hands on him in the prison. Meanwhile Pérez was writing letters to Philip offering to keep out of public life if his future safety could be guaranteed and his wife and children released (they had been flung into a Madrid gaol). Philip disregarded the letters and with the cool determination which characterised him when he felt in danger he pressed on with his subtle schemes to trap Pérez once and for all. In July he had him condemned to death as a common criminal in Madrid. Pérez acted at once. He made a statement before the Justicia at Saragossa admitting his role in the Escovedo murder but adding that he had simply carried out Philip's orders. This statement alone would not have created a sensation. But he produced the state papers which Philip had been trying to lay his hands on for so long. They were letters in Philip's own hand. They showed clearly that the order for murder had indeed come from him. The whole of Saragossa knew about it in a few hours, the rest of Spain in a few days. The news spread quickly to foreign courts, and Philip's standing in the world was lower than it had ever been. He now tried another charge—that Pérez had been disloyal to the crown. But the Justicia barred this too. It was clear that where clean methods had failed, a foul one would have to be used.

And the foul one Philip chose worked through the Inquisition.

Two pictures reproduced from Baron Eytzinger's De
Leone Belgico, *published in Cologne in 1583.*
*Tortures at Antorff in 1576 (Top). Spanish troops leave
Maestricht, 21 April 1577 (Bottom)*

He did something his father would never have done. Together with the grand Constable, the count of Chinchon, and his man in Saragossa, the duke of Almenara, he prepared a statement for the Inquisition claiming that during his imprisonment in Madrid Pérez had talked like a disbeliever. He had even practised black magic. He was possibly a homosexual too! He had once administered poison under the guise of medicine to an astrologer, and killed him.

Philip calculated that horror of the atheist was so great in Spaniards of all classes that Pérez would soon be without a friend even in Saragossa. The priests then got to work. They demanded of the Justicia that he hand Pérez over at once. The Justicia gave way. But the people of Saragossa came out against him. They poured into the streets when the tocsin sounded for Pérez's removal to the Inquisition prison. There were even priests among them. The Inquisition seemed to them a Castilian invention. The crowds appealed to the Justicia to prevent the transfer, but he refused. They surrounded the duke of Almenara's palace yelling 'Liberty!' The Justicia went inside to escape them. Almenara was all for defying the mob but his front door was pushed down. The Justicia rushed on to the balcony and promised the mob that the duke of Almenara would himself be taken to the *carcel de los manifestados*, on one condition: that the duke suffer no harm on his way there. The crowd seemed to agree, but when the duke emerged he was stabbed almost to death. He died two weeks later. Meanwhile another crowd gathered at the Inquisition prison to demand Pérez's release. In the late afternoon he was delivered to the crowd. He made another triumphal procession, back to the *carcel*.

Philip did not invade Aragón, principally perhaps because it would reveal the extent of his alarm. Nor could he rely on sympathy abroad. So he trod stealthily. He began to isolate Saragossa diplomatically. He played on the feeling in the other towns of Aragón that they did not want to be ruled by a Saragossan mob. They preferred royal protection. But then the Justicia in Saragossa died. His son, who felt much less inclined to give way either to Philip or to the Inquisition, took over. When Philip issued a second order (24 September) that Pérez must be conducted back to the Inquisition

10

prison another crowd assembled and the violence started all over again. This time Pérez got away from the *carcel de los manifestados* to the house of the rebel leader, Diego de Heredia. The duke of Villahermosa too was in the rebel movement. After all, Philip had caused him to become virtually a pauper.

Saragossa was now ready to fight Philip. And Philip at last had the excuse he needed to enter Aragón with a Castilian army. Order had to be restored. The Church too had been flouted in the persons of her own inquisitors. Luckily for him the Aragonese rebels failed to get support from Catalonia and Valencia. And the rebels were divided among themselves. Heredia made the mistake of putting round a rumour that the young Justicia and the duke of Villahermosa were planning to go over to Philip. Villahermosa had to leave the city hurriedly. The Justicia was sent to forbid entry to Philip's invading army. This was led by Alonso de Vargas from the Estremadura, who had had experience of rebellion in the Netherlands. Since Vargas had a much superior force (12,000 against 400) the Justicia could only protest and let him in. The rebel movement broke up at once.

Again Pérez escaped. Vargas occupied the city peacefully, showing every respect to the very people he knew to have been enemies not an hour before. Saragossa settled down to normal life again, and it seemed that Philip had achieved all he wanted without ugly reprisals. The rebel movement—now at Epila, under the ex-Justicia and the duke of Villahermosa—looked quite tame, despite its efforts to get help from France. The leaders began to think of returning to their native city, which seemed to have forgotten the recent riots, so peaceful was its atmosphere. That was precisely what Philip intended. The rebels returned. And he sprang like a tiger. A messenger arrived in Saragossa from Madrid on 12 December 1590 with a letter for Vargas. It contained an order to behead the Justicia. Vargas is said to have wept.

When the twenty-six-year-old Justicia was told that he was to die as a traitor (under the windows of his own house) he said 'Traitor, *no*—badly advised, *yes*.' He was executed eight days after the order arrived.

The Justicia being the symbol of Aragonese independence, it looked as though that independence too was dead. Philip could not have asked for a better denouement. Saragossa was terrified into silence. The remaining rebel leaders were caught and tortured. The evidence they gave before they were put to death was used to incriminate the duke of Villahermosa. He had already been arrested in Madrid. Like his associate, the count of Aranda, he died in prison. No one knew how. But the trial against him went on for a number of years. Eventually, in the reign of Philip III, he was posthumously acquitted.

When he came to discuss Aragón's future Philip was careful not to abandon strict legality. To tamper with Aragonese autonomy in an official way would have been dangerous. Besides, it would have meant tampering with Valencia and Catalonia too, and both these provinces had been loyal to him. What he did was to keep his troops in Aragón as long as he decently could. Not until December 1593 was the province free of Castilians, and this on condition that a royal garrison be left at Aljaferia. The official excuse for this was that the officers of the Inquisition had to be protected. So Aragón kept its separate government while absorbing the message that the real authority lay in Madrid. Philip saw to it that the Aragonese had less control over their finances and their army in future, that the Justicia could be removed at the royal pleasure, that no special privileges could be claimed against Madrid law, and that in the Cortes majority decisions should replace unanimous decisions. All this was passed by the Aragonese Cortes itself.

But Philip's most telling thrust was his clause about unanimous voting. The whole point of unanimity in the Cortes had been to see that *all* the deputies were satisfied with a decision. Now, with majority voting, bribery and persuasion by force could work much more effectively. Fear of being included in an intimidated minority might sway a vote. It became clear that the autonomy of the Spanish provinces was a ghost, many years before it was formally ended in 1707.

As for Pérez, he got away to France, with Philip's agents hot on his heels. Philip tried to draw him back over the Pyrenees with promises. But Pérez knew his man. Instead he accepted Henry IV's offer to meet him at Tours (1598). The French king (like his predecessor aching to release himself from the shackles of the Spanish embassy) needed a man who knew Philip's mind, and the real state of Spain. And Pérez carried a mass of state secrets in his head.

Philip tried murder again. A plot involving three Spanish assassins failed in Navarre. A lovely young woman was engaged to lure Pérez into a trap. She fell in love with him instead. When he was sent by Henry IV to England, to persuade Elizabeth to make an alliance with France against Spain, two Irishmen tried to do Philip's bloody work for him but were caught and executed.

Pérez failed to persuade the queen of England but he did win over the earl of Essex. And he received a small pension from the English government. When he returned to Paris the following year the Baron de Pinilla, a paid agent of Philip, tried to shoot him but failed. The name Pérez became a legend everywhere in Europe, partly because of his powers of survival. He and the Portuguese Don Antonio succeeded in blackening Philip's name for four centuries to come—until the historian von Ranke tried to adjust the balance.

Philip was if anything more humane than the rulers around him. Often he let a man go free when he could legally have held him. There is the story of the abbot who was brought to him on the charge of sheltering a wanted man in his monastery. When Philip asked him for an explanation the man replied, on his knees, 'Charity'. The king is said to have taken two steps back with surprise and repeated the word to himself. He gave orders that the friar be sent back to his monastery loaded with gifts. As for the wanted man (a courtier who had slept with one of his ladies-in-waiting) his sentence was commuted to one of exile.

Philip did not exact vengeance on the Princess Eboli for her loyalty to Antonio Pérez. But he expected 'truth and good faith' (his own words) in the men who served him. And Pérez was an unscrupulous man. He made a good life in Paris and London with his slanderous stories about Philip, though he did die in misery and poverty, being no longer necessary to the politics of either country. He had a great influence abroad—on the French language, even on French manners. He brought with him an inside knowledge of a feared and legendary power which no one else had. It gave him a fascinated and generous audience for many years. He died long after Philip, in 1616.

Philip was now ready to invade France. He sent 3,500 men to Brittany under Don Juan del Anguila (September 1590). Officially it was because the reigning Duke de Mercoeur (brother-in-law of the late Henry III) had asked for his help. Being descended from the dukes of Burgundy Mercoeur could argue a family connection with Philip that might justify Spanish soldiers in France. He could also claim Brittany as his own through his wife, who was heiress to the possessions of the Penthièvre family. And he calculated that he could get rid of the Spaniards after they had won his battles for him, precisely as Philip calculated that he could get rid of the duke. He wanted his daughter Isabella Clara Eugenia on the French throne. But if this did not prove possible he had no objection to dividing France up. Then he could claim Brittany for his daughter as the descendant of Queen Claude, duchess of Brittany. And he would claim the duchy of Burgundy for himself, through his connection with Charles the Bold. Provence too might be his, if his rights as count of Barcelona were recognised.

Henry of Navarre, declared Henry IV of France by the dying Henry III, had defeated the duke of Mayenne at Arques, and had begun to overrun Normandy. He was not yet recognised as king, naturally enough. But neither the pope nor Venice was averse to recognising a heretic king of France if it would help to keep Philip out of the country. Henry besieged Paris with only 12,000 soldiers against at least six times that number. After failing to get forward by assault he decided to starve the city out. Wheat supplies soon ceased (June 1590). Horses, rats, cats and dogs were eaten in the city. Bodies were disinterred in the burial grounds and their bones ground down. The Spaniards and the papal legate helped with supplies as much as they were able. Spanish soup-kitchens were set up in the streets. Paris held out for four months. Thirteen thousand people died of starvation.

Once in Brittany Philip injected it with a lot of money to sweeten the inhabitants (a possibility that the duke had overlooked). The invading army quickly became an army of occupation. At the beginning of 1591, while the case for Isabella Clara Eugenia was being argued between Spanish and French jurists, Mendoza managed to slip a Spanish garrison into Paris from the Netherlands, so that the occupation army in Brittany now had a headquarters. And the presence of the garrison helped to give the legalistic arguments in favour of the Princess Eugenia just that extra bit of force.

The duke of Mayenne resented the invasion but for the moment could do nothing about it. Mendoza—old and nearly blind now— was hardly his friend. Philip's money failed to sweeten the Bretons for long. It failed to put them against Mercoeur. Then Mendoza's successors in Paris—Juan Bentista de Tassis (ambassador) and Diego de Ibarra (a diplomat locally described as 'vile and haughty') —made a complete ruin of political relations with France and managed to unify the country against Spain where Henry of Navarre had failed.

Philip was now anxious for Alexander of Parma to make a full-scale invasion. Paradoxically, he was supported in this by the duke of Mayenne, who—apart from being under pressure from the Parisians to protect them—hoped to snatch something for himself (such as the French crown) out of the chaos. Parma received orders to cross the French frontier in August 1591, and Henry of Navarre raised the siege in order to go and meet him, hoping to deal him a deadly blow in open battle. But Parma managed to avoid an engagement and slip two of his regiments across the Marne and establish contact with Paris. Twelve hundred Spanish and Neapolitan troops were garrisoned in the city.

Rouen, also besieged by Henry of Navarre, was relieved by the spring of the following year. François de Bourbon, the prince of Condé, was defeated at Craon by Spanish and Breton forces together. Meanwhile the diplomatic pressure to get the Spanish princess on to the French throne was stepped up. Philip hoped to extract an answer to this while the guns could be heard at the gates of Paris, so to speak.

In the spring of 1592 Parma was wounded and retired to the Netherlands. Philip's suspicion of his brilliant qualities had now come to a head. He decided to break him. The duke of Medina Sidonia had already begun to feed Philip with all kinds of seductive malice against Parma, whose campaign in France had cost him his hold on the Netherlands, precisely as he himself had predicted. Maurice of Nassau (William of Orange's son) had been quick to take advantage of Parma's absence.

Parma wanted to retire from public life but remain in the Netherlands. Philip wanted him back in Spain, where he would be a subject and no longer the equivalent of a king. In the summer of 1592 he sent the count of Fuentes to Brussels as an interim governor, but without letting Parma know what his intentions were. In fact he wrote him a letter at the time congratulating him on the fall of Rouen. In other letters he assured him that he still enjoyed his full confidence, and that the libels being spoken against him were falling on deaf ears. But Philip's work of getting rid of Parma was done for him in another way. Parma died naturally at Arras on the night of 2 December 1592.

There was no one of his calibre to succeed him. The count of Mansfeld, who took over the French command, had nothing like his hold on the situation. The duke of Mayenne did not fear Mansfeld, for one thing. The result was that the Estates-General stiffened in their negotiations with Philip. He intensified his war and captured Noyon on 30 March 1593. This was designed to intimidate the French while negotiations for the throne were still on. He also sent Lorenzo Suarez de Figueroa, duke of Feria, as his special envoy in Paris. He was to press four claims—those of the princess, the two brothers of the emperor Rudolf, and lastly the duke of Guise or the cardinal of Lorraine, in that order.

In the spring of 1593 Feria and Mayenne reached a compromise whereby the latter would take the Princess Isabella as his queen in return for Spanish money, which he needed badly. Feria then appeared before the Estates-General and reminded them, in the blunt way great powers sometimes find useful, of the 'help' that Philip had recently given France. This only served to hold the French together—citizens and Estates-General and Henry of Navarre. But Henry of Navarre would clearly never do as king of France. The Estates-General would not have a protestant on the throne (even if Philip tolerated it). But then Henry of Navarre suddenly stopped being a protestant. He took the wafer again at the cathedral of St. Denis on 25 July 1593.

Philip was thrown but not knocked out by this. He set about trying to get Pope Clement VIII to refuse to accept Henry back into the Church. But his representative at the Vatican was the duke of Sesa. Here again mediocrity lost him what brilliance and tact could have won. Sesa threatened to withdraw to Naples if the pope received an envoy from Henry of Navarre, which only stiffened Clement's will in the opposite direction. He received Henry's envoy (November 1593), though without granting Henry absolution.

Meanwhile Philip spent over 20,000 crowns in bribes among the deputies of the Estates-General. Realising that they were determined to have a Frenchman as king, he got Feria to say that this was acceptable provided that he himself could choose him. Secondly the queen must be Isabella. She must share the throne. Apart from the duke of Mayenne, the young duke of Guise was suggested as an alternative.

On 27 February 1594 Henry of Navarre was crowned king of France at Chartres. He still had to win Paris—which meant pushing out the duke of Mayenne. He sought ways of doing this without an armed attack. Cutting down his own subjects was not the best way for a king to start his reign. As it happened, Mayenne was at that moment out of Paris. He had gone to the Netherlands to discuss with Mansfeld the possibility of another attack on France from the north. This gave Henry the chance he was after. Count Brissac, a catholic extremist and apparently well in with the Spaniards, had taken Mayenne's place as marshal of France. Henry got access to Brissac and managed to persuade him—with the help of a heavy bribe—that the Parisians had a right to receive their own king peacefully. Brissac managed to get three of the city's gates opened, despite the fact that the duke of Feria had got wind of the arrangement some hours before and had acted at once. Without the smallest fuss Henry's troops entered Paris and surrounded the Spanish garrison. Instead of massacring them Henry sent a message to Feria that if he and his troops were out of the city by the following day, with a promise never to return, all lives would be spared.

The next day the entire Spanish garrison marched out in good order. Henry's forbearance made a great impression on the Parisians. Yet he was still, from the pope's point of view, a heretic. By September of the following year that was no longer true. He was given the papal pardon. But Spanish troops were still in Brittany. And there could still be an attack from the Netherlands. It looked as if Philip had failed in only one respect; he had not succeeded in dividing the French. The time was coming for open war, with the legal aspects thrown aside. The pacification of the Netherlands, France and England was now one operation.

Chapter 14

The Last Act

A full-scale campaign against England was read by the English into Philip's occupation of Brittany. If the Channel ports had fallen into his hands the situation would have become most dangerous for Elizabeth. This had forced her to give Henry III all the support she could.

Philip was certainly itching to get at England again. He was still willing to have Elizabeth murdered. On the other hand he had not entirely despaired of bringing her inside the Spanish orbit. He still wrote to her. And his recent setbacks in France may have given him an incentive to be friendlier towards her than usual.

But at the beginning of 1594 Essex made loud claims that he had discovered a new murder plot. It involved Rodrigo López, the queen's doctor and a Portuguese Jew. López was said to have offered to poison the queen in return for a large sum of Spanish money. The charge was never proved. And the queen never really believed it. Behind it all was no less a celebrity than Antonio Pérez. For some time he had been living in London as López's guest. But they had quarrelled. Pérez had obtained a pension from the queen through the good offices of his friend Essex, and it may well have been he who started—or perhaps only amplified—the trumped-up charge. López was almost certainly innocent. When Essex saw that his accusations against 'the poor man' only made the queen angry he got angry himself. He worked even harder to get López executed. The queen held the accused in the Tower under her own protection. But somehow he was condemned, and publicly hung, drawn and quartered. Essex, as leader of the war-party ('attack Spain now'), clearly needed a public scare at the time, and was not above creating one out of nothing. He may well have known that Elizabeth was writing to Philip on the subject of a future peace-settlement. There is nothing like the discovery of a murder-plot to throw all parties back to their political start-lines.

Whatever Philip might have wanted or thought possible, his system was now what decided policy. It had developed too far to make anything like a carefully constructed peace possible, despite the fact that the state of the country and his vast debts made peace essential. Like his father, he had too many commitments abroad to draw back now.

Drake and old Sir John Hawkins's son Richard had been harrying Spanish ports on the other side of the Atlantic with the queen's permission. Then Richard had been taken prisoner in the Bay of San Mateo in July 1594. On the pretext of avenging him, Drake and the young man's father got permission for a voyage (which proved to be ill-fated) via the Canaries and Las Palmas to the Antilles, where the Spaniards were waiting for them. Hawkins fell sick and died on 22 November 1595. Drake died in February of the following year. That was a tremendous shot in the arm for Philip. He felt he would soon be able to drive the English fleet off the seas, especially with his new fast ships. The English had failed to get control of the trade routes across the Atlantic. They had failed to seize Spanish treasure-boats.

Essex and his war-party got their way in June 1596. In command of 10,000 men (plus 5,000 Dutch under Louis of Nassau) he set sail for Spain. The fleet of sixty vessels was under the command of Lord Howard of Effingham. Their target was Cádiz. The old Armada commander, Medina Sidonia, was again made commander, and found on his arrival that the harbour's defences were feeble. The English landed with ease, and the best the Spaniards could do was to set light to all their merchant ships to prevent them being taken. The city was plundered (for sixteen days) and gutted by fire. Essex then returned to England. The whole thing had taken little more than a month.

Philip, ill at Toledo during the English attack and thought to be dying, decided on war at once. It revived his old stamina and concentration. He was at his desk again for long hours together. He ordered a new invasion fleet to be fitted out at Lisbon and San Lucar.

But this was easier said than done. He had to replace Medina
Sidonia with another man. But that did not get the ships fitted any
faster. Even by October 1596 the fleet was not ready. But it was
Philip's deadline, and he made the fleet sail just the same. A storm
wrecked it the moment it put its nose outside harbour. Two
thousand men were lost, and a third of the ships. The invasion had
to be abandoned.

In July of the following year (1597) Essex tried to repeat his Cádiz
success. But he too was caught by a storm and had to return to
harbour. Meanwhile Philip was preparing a third invasion, hoping
to find English ports empty of ships while Essex was safe in the
Azores. But once again delays removed all chance of using the un-
foreseen to advantage. By the time the Armada was at the mouth of
the Channel Essex was just sailing in from the opposite direction,
and stiff winds gave him the protection he needed for slipping back
into port, while the same winds dispersed the Spanish fleet.

Philip's tendency to think of England, France and the Netherlands as essentially one enemy-problem had the natural effect of
bringing those three countries closer together than ever before. The
protestant elements in the Netherlands hoped for a leader in
Henry IV, the new French king. Maurice of Nassau, the new
Netherlands leader, had made Holland, Utrecht and Zeeland safe
on their southern borders and rescued Gelderland from the isolating
grip of the Spanish. The Mansfelds (father and son) had proved
themselves incompetent to take Alexander of Parma's place. In fact,
under the disguise of power and success (which in the end were the
shadows thrown by the past over present chaos) the Spanish empire
was disintegrating as fast as possible. Philip was already showing
signs of the agonising disease that killed him. He was less capable of
long and concentrated work. He drove himself pitilessly. He had
no hopes of his son, who was seventeen at this time. The future
Philip III seemed to have no ideas in particular; his favourite Don
Francisco de Sandoval y Rojas, marquis of Denia, did his thinking
for him, in his lax and pleasant way. It was clear that both the future
king and his favourite would live on the capital of the past when
they came to power.

Philip's choice of the count of Fuentes to govern the Netherlands (or what was left of them) was not only a preference for mediocrity. He needed another Alva. The count was the late Alva's brother-in-law, and it looked as if he would fit the role admirably. As to the successor of the late Alexander of Parma, that was to be another nephew, the Archduke Ernest of Austria. Fuentes was to govern in the meantime.

His method of governing was to put the clock back to the time before the peace of Arras. The Italian and Belgian advisers that had surrounded Parma were sacked. A decree went out that in future no prisoners were to be exchanged with the United Provinces (as the new protestant Netherlands were called) and that any prisoners taken should be sentenced to death automatically as traitors. In other words, the resentment of the early years of the Netherlands struggle was to be dragged up again. In a matter of weeks all Parma's tactful and healing work was undone. Fuentes did a good soldier's job. He awakened rebellion even in the Spanish Netherlands. The catholics and the protestants were on the point of uniting again. Spanish troops were disgruntled. There were the old delays in pay. Mutiny had broken out again. What strength Fuentes could have mustered against Maurice of Nassau was concentrated on the French border, awaiting orders from Philip for an attack south. Meanwhile Maurice of Nassau's campaigns in Holland and the far north were going well. He was a reserved and detached young man. His main interest was mathematics and by the methodical training of his relatively small number of troops (20,000 infantry and 2,000 cavalry) he managed to produce mobile groups that confounded the opposing armies, who based their movements on the old strategy. In fact his strategy was older than theirs, being drawn from ancient models. The city of Groningen surrendered to him on 24 July 1594. The following January Henry IV of France declared war on Spain.

Fuentes effectively stopped Henry joining up with Maurice of Nassau. His action was quick and unhesitating. He moved his army across the French border and took Le Catelet. Then he took Cambrai. But in Franche Comté the battle between Henry IV and the duke of Mayenne (who had help from the Spanish governor of

Milan, with 15,000 men) went badly, and Mayenne's defeat at Dijon took him over to the side of the king. In Britanny there were the results of full Spanish occupation: collapse of the civil authority, and a predominance of crime. In the meantime Ernest of Austria had died, before he had taken over the Netherlands, and Philip chose his younger brother, Albert (even more Castilianised than Ernest, and even more aware of every thought in Philip's brain) to replace him.

Albert got more money than Fuentes. His generals captured Calais (17 April 1596) in a sudden swoop, when Henry was expecting them to try to relieve his siege at La Fere, on the Paris–Brussels road.

Calais had been completely undefended. It looked as if the invasion of England could now take place, although no one—including Elizabeth—expected the Spanish to be able to hold out in Calais for long. If anything Elizabeth was more afraid of Calais becoming French. Reluctantly she gave Henry IV the help he asked for, small enough though it was. In fact the Spaniards could have beaten Henry easily and divided France again, if only they had not been obliged to return to the Netherlands to deal with Maurice of Nassau. During 1597 Nassau captured one town after another in the northern part of the Spanish Netherlands. In France, Amiens was wrested back from the Spanish by the Marshal de Biron (September 1597).

There was nothing for it but to make peace. Spain was in any case by now bankrupt. The silver that had poured in from the Americas was no longer sufficient to finance an empire. It amounted, plentiful though it was, to only a quarter of the exchequer. Less than half of the total revenue of the crown was now real income; the rest went to pay interest. The same was happening in Spain as had happened in Portugal. People had been leaving the land in thousands for some time. The towns (except for those in northern Castile, which were hit most by the bankruptcy) were growing at the expense of agriculture. The depressed state of the land meant scarcity of produce and therefore higher prices, aggravated by the need to import (for instance grain from northern Europe). To some extent this was the pattern all over the Mediterranean in the second half of the sixteenth century. But the fact remained that the country's finances were in chaos, and that much-needed subsidies for agriculture—the only way of saving it—were not made available. And the people were exhausted. They were taxed beyond the point where their initiative and zeal could survive. Castile alone yielded over three times as much money annually as came from the Americas in silver. Philip's embargo of 1585 on all Dutch ships in Spanish or Portuguese ports had also been fatal—though not to the Dutch. They found the salt for their herring industry in Spanish America now, together with much other produce that Spain could have given them. They seized the salt island of Araya in 1599. And they now had an Atlantic fleet. They found their spices in India and brought them home themselves. A Dutch empire was the result.

Philip had to stomach Henry IV's Edict of Nantes, by which the Huguenots were recognised to have human rights. And he signed a treaty with Henry, on 2 May 1598, by which he agreed to clear out of Calais, Britanny and Picardy, where his hated and unpaid troops were still lingering. He agreed not to go to war to support his claims to Burgundy. His father's lifelong concern was at last given up. By what he considered to be this act of generosity Philip hoped to stop Henry IV supporting the rebels in the Netherlands. But it did not work. Henry signed a pledge not to help them, then disregarded it. He now did secretly what he had hitherto done openly.

In the Netherlands too Philip had to face facts. His way of making a peace settlement was by marrying the Archduke Albert to the still unmarried Infanta Eugenia, and thus securing the Netherlands as a Spanish dominion after his death. Albert and Eugenia were to be king and queen. In the event of their marriage being barren, the Netherlands crown was to revert to Spain.

It did little to alter the situation. The one positive result was that there were no wars going on. The rebels of the Seventeen Provinces were not formally recognised, but they were not attacked either. What Philip could say—in this last year of his reign—was that much of Europe was now catholic, whereas it could easily have been wholly protestant by now. The pope could never have done the job alone.

But even as a 'catholic restoration' it did not amount to much. Protestant states had come into being. The Church had not healed the most terrible schism of its history. Above all a secular world had emerged to which Philip and the pope were strangers. Yet Philip had pioneered that world. He had made war while hating war. He had acted outside the law while hating illegality. The contradiction was perhaps inevitable, arising as it did from the fact that for spiritual ends he used worldly means, and seemed surprised (like his father before him) that only worldly ends were achieved.

He had centralised the government of Spain in himself, but by so doing he had helped to centralise foreign governments too—against him. To deal with his agents and armies and governors and viceroys, they had been provoked to unity. Thus the later strength of England, France and the Netherlands was to a large extent achieved by means of him.

A Venetian ambassador once described Philip as 'the Prince who fought with gold rather than with steel, by his brain rather than by his arms'. To a remarkable extent his system of governing succeeded and survived. His power did not. He made government a matter of calculating. It became a balance sheet of interests (unfortunately the financial side of his balance sheet was missing). He provoked other rulers into calculating too. Elizabeth would not have been so clever without him. More than anyone perhaps he introduced modern diplomacy. Honeyed words now masked power-interests. He juggled, he spun, he concealed. And from this, far more than from his pillaging armies, came the terror that he spread. Machiavelli had once written of Ferdinand of Aragón (without divulging his name) that he never talked of anything but peace and good faith, 'yet had he ever observed either he would several times have lost his credit and his estates'. The same applied to Philip II on a global scale.

England remained uninvaded. Protestantism in the Netherlands remained undiscouraged. It would not take many years for the Spanish empire to dwindle to a simple matter of Castile and the 'New Spain' across the Atlantic. But New Spain too looked like becoming independent, as a matter of fact rather than of design or hope. It too had its difficulties. A series of terrible diseases had reduced the Indian population of Mexico from about 11,000,000 at the time of the first voyages to about 2,000,000 by the end of the sixteenth century. The country's labour force had therefore collapsed. Less silver came to Spain, fewer immigrants arrived in New Spain. The ceiling figure reached by bullion imports had been, in the equivalent sterling, over £20,000,000 annually (between 1591 and 1595). By the middle of the next century it was down to £2,000,000 annually. New Spain could not afford Europe's articles any more, and transferred its custom to the Orient. It developed its own cloth industry, as Peru produced its own wine and oil and grain; all these things had at one time been imported from Spain. So new countries had come into being without the slightest breath of heresy or un-Spanish behaviour.

Philip died on 12 September 1598. He had been king of Spain for forty years. He died slowly at the Escorial, in terrible pain, his body covered with suppurating sores that filled his room with an unbearable stench. He insisted on having his coffin placed beside his bed, and on a table before him there was a skull with a crown of gold, to show him in a last vivid image how little all the power in the world counted. Really he had always had that image before him. He also asked for the scourge with which his father had whipped himself, so that he could touch it, as a last reminder of sanctity from the man he had worshipped and respected above all others. He died gazing at a crucifix. Characteristically he never once uttered a word of complaint.

Philip had said of his son in 1582, 'God who has given me so many kingdoms has denied me a son capable of ruling them. I fear that they will govern him!' But it is doubtful if any ruler, however capable, could have stopped the later disruptions. Living on credit had become a feature of government everywhere. As ideas began to actuate policies rather than clearly identified dynastic interests, so finances were stretched to meet grandiose schemes. Political and commercial projects, increasingly hand in hand, began to outpace

work done and reward earned. It produced a basic condition of
impoverishment, paradoxically written into wealth as its necessary
part. Violence of all kinds—wars, revolutions, assassinations,
pogroms, colonial decimations—were no longer an accident or
side-effect but the very basis of life, the means by which it worked
and survived. Gradually after the sixteenth century the Christian
state became to all intents and purposes a war machine. War itself
became not simply a principal industry but a principal means chosen
by society for devising new techniques of production and organisation. When history did not move fast enough war came along to
discard the creatures of a former power and to bring into prominence
those of a new one. Each war produced a different class situation
from that with which it had started. By the twentieth century it
had become clear that war, disguised as a distressing accident,
was in fact a technical reservoir on which the whole of society
fed.

But war is only the end-product of Christendom's—now we must
say the world's—essential state of violence. England's industrial
revolution towards the end of the eighteenth century, which changed
human life everywhere, was no less an expression of the violence
than the protestant revolution of the sixteenth century, the Crom-
wellian revolution of the seventeenth, the French revolution of the
eighteenth, to name only a few of the perennial upheavals. They
were all elements in the same process. The growth of industry
caused changes in English life no less drastic and perhaps in the
end no less bloody than the revolution in France. They were made
urgently necessary in England by the Napoleonic wars. More had
to be produced in a shorter time than ever before, to cope with a
desperately tightened supply situation; just as the Napoleonic wars
were a military attempt to solve the same problem in France. The
industrial revolution was no less of a violence done to the human
creature than those wars, and eventually it extended to the whole of
nature. It expanded to embrace the world, not because it was considered beneficial by other countries to produce more commodities
more quickly; not because people found such a system with its often
degrading conditions of work, its smoke and its noise, more ad-

vanced than what they had known before; but because of similar conditions of compulsion, written into their own commercial system as they came to adopt it themselves. Only today is it recognised (what the first industrial workers recognised at once in their Luddite or machine-breaking movement) that the industrial revolution, like all the revolutions that rocked society since the collapse of the Middle Ages, was essentially an act of violence, mounting in our day to what looks to some people like a triumphant exploitation of nature and to others a universal war on nature which promises the most disastrous global consequences.

The constant upheavals of Christian history since the sixteenth century are exact reflections of its financial upheavals, suffered by states and individuals alike. The 'financial crisis' was born with banking. In the 1420s and 1430s there was a prolonged crisis in Florence, just at the time when Giovanni di Averardo de' Medici was building up the family banking business on an international scale. His great-grandson Lorenzo, despite (or rather because of) the fact that he was the invisible head of state and ran the foremost banking business in Europe, on which other heads of state were uncomfortably dependent, was often in need of ready cash. At the time of his daughter Maddalena's marriage in 1488 he was unable to pay her dowry of 4,000 florins as a down payment, as he had promised. Yet not a year later he and his branches at Bruges and Lyons were flourishing. Profit was made quickly, at great risk, and the results were bound to be spectacularly uneven.

What is not so immediately obvious is that these sudden and unexpected plunges into near-bankruptcy, and the equally sudden rises to extravagant gain, sometimes within months of each other, had serious repercussions on the lives of people working with their hands or managing modest businesses. We know that in Florence's first big crisis nearly half the master craftsmen working on the cupola of the cathedral had to be laid off, and we can assume from this that thousands of less skilled labourers were out of a job too. Yet a little later the republic passed through one of its happiest and most prosperous periods. The very fact that finance had become the key factor to human operations meant that these operations were in a constant state of upheaval and uncertainty. Nothing could be more conducive to violence.

During the whole period of the Medicean republic, Florence changed constitutions, leaders, electoral systems so frantically that it was a wonder any government resulted at all. There were *coups d'état*, assassinations, endless factional disputes. Committees of reform were almost always in session. Yet the Florentine believed in peaceful policies. He recoiled on the whole from brutalities. Piero de' Medici endeared himself to the people by sparing his enemies after he had squashed their conspiracy. The republic had no army; it liked to use other people's. Yet it went from one crisis to another. It was in a constant state of distraught nerves. Inevitably its daily life reflected the violence of the operations on which it depended for its place in the world—namely financial ones. These were like messages written on the wall of the future. No one could read the real meaning, even the signatories of the loans, until the time came for them to be read out in war, conspiracy or revolution.

And Florence's highly modern predicament became the world's. A strange unreality entered life, dividing thought, projects, hopes from actuality. Art and philosophy and even religion began their journey of increasingly artificial detachment from 'real' life. And this 'real' life was in the nature of a promissory note which could never be honoured. Idealism came into being—a bemused state of hope for the unrealisable. The Renaissance failed. It left behind it a marvellous record of a hopeless bid for civilisation which we mistakenly read for the civilisation itself. And it left behind many cold neo-classical façades and arches and chapels covering up the throbbingly intimate work of the Middle Ages, whose world had at least been made by men and women on the basis of their lives, and not on notions of symmetry and balance.

This naturally influenced the way people studied nature. The tendency to create an ideal and intellectual world remote from the fierce upheavals of daily life produced a science which often took the intellectual analysis of matter for a description of its nature and even origin. This science even began to pose as a complete knowledge of life. An analysis of the body in terms of bloodstream and nervous system and skeletal structure was soon in danger of being taken for a 'real' description of the person. There was too a crude reliance on the field of what could be seen and touched as the only 'real' world—a tendency which began to break down only in the twentieth century, with the discovery of invisible vibrations, particularly in the matter of sound. Mathematics—a method of analysis —began to seem the 'truth' about the relations between things. It hit rather hard the perhaps callow religious beliefs of the Christian world, with its barbarian system of reward in the form of heaven and vengeance in the form of hell. These 'realities' of analysis could not be seen or heard; and religious experience had not gone deep enough to show that no amount of analysis could challenge the kind of knowledge reached by an altogether different process than the reason. Unfortunately religion had tried to prove itself rational. And it was only a matter of time before the rationalists knocked it all down.

In the strangest way science followed the money operations in its remoteness from life as a whole system, and in its savage effects. The promissory note of the scientific world offered a more rational world in the future, but its effects were in the form of mad upheaval. The industrial revolution, which was its child, turned Europe upside-down more quickly than a war could have done. It came about blindly and haphazardly, with the minimum of the promised rationality. Apparently this science was closely allied to gain, which made its connection with money operations even stronger. In the end, under the protection of vast military programmes, it was making war on everything from 'experimental animals' to the outer atmosphere. Its advances have produced an unhealthy globe, which may soon be unfit to live on.

The future never happened in quite the way the scientists predicted. In fact, under the disguise of the tightest intellectual control ever, men lost control of life. It seems curious to say that in mediaeval times life *was* controlled. This does not mean that the churchmen knew all the answers, or even that their religion was 'universal' as they themselves thought. But still, human life was within a human scope. Less and less could that be said after the sixteenth century.

The Middle Ages came into being as a result of the wave of barbarian terrorism that rocked the Roman empire. The Renaissance seemed to revive that terrorism, until by the twentieth century it became a recognised feature of society.

When Florence passed into the hands of foreign armies, and its Medici became grand dukes of Tuscany, life in the city itself was quieter; it had become a backwater, and the big promissory operations were taking place elsewhere, for instance, in Madrid.

The influx of bullion ruined the Spanish economy while seeming to be giving it vigour. Inflation was the result. Nowadays such inflows of money are a daily affair in almost every country, and the inflation is usually short-term; the increased spending power entails daily adjustments, sometimes in the form of price- and wage-controls. But society is still credit-based, and to this extent 'bullionism', though exploded time and again by the economic theorists, has been accepted. Money became confused with wealth. The basic problem of sixteenth-century life (and the resultant terror, at that time disguised as an argument about religion as ours today is disguised as an argument about politics), far from having been solved, has only been sophisticated to the point where no solution is possible, only short-term adjustments to stave off disaster. The need for empire, which in monetary terms is the search for more power to buy, grows accordingly, inducing not simply a constant threat of war and massive defence industries but a state of violence at the heart of society, which in the end is to say the human heart.

The conditions of sixteenth-century Spain were thus embryo conditions. The hunger for bullion was shared by the English, the French and the Dutch, who in turn created their empires. Society became a race for wealth. Banks became the key-institutions they are today. The possession of money even became a mark of personal integrity, so far had society sunk from its first Christian premises. Bullionism, far from having been displaced by something more realistic, became the dominant human obsession.

It was inevitable that one day all society, every class and every type of worker, should join in the race for wealth. Francesco Guicciardini, Florence's sixteenth-century historian, wrote that the people, driven by a hunger for riches, 'follow their own private interests' and 'are ill-adapted to uphold the liberty of the city'. A certain hollowness of life was a result, as every human enterprise became encapsulated in a profit-and-loss account. The Florentine humanists always held that the state deserted by 'philosophy' (we would say 'thought') becomes corrupted and falls.

The period of small wars in and around Germany in the seventeenth century, sometimes called the Thirty Years War, was perhaps the first convulsion resulting from this state of affairs. These wars were really one war of Europe, not by any means a war of the German states alone. The protestant-catholic struggle inside Germany was simply exploited from outside. The war was a secular struggle for power. The new national groupings were its cause. It was a struggle between the Bourbon and the Hapsburg houses. The entire ecclesiastical setting of the mediaeval world was with pain and confusion penetrated everywhere with the new principle that government was the exercise of power for the accumulation of further power. 'Interests' as meaning something quite nakedly self-seeking, without the intrusion of doctrine or conscience, came into being for the first time. The long-term result was a period of cynicism and pseudo-rationalism in the eighteenth century, which ended by bringing down the aristocracy everywhere, together with the so-called *ancien régime* it was supposed to represent. But the impossibility of an aristocracy without a Church behind it had been demonstrated long before; and the *ancien régime* had ceased to exist long before the French revolution and Bonapartism came about. These were if anything the climax of eighteenth-century life and thought, rather than their decapitation. The so-called *ancien régime* was already capitulating in the sixteenth century. In almost every country of Europe, even in the conservative republic of Venice, a moneyed class had become the effective power long before the 'age of reason' closed itself in massacre and industrialisation. That class had in fact brought the 'age of reason' into being.

Philip III preferred pleasure to politics. The result was that ministers and favourites did the ruling. For more than twenty years the
marquis of Denia, now the duke of Lerma, filled his court with the
grandees Philip had kept away. He made himself the centre of an
enormous system of bribery covering the Church and every class of
society except the very poor. One of the first acts of the new regime
was to release the Catalonian rebels still in gaol. Philip III bought
his popularity.

There was a sudden dip into self-indulgence and luxury. Any
excuse would do for a public celebration—a noble birth, a marriage,
a canonisation. Processions and free food and drink for a day or two
helped to quieten the increasing armies of the starving.

Another Armada was sent against England in 1601 but was ruined
by a storm. Lerma tried to exploit the Irish troubles, and the Irish
even recognised Philip III as their king. He landed 3,000 men at
Kinsale, but his forces got divided. Spanish plotting in England
went on as in Philip II's day. The latest plan was to put the catholic
Arabella Stuart on the throne after the death—if possible, murder—
of Elizabeth. But now Spain had less money to keep its plots turning.
Elizabeth died on 3 April 1603 and since James I was rather more
tolerant of Spain than she or her subjects had been, a period of peace
between the two countries followed. The Treaty of London was
signed despite Sully's efforts to arrange an Anglo-French treaty
directed against Spain. Spain's finest diplomat, the count of
Gondomar, became James I's best friend, and managed to secure
the execution of Raleigh for his piracy in the Orinoco. For a time
there was a plan to marry the Spanish infanta to the Prince of Wales.
James hoped (with Gondomar's encouragement) that he might
become the chief arbiter of European affairs in this way. It was an
absurd revival of Henry VIII's dream. As for the Dutch, a truce
lasting twelve years was signed with them in 1609. Lerma check-
mated Henry IV of France by establishing an effective system of
espionage at the French court, working mainly through bribery.
Spanish money bought the king's favourite, the marchioness of
Vermeuil, and plot after plot was directed against Henry's life.
Finally the dagger of a man called Ravaillac got him in 1610, with

the result that his widow, Mary de' Medici (who was pro-Spanish!), ruled France for her son, Louis XIII.

One of the most notorious plots of the age came about in Venice, called 'the Spanish plot' by most historians despite the fact that no one has ever proved that the Spanish had anything to do with it. Henry Wotten, the English ambassador in Venice at the time, called it the 'French plot'. Between 300 and 500 men (said to be mostly Frenchmen) were strangled or secretly drowned during May of 1618 on the orders of the Venetian government. The citizens of Venice were horrified to see unexplained corpses swinging 'between the columns' on the Molo every morning. No one provided any explanation. But it seems that a Frenchman called Jacques Pierre had some months before gone to Venice after serving with the Spanish viceroy in Naples, the duke d'Ossuna. Pierre revealed to the Venetian government that he himself was the chief agent in a plot of the duke's to massacre the entire noble class of Venice and overthrow the republic, so that the republic could then be transferred to the Spanish crown. The odd thing is that the Inquisitors (Venice's secret council of three) did nothing about Pierre's report for ten months. At the end of that time they arrested and murdered masses of foreigners in the city. Finally, Pierre himself was secretly drowned.

Comte Daru in his *History of Venice* made a subtle interpretation of these events. He claimed that the duke d'Ossuna and the government of Venice were in a joint plot (perhaps with France as a third conniving party) whereby Naples was to be wrested from Spain and given to the duke as king. Jacques Pierre, the duke's agent, was briefed to go to Venice to win over the Dutch troops at that time stationed there, without being given the reason. He assumed that it was to overthrow the Venetian state, and in fright gave away the plot to the Inquisitors, who then saw that the secret was out and that those implicated must be done away with so as to hide all traces from the foreign world. The best way to do this was to make it look like a Spanish plot, especially as the Spaniards were the most notorious plotters of the age and no one would wonder twice about it. The Spanish embassy in Venice was more or less besieged by mobs for days. In the Inquisitors' report Jacques Pierre's deposition was only mentioned in so far as it helped the case; and the whole report looked like an official piece of case-making after the event. To support Daru there is the fact that the duke d'Ossuna was recalled to Spain, and that later he was murdered, some say by the Jesuits (for heretical remarks he had made years before in Naples). Venice was so secretive about this whole affair that James I said jokingly that whenever he talked about it to the Venetian ambassador he was made to feel that he himself had been one of the plotters.

Spain was still looked on as the greatest power on earth, and during this period at the beginning of the seventeenth century its foreign affairs still had an aura of glory. Internally it was the opposite. The *moriscos* now turned to other Christian powers for support where they had once turned to the Turks. In 1602 they promised to assist a French invasion of Spain, in return for help. The Duke de la Force had been discussing this with Henry IV in the royal carriage when Ravaillac's dagger fell. The Archbishop Ribera's fanatical preaching against the *moriscos* (their hard work was held to be a sign that they wanted to milk Spain of her wealth) got a powerful stimulant from a letter of James I to Philip III claiming that correspondence between the late queen of England and the *moriscos* had come to light. A rebellion in Spain had been plotted between them, he said. In Valencia there were now nearly 30,000 *morisco* families on whose work the wealth of the area largely depended. Lerma persuaded Philip to get rid of them all. They were shipped off to Barbary, mostly with no more than the clothes they stood up in. After the expulsion the failing economy degenerated even more quickly.

A reputation for crime began to surround the government. An obscure figure in the Madrid underworld was killed, it was thought by Rodrigo Calderón, one of Lerma's favourites. There was a great uproar about it and Calderón ended in gaol for something he had probably not done. He was executed and Lerma fell in 1618. Philip died before he was thirty.

The reign of Philip IV was a kind of epilogue, even an epitaph to Spanish power. The Dutch destroyed his fleet at the Battle of Downs in 1639 and in the four-day battle off the coast of Pernambuco in 1640. That was really the end of the Spanish empire. Sixty years of union with Portugal had only embittered the relations between the two countries, especially as Spain had lost Portugal's eastern empire for her. Olivarez, the king's minister, was no politician, and turned errors into disasters. He persuaded Philip IV that new wars might revive Spanish glory. They only brought crippling debts. When his taxes became intolerable to Barcelona he moved his troops in. The result was the revolt of all Catalonia in 1640. The rebels elected Louis XIII as the count of Barcelona, and put themselves formally under the protection of the French. The Portuguese were encouraged by this, and also rebelled. And twenty-eight years of futile warfare between Portugal and Spain was the result.

Without power and intelligence, or the energy that comes from self-denial, there could be no social cohesion, let alone wealth. Gradually the legend of 'the greatest country on the earth' faded. The haughtiness faded, and so too the fear of it faded.

Select Bibliography

The following is a short list of books selected from a great many consulted and contains the essentials of the story of *The Spanish Terror*.

ARMSTRONG, EDWARD: *The Emperor Charles V* (Macmillan, 1902)

BAUDIN, LOUIS: *Daily Life in Peru at the Time of the Last Incas* (Allen and Unwin, 1961)

BERTRAND AND PETRIE: *The History of Spain* (Eyre and Spottiswoode, 1934)

KARL BRANDI: *The Holy Roman Empire* (Cape, 1939)

CADOUX, CECIL JOHN: *Philip of Spain and the Netherlands* (Lutterworth Press, 1947)

CAMERON, RODERICK: *Viceroyalties of the West* (Weidenfeld and Nicolson, 1968)

CHADWICK, OWEN: *The Reformation* (Pelican Books, 1964)

DAVIES, R. TREVOR: *The Golden Century of Spain* (Macmillan, 1937)

DIAZ, BERNAL: *The Conquest of New Spain* (Penguin Books, 1963)

DICKENS, A. G.: *Reformation and Society* (Thames and Hudson, 1966)

ELLIOTT, J. H.: *Imperial Spain 1469–1716* (Edward Arnold, 1963)

HAMILTON, EARL J.: *American Treasure and the Price Revolution in Spain* (Harvard Economic Studies, 1934)

HEER, FRIEDRICH: *The Holy Roman Empire* (Weidenfeld and Nicolson, 1960)

HUIZINGA, J.: *Erasmus of Rotterdam* (Phaidon Press, 1952)

HUME, MARTIN: *Philip II of Spain* (London, 1897)

HUME, MARTIN: *Spain, its Greatness and Decay* (Cambridge University Press, 1925)

KAMEN, H. A.: *The Spanish Inquisition* (Weidenfeld and Nicolson, 1965)

LEA, H. C.: *History of the Inquisition in Spain* (New York, 1906/7)

MCLUHAN, MARSHALL: *The Gutenburg Galaxy* (Routledge and Kegan Paul, 1962)

MERRIMAN, R. B.: *The Rise of the Spanish Empire* (Macmillan, New York, 1925)

NEALE, J. E.: *Queen Elizabeth* (Cape, 1934)

New Cambridge Modern History, Vol. 2, The Reformation 1520–59 (Cambridge University Press, 1958)

PEERS, E. ALISON: *Spanish Mysticism* (London, 1924)

PETRIE, SIR CHARLES: *Philip II of Spain* (Eyre and Spottiswoode, 1963)

PIRENNE, HENRI: *A History of Europe* (Allen and Unwin, 1939)

PRESCOTT, W. H.: *History of the Conquest of Peru* (New York, 1847)

ROBERTSON, WILLIAM: *History of the Reign of Charles V* (Routledge, 1857)

STEINBERG, S. H.: *The Thirty Years War* (Edward Arnold, 1966)

TREND, J. B.: *The Civilisation of Spain* (Oxford Unversity Press, 1944)

Index

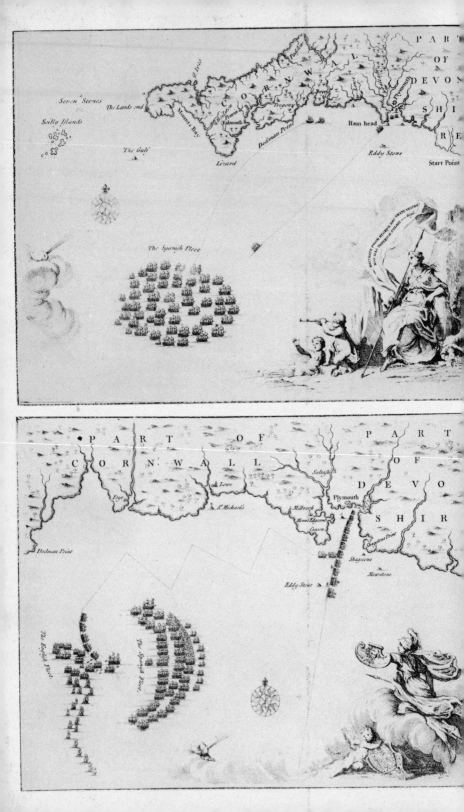